A HISTORY OF THE RUSSIAN CHURCH TO 1448

D1596736

A History of the Russian Church to 1448

John Fennell

Longman
London and New York

Longman Group Limited
Longman House, Burnt Mill,
Harlow, Essex CM20 2JE, England
and Associated Companies throughout the world.

Published in the United States of America
by Longman Publishing, New York

© John Fennell 1995

First published 1995

ISBN 0–582 08068 1 CSD
ISBN 0–582 08067 3 PPR

British Library Cataloguing-in-Publication Data

A catalogue record for this book is
available from the British Library

Library of Congress Cataloging in Publication Data

Fennell, John Lister Illingworth.
    A history of the Russian church to 1448 / John Fennell.
    p.   cm.
    Includes bibliographical references and index.
    ISBN 0–582–08068–1 (hard). — ISBN 0–582–08067–3 (pbk.)
    1. Russkaia pravoslavnaia tserkov ´—History. 2. Orthodox Eastern
    Church—Russia—History. 3. Russia—Church History.
    BX485.F45 1995
    281.947'09'02—dc20

                                                        94–16348
                                                        CIP

Set in 10.5/12 pt Monophoto Bembo
by 15B
Produced by Longman Singapore Publishers (Pte) Ltd.
Printed in Singapore

Contents

PART TWO

List of abbreviations used in the text and the bibliography

AED	Antifeodal'nye ereticheskie dvizheniya
AFZ	Akty feodal'nogo zemlevladeniya i khozyaystva XIV–XVI vekov
AHE	Die altrussischen hagiographischen Erzahlungen und liturgischen Dichtungen uber die heiligen Boris und Gleb
AI	Akty istoricheskie
APC	Acta patriarchatus Constantinopolitani
CD	Codex diplomaticus nec non epistolaris Silesiae
Cherepnin, RFA	Cherepnin, L. V., Russkie feodal'nye arkhivy XIV–XV vekov
CSHB	Corpus scriptorum historiae byzantinae
DDG	Dukhovnye i dogovornye gramoty velikikh i udel'nykh knyazey XIV–XVI vv.
GVNP	Gramoty velikogo Novgoroda i Pskova
Golubinsky, IRTs	Golubinsky, E. E., Istoriya Russkoy Tserkvi
LPS	Letopisets Pereyaslavlya-Suzdal'skogo
LRD	Letopisi russkoy literatury i drevnosti
MGH, SSRG	Monumenta Germaniae historica, Scriptores rerum germanicarum
MIL	Des Metropoliten Ilarion Lobrede auf Vladimir den Heiligen und Glaubensbekenntnis (L. Müller)
OED	Oxford English Dictionary
NPL	Novgorodskaya pervaya letopis' starshego i mladshego izvodov
PG	Patrologiae cursus completus, Series Graeca
PL	Pskovskie letopisi
PLDR	Pamyatniki literatury Drevney Rusi
Proceedings	Proceedings of the International Congress Commemorating the Millennium of Christianity in Rus'-Ukraine
PRP	Pamyatniki russkogo prava
PSRL	Polnoe sobranie russkikh letopisey

PVL	*Povest' vremennykh let*
RIB	*Russkaya istoricheskaya Biblioteka*
TL	*Troitskaya letopis'*
TODRL	*Trudy Otdela drevrusskoy literatury*
Tserkov'	*Tserkov', obshchestvo i gosudarstvo v feodal'noy Rossii*

Preface

About three weeks after John died, Andrew MacLennan telephoned me to ask about John's unfinished book. I realized, of course, that *The History of the Russian Church* had to be published but I did not know what steps to take. Two people came to my help at that time: my son Nicholas, who gave me his love and total support when I needed it most, and Michał Giedroyć, who at once offered advice and guidance. I must say that words cannot adequately express my gratitude to Michał. His concern, interest and friendship throughout have been invaluable. In spite of grave personal circumstances he generously gave of his time to read the manuscript and to advise me. He subsequently became one of the advisers to the editors.

I am also greatly indebted to Professor Wladimir Vodoff of the École Pratique des Hautes Études in Paris; he undertook the bibliography – an incredibly painstaking task, a true labour of love. I am grateful to Mr David Howells, the Taylorian Institute Slavonic Librarian, for offering to compile the index. My special thanks go to Mr Paul Foote, for many years a close friend of John's and mine, who kindly agreed to read the proofs.

The History of the Russian Church could not have been published without the selfless devotion and effort of our friends.

Both the editors, Virginia Llewellyn Smith, who was once John's student, and Dorothy McCarthy, were sensitively efficient, and showed kindness and understanding. Finally, I must thank Andrew for his tact and patience in helping me to bring John's book to final publication.

Marina Fennell

Editorial Introduction

At the time of his retirement in 1985 from the Chair of Russian at Oxford, the late Professor John Fennell had already laid plans for his next major undertaking: the writing of a history of the Russian Church. He intended to take it to the end of the sixteenth century. Those familiar with Fennell's work on Russian history will recall that in his efforts to find the roots of Russia's statehood, he had moved backwards through time, from Ivan Grozny to pre-Mongol Rus'. In this book he was to make this journey in reverse.

Those who knew of the project had little doubt that once again John Fennell would offer his readers a full, objective, and original account of his subject, rigorously based on the study of primary sources. But those closer to him sensed that this time something more might be in prospect: Fennell's credentials, apart from his brilliant record as an historian, included his personal commitment to Orthodoxy. Of course, the book would be a product of a detached perspective and rigorous scholarship; but of scholarship enhanced and sharpened by the deep understanding he had of his Church.

Early in 1992 the project was known to be well advanced. A self-contained volume was emerging covering the period from the earliest beginnings of Christianity in Rus' to 1448, the crucial year in which the hierarchy of Muscovy unilaterally elected its new Metropolitan without reference to the Pariarchate of Constantinople. A plan was also emerging for a second volume which would cover the following century and a half.

John Fennell died suddenly in August 1992. The reaction of his publisher, Andrew MacLennan of Longman, was that every effort must be made to have Fennell's last work published with the least delay. This view was shared by his colleagues in Russian studies and by the late author's family. Here was a fitting monument to this distinguished historian; and furthermore a contribution towards a dialogue between the two mainstreams of Christendom, Orthodox and Latin. The question still remained of how close Fennell's text was to its intended final form. This required a fine judgement from those who best knew him, and his work. Andrew MacLennan invited two of Fennell's colleagues – one a valued collaborator and friend of long standing and the other a former pupil – to read the typescript and offer an opinion. The message from both, Professor Andrzej Poppe of Warsaw University and Dr Jonathan Shepard of Cambridge, was not merely that the project must go ahead, but that Fennell's text was virtually ready for the press.

There remained several tasks: the checking of references; the transliteration of Cyrillic in the footnotes and in the text; the preparation of the bibliography. These were important in themselves, but involved no impingement on Fennell's main text. Professor Wladimir Vodoff of the Sorbonne undertook to check the references and prepare a bibliography; Virginia Llewellyn Smith, herself a one-time pupil of John Fennell, dealt with matters concerned with the Russian language, including transliteration from Cyrillic. Professor Vodoff kindly made himself available throughout the editorial process to resolve any queries on the subject matter, and to provide any further clarifications.

Dorothy McCarthy was invited by Longman to assume the responsibility for copy-editing. This was a delicate task, calling for an intervention minimal yet sufficient to achieve a finished product that the author himself would have wished for. Ms McCarthy's response to this not inconsiderable challenge was finely weighed and assured. Amendments to Fennell's original text were made only on the rare occasions when revision appeared necessary for the sake of clarity. Ms McCarthy devised a set of succinct chapter headings to accord with the author's style and his own suggestion for the subdivision of the narrative. The only change to the structure of the book was the reversal of the order of the last two chapters. This Ms McCarthy did, after consultation with me, principally in order to maintain the same chapter sequence in the two parts of the book. The designation of Grand *Prince* applied by Fennell to the rulers of the Grand Duchy of Lithuania instead of the generally used title of Grand *Duke*, was retained by the publisher for reasons of consistency with the author's earlier books.

Here then is the result of this sympathetic and at the same time minimalist editorial enterprise. Readers familiar with John Fennell's writing will at once recognize the elegance of the scholarly exposition, the style, and the occasional touch of dry humour. It is all there, undisturbed. And those familiar with the pattern of Fennell's search for the essence of medieval Rus' will also recognize this, his last book, as a natural, indeed inevitable outcome of the indivisibility of that search and of his personal spiritual journey.

Michał Giedroyć
Oxford, 20 April 1994

PART ONE

CHAPTER ONE

An Outline of Kievan History, to 1240

1

It is difficult to become acquainted with the history of the Russian Church without some background knowledge of at least the bare outlines of the political and social history of the Russian State in each of the periods under investigation. But in this, the first period, where to begin?

Perhaps the first question we ought to put is: who were the Russians? Where did they come from? The prehistory of the Eastern Slavs, however, is complex and largely conjectural. Rather, therefore, than inflict upon the reader a summary of the often conflicting views of scholars on the subject, it is proposed here to start with the mid-ninth century when the Varangians or Vikings from Scandinavia began to penetrate the vast complex of Slavonic tribes, as well as some of Finno-Ugric and Baltic extraction, which inhabited the lands watered by the upper reaches of the Dnepr, Volga, Western Dvina and Western Bug rivers and the east bank of the Dnestr, an area stretching from the Gulf of Finland and Karelia in the north to the Carpathians in the south-west. The aim of their penetration was Byzantium, and their route the Dnepr down to the Black Sea.

Now, in the earliest Russian chronicle (the so-called *Tale of Bygone Years* or, as it is now more commonly known, the Primary Chronicle), the final editing of which dates from the second decade of the twelfth century, we are told how in 859 the Scandinavian Varangians came from over the Baltic Sea and began to levy tribute on the northern tribes. Three years later these same tribes chased out the Varangians, but owing to their inability to rule themselves, decided to send for their previous masters: 'They went beyond the [Baltic] Sea to the

Varangians, to the Rus′, for these Varangians were called Rus′, just as other Varangians are called Swedes, and others Norwegians, Angles, and others Gotlanders – so too these [were called Rus′].' Their request was simple and it smacks of folklore, as does the reaction of the Varangian 'Rus′':

> 'Our land is great and abundant, but there is no order in it. Come and rule and take command over us.' And three brothers were chosen with their clans and they took all Rus′ with them and came. And the eldest, Ryurik, settled in Novgorod; the second, Sineus, in Beloozero [the White Lake district north-east of Novgorod] and the third, Truvor, in Izborsk [south-west of Novgorod]. And from these Varangians the Russian land got its name.[1]

This naïve-sounding tale of the origins of the Russian State has given birth to one of the greatest and longest-lasting of all scholarly conflicts in Russian historiography – the so-called Normanist Controversy. It has worried and divided historians and linguists ever since the mid-eighteenth century. What role did the Varangians-Vikings-Normans-Norsemen from Scandinavia play? Were they 'summoned', as the chronicler would have us believe? And were *they* the Rus′ as the chronicle insists? Or were the *Slavs* the Rus′? Did Ryurik and his two 'brothers' actually exist? Was the dynasty of the ruling princely family which stemmed from the chronicle's 'Ryurik' predominantly Scandinavian or Slavonic? It would be tedious in the extreme to outline the by now tired arguments of both sides: of the 'Normanists', who tend to believe the general message of the chronicle; and the 'Anti-Normanists' (mostly Soviet), who consider that *Rus′* means Slavs, that the chronicle story is a dismissable myth and that the 'summoning' of the princes is merely a reflection of the tendency in medieval historiography to attribute the origins of the ruling dynasty of a nation to a foreign State (for example, the Venerable Bede's tale of the invitation of Hengist and Horsa to fight the Picts; *terra lata et spatiosa* ('a wide and spacious land'), they were allegedly told).[2]

Taking a 'Normanist' standpoint, this writer considers that the most reasonable and probable solution of the problem is as follows: in the first half of the ninth century, *Rus′*, from which *Russia(n)*, or, as some modern historians would have it, the ugly-looking '*Rus′sia(n)*', derives, clearly meant Scandinavian Varangians not only to the scribes and

---

1. *PVL*, vol. 1, p. 18.
2. For A. D. Stokes's brief outline of the controversy in English, see Auty and Obolensky (eds), *An Introduction to Russian History*, pp. 53–5, and p. 76 for a short bibliography.

editors of the Russian Primary Chronicle but also to contemporary and near-contemporary Greek, Arab and Latin writers.[3] It is unlikely that these Varangian-Rus' 'founded' any State on arrival (as some 'Normanists' claim), nor did they find a ready-made Slavonic State (as some 'anti-Normanists' think). One cannot talk of the establishment of anything more than a loose federation of tribes which came under the eventual overall control of the Varangians in the second half of the ninth century. But were these Varangian-Rus' 'summoned' in the first place? Or did they simply invade? Perhaps the anti-Normanist view of the mythical element in the summoning story of the chronicle is the correct one. But it matters little whether they came invited or whether they invaded. What does matter is that they stayed in the Russian land, that their leaders formed the ruling dynasty, their Scandinavian names becoming slavonicized (Helgi – Oleg; Ingvarr – Igor'; Helga – Ol'ga; perhaps Valdimarr – Vladimir, etc.), and that in a remarkably short time they were absorbed in the great Slavonic sea, just as the earlier Asiatic Bulgars, who in the seventh century had migrated to the predominantly Slavonic region near the mouth of the Danube, were absorbed by the native population.

Very little is known either of Ryurik's ethnic origins (was he Swedish, Danish?[4]) or of his career in Russia. It would appear that he settled in Novgorod in about 856 and quickly spread his authority over much of the north of present-day European Russia. As for Sineus and Truvor, no more is heard of them except that they died in 858. In the year after Ryurik's arrival in Russia, however, two members of his entourage, Askol'd and Dir, 'asked permission [to go] to Constantinople'.[5] On their way they seized the Slavonic settlement of Kiev on the Dnepr, subjugating the local west-bank tribe of the Polyane. In 860 they ineffectually besieged Constantinople and returned to consolidate their control over Kiev and its district.[6] Ryurik did nothing to

---

3. e.g. Constantine Porphyrogenitus in his *De administrando imperio*, pp. 58–9, gives the names of seven of the nine Dnepr rapids in 'Russian' (‘Ρωσιστί) and 'Slavonic' (Σκλαβηνιστί), and the Russian names derive from Old Swedish; a number of Arab ninth- and tenth-century travellers and geographers distinguish between 'Russians' (Rūs) and Slavs (as-Saqāliba); the ninth-century *Annales Bertiniani*, p. 31, record that a party of *Rhos* amongst the Byzantine ambassadors to Louis the Pious at Ingelheim on the Rhine admitted under interrogation that they were Swedes, while in the tenth century the Italian author Bishop Liutprand of Cremona in his *Relatio*, p. 9, calls the *Russios Nortmannos'* ('Constantinopolitana urbs habet ab Aquilone . . . Russios, quos alio nomine Nortmannos appellamus . . .').
4. Vernadsky identifies Ryurik with Rorik of Jutland (*Ancient Russia*, pp. 337–9).
5. *PVL*, vol. 1, p. 18.
6. See below, pp. 22–3.

interfere with their rule in the south, but after his death in 879, his kinsman Oleg, who seems to have been appointed as regent for Ryurik's son Igor', killed Askol'd and Dir, took Kiev and made it the capital of his realm, thus uniting the whole of Rus' from the Gulf of Finland to the lower reaches of the Dnepr river. One after another the neighbouring tribes to the north-west, the north and the east of Kiev were brought under Oleg's control.

Why did Oleg abandon the security of Novgorod, close to the source of Varangian mercenaries in Scandinavia? The answer must be found in the lure of Constantinople. For after some twenty-five years of consolidation Oleg attacked Constantinople (907) and obliged the Greeks to sign a treaty which opened the Black Sea for Russo-Varangian commerce with Byzantium and perhaps even gave Oleg a foothold in what was to become for Russia the important centre of Tmutarakan' on the Kuban' peninsula.

Concerning Igor''s reign (913–44), only fragmentary information is available. Little is known of his dealings with the subject tribes: the chronicle does not tell us how they were administered or what their relations with Kiev were. All that we know is that the neighbouring Drevlyane killed Igor' as a result of his extortionate demands for tribute: 'he was tied to two trees', according to the tenth-century Byzantine historian Leo the Deacon, 'and torn into two parts'.[7] His wife Ol'ga is said to have avenged his death by slaughtering a large number of Drevlyane in various bizarre and bloody ways.[8] Abroad he undertook two raids on Byzantine territory (941 and 944), the second of which ended with yet another trade treaty similar to that of Oleg in 907.

Igor''s successor to the throne of Kiev, Svyatoslav, was the odd man out amongst all the rulers of Russia from his grandfather Ryurik to Ivan the Terrible: glamorous, tough, adventurous, militarily highly successful, the archetypal warrior-prince:

> His gait was as light as a panther's and he waged many a war. On his campaigns he took no waggons with him, no kettles, nor did he boil his meat; but he would cut thin strips of horse-flesh or the meat of wild beasts or beef, cook them on coals and eat them. He had no tent, but would spread a piece of saddle-cloth beneath him and would use his saddle as a pillow.[9]

7. Leo Diaconus, *Historia*, p. 106
8. *PVL*, vol. 1, pp. 40–2. See below, p. 27.
9. *PVL*, vol. 1, p. 46.

Describing his meeting with Emperor John Tzimisces, Leo the Deacon gives us the following picture of his physical appearance:

> He was of medium height, neither too tall nor too short, with bushy eyebrows, blue eyes, a flat nose, a shaven beard, with thick long hairs hanging down from his upper lip. His head was completely shaven – on one side, however, a lock of hair hung down signifying nobility of birth. His neck was thick, his shoulders broad, and his figure was well-proportioned. He appeared gloomy and fierce. From one ear there hung a gold earring adorned with two pearls and a ruby inserted between them. His clothing was white and in no way different from that of the others with him – except for its cleanliness.[10]

His foreign adventures – and this is practically all we know about his activities in general – were on a far grander scale than those of his predecessors. It would appear that his eastern campaigns (966–67) were aimed at clearing the Volga of hostile forces, opening up trade routes with the east, penetrating the Caucasus and perhaps even gaining a foothold on the Byzantine possessions in the Crimea. I say 'it would appear', because in fact all we have are the barest details: an attack on the Moslem State of 'Old Great Bulgaria' at the junction of the Volga and Kama rivers;[11] war with the vast Khazar Kaganate stretching from the Volga in the east to the Don and the lower reaches of the Dnepr in the west – war which ended with the defeat of the Khazars and the fall of their capital Itile on the estuary of the Volga; victory over the north-Caucasian Ossetians and Circassians which presumably brought him to the Taman' peninsula on the east bank of the straits of Kerch.[12]

But can we believe that such a vast campaign was possible in the course of two – or even three or four – years? How many warriors did Svyatoslav have at his disposal? How many boats, waggons? How did he cover the huge distances: Kiev to Bulgary (he is said to have sailed up the Oka and Volga rivers[13]), Bulgary to the Caspian, the Caspian to within striking distance of the Sea of Azov and the eastern promontory of the Crimea? Did he overcome the whole of Khazaria? Owing to the paucity of the sources, these questions are impossible to answer. We can, however, gauge the long-term results.

Certainly the attack on Bulgary, if it ever took place, does not seem to have been decisive, for the Old Bulgar State continued to be a

10. Leo Diaconus, *Historia*, pp. 156–7.
11. The only details come from an Arab source, Ibn Hauqal, who gives the year as 969 (*PVL*, vol. 2, pp. 310–11). The Primary Chronicle makes no mention of the attack on Bulgary.
12. *PVL*, vol. 1, p. 47.
13. Ibid., p. 46.

thorn in Russia's side for many a year. Nor do we hear of any lasting results of Svyatoslav's conquest of the Ossetians and Circassians. But Khazaria appears to have been disastrously debilitated by Svyatoslav's invasion, and, as historians never tire of pointing out, the virtual destruction of the great buffer State on the south-east borders of Russia opened the floodgates to the nomadic Turkic hordes from the east who were to plague the Russians for centuries to come.

But the most immediate result of Svyatoslav's eastern campaign was the fact that his conquests brought him into close contact with Byzantine possessions on the north of the Black Sea. Whether he intended to round off his expedition by attacking the Crimea we do not know. But evidently the emperor Nicephorus Phocas considered that the situation was a highly dangerous one for Byzantium. In early 967 he urged, and heavily bribed, Svyatoslav to attempt an easier military objective – trans-Danubian Bulgaria, the old enemy of Byzantium. The lure was great: not only was Svyatoslav attracted by tales of the fabulous wealth of the country, but also he realized that the conquest of Bulgaria could bring him to the very gates of Constantinople.

His first Balkan campaign (967) was immediately successful: a Bulgarian army was defeated, a number of towns on the Danube were captured (eighty, according to the generous reckoning of the Primary Chronicle) and he established his headquarters in Little Preslav (*Pereyaslavets* is the Russian version), probably near the influx of the Prut into the Danube, i.e. in the extreme north-east corner of Bulgaria. Worried by Svyatoslav's initial successes, Nicephorus made peace with the Bulgarians and in all probability set the nomadic Turkic Pechenegs on Kiev (968). Leaving his army in Little Preslav, Svyatoslav hastened home, defeated the Pechenegs and spent a year in Kiev appointing his sons as viceroys, but mainly collecting reinforcements for Bulgaria. In August 969 he was back. Having captured the capital city, Preslav, he moved south, sacked Philippopolis on the Maritsa river and reached Adrianopolis in Byzantine territory. In the spring of 971 the new emperor, John Tzimisces, invaded Bulgaria and occupied all the territories seized by Svyatoslav's army. Svyatoslav was forced to acknowledge defeat. He withdrew with the remnants of his army. At the Dnepr rapids he was attacked by the Pechenegs – sent again, no doubt, by the Greeks – and was killed by them in the spring of 972.

So Svyatoslav's Bulgarian venture which had started so gloriously ended in abject failure. It was the severest military setback ever experienced by Russo-Varangian forces. There was no wealth in it for Svyatoslav, and although at one time he was close to Constantinople there was no opportunity of besieging or attacking it. But from a cultural and a religious point of view the results were inestimable; for many were the Russians – fighters, non-combatants, camp-followers, male and female – who stayed in Bulgaria and settled there, and many the Bulgarians who found their way to Russia either as prisoners of war or as refugees. Needless to say, the exchange of cultures was all to the Russians' benefit. Preslav, the capital, which Tsar Simeon (893–927) had attempted to convert into a second Constantinople, was the centre of Bulgarian Orthodoxy (accepted in 864 from Byzantium) and the cradle of Old Slavonic literature – albeit mostly in translation from the Byzantine Greek – which the Russians were to borrow from at a later date. And many a Russo-Varangian had witnessed the glory of Preslav. Could they have failed to be impressed and influenced?[14]

Svyatoslav's successor on the throne of Kiev, his eldest son Yaropolk (973–78), may well have been one of the beneficiaries of the Bulgarian campaigns, for not only was his Greek wife a former nun imported by Svyatoslav himself from Bulgaria, but, as will be seen in the next chapter, he may even have been converted to Christianity. Practically nothing is known of his brief reign, except that towards the end of it he was master not only of Kiev but also of the land of the Drevlyane (the domain of his brother Oleg, who had died after being defeated by him), of Novgorod (abandoned by his half-brother Vladimir, who had 'fled' to Scandinavia to collect an army of Varangians having learned that 'Yaropolk had killed Oleg'[15]) and probably of most of the districts of the future Kievan State. Of more interest is the information reported in the sixteenth-century Nikon Chronicle to the effect that Yaropolk, having 'defeated the Pechenegs and levied tribute on them', took the wise step of receiving into his service a Pecheneg khan ('Prince Ildey' in the Russian text). 'And he gave him cities and districts, and held him in great honour',[16] thus initiating the practice of so many of his successors of allying themselves with various Turkic aggressors and using their troops to defend their frontiers against the nomads themselves.[17] His life ended violently: his half-brother Vladimir had him assassinated in 978, took possession of his Greek wife and sat upon his throne.[18]

14. For the importance of Russia's Bulgarian links in the propagation of Christianity in Kiev, see below, p. 44.

15. *PVL*, vol. 1, p. 54.

16. *PSRL*, vol. 9, p. 39.

17. Note that when Vladimir in 978 attacked Yaropolk in Kiev, Yaropolk was advised by a retainer to flee to the Pechenegs and bring back an army to confront Vladimir. *PVL*, vol. 1, p. 55.

18. *PVL* (vol. 1, pp. 55–6) has 980 as the date of his murder. But it also states (p. 17) that Vladimir (d. 1015) ruled 37 years, i.e. from 978. See Nazarenko, 'Rus' i Germaniya', p. 66 n. 88.

2

The outstanding spiritual and cultural achievement of Vladimir's long reign (978–1015) was of course his acceptance of Christianity and his mass baptism of the Russian people, which are discussed more fully in the next chapter. But his political achievements, both at home and abroad, were also considerable.

His first recorded act as ruler of Kiev was to rid himself of many of his Varangian mercenaries who had facilitated his return to Russia from Scandinavia: those who were anxious to enrich themselves at the expense of the local Kievan population were sent packing to Constantinople where they could serve, out of harm's way, in the emperor's army. The loyal and useful members of his entourage ('the good, the wise and the brave'[19]) he settled in outlying towns, probably to stiffen the resistance of the southern and south-eastern frontiers against the Pechenegs.

He lost little time in consolidating his position by militarily bringing to heel the recalcitrant, troublesome tribes to the north and the east of Kiev (the Radimichi and the Vyatichi)[20] and by establishing a defensive line of fortifications against steppe marauders. In the west he seized the important centres of Cherven' and Peremyshl' (981)[21] at the expense of Bohemia – both vital trade points with Cracow and Prague and the source of the bulk of Kiev's salt import. Two years later he conquered the Baltic tribe of the Yatvingians[22] on the upper Neman and Western Bug rivers, perhaps with the aim of finding an outlet to the Baltic Sea. And in the north-east he defeated the Volga Bulgars in 985,[23] previously attacked by his father Svyatoslav in 966,[24] and concluded a pact of friendship with them, thus securing the Oka and the upper reaches of the Volga from invasion.

Apart from the momentous events surrounding Vladimir's acceptance of Christianity – the initial pagan revival, the choice of faiths, the baptism, the Byzantine bride, the Cherson campaign – and apart from the above-mentioned political and military achievements, very little is known about his activities, especially in the latter part of his reign.

19. *PVL*, vol. 1, p. 56.
20. Ibid., pp. 58, 59.
21. Ibid., p. 58.
22. Ibid.
23. Ibid., p. 59.
24. See above, p. 7.

The chronicle is singularly reticent. Indeed, of the sixteen years from 998 to 1013, eleven are left blank and only the most superficial jottings are contained in the remaining five. Either whoever compiled the record of Vladimir's last years ran out of steam, which is unlikely when one considers how much adulatory material was crammed into the first nineteen years, or perhaps a later editor simply excised events which did not redound to his credit or, more likely, to the credit of his famous and glorious son Yaroslav, called 'the Wise'. For in 1014 Yaroslav, by then ruler of Novgorod, began withholding tribute to his father in Kiev, and, learning of Vladimir's intention to march against him, imported Varangian mercenaries from 'over the sea' to oppose him. For the time being Russia was saved from the first of its many bouts of internecine war only by Vladimir's death in 1015.

The year 1015 marked the beginning of a period of mayhem, murder and eventually civil war. It was perhaps inevitable that Vladimir's death should be followed by a relentless struggle for power amongst his sons. For, as can be imagined, his many marriages – and even more liaisons – spawned a large number of descendants, most of whom were only too anxious to grab what power, land and wealth they could. Little seems to have been done by Vladimir himself to forestall the inevitable chaos other than to settle a number of his sons in various parts of the country; but what their political allegiance to their father consisted of is unknown: unless it was simply the collection of tribute and the dispatch of part of it to Kiev. Nor do we have any firm idea who if anyone was designated by him as his successor; it is not even certain who *was* his eldest descendant, legitimate or otherwise. Three sons (Boris, Gleb and Svyatoslav) were murdered – by whom it is not certain, though the hagiographers of the first two, who were both later canonized as martyrs (or 'passion-sufferers'), lay the blame fairly and squarely on the shoulders of a convenient scapegoat in the person of Svyatopolk (son of Yaropolk or of Vladimir?[25]), who occupied the throne of Kiev on Vladimir's death. The internecine war

25. After Vladimir had had Yaropolk murdered, he 'lay with his brother's Greek wife, and she was pregnant . . . and from her was born Svyatopolk . . . Vladimir lay with her not in marriage, for he was an adulterer. For this reason his father [i.e. Vladimir] did not love him, for he was from two fathers, Yaropolk and Vladimir' (*PVL*, vol. 1, p. 56). Note that 'was pregnant' could be either '*became* pregnant' or 'was already pregnant': the verb *bě* is aorist, but is also frequently used in early texts as an imperfect. The passage quoted was almost certainly composed during Yaroslav's reign (1036–54), hence the harsh appraisal of Vladimir.

which followed only ended in 1019 when Svyatopolk died in exile having been defeated by Yaroslav, the then ruler of Novgorod.

Yaroslav, however, was not the eldest surviving son of Vladimir, and it was not until 1036 that he emerged as the sole and undisputed ruler of Rus'. All his many brothers had by then either died or been otherwise disposed of – with one exception, the unfortunate Sudislav, who in 1036 was thrown into gaol, where he remained until after Yaroslav's death. What had happened to all the other brothers we shall never know, for the only source of events from 1015 to Yaroslav's death in 1054, the Primary Chronicle, clearly went through a very strict editing process before or just after Yaroslav's death. All we are left with are the glorious achievements of Yaroslav 'the Wise': his wars against Pechenegs, Yatvingians, Lithuanians, Poles, Finns, Greeks; his great building programme of monasteries and churches; his embellishment and transformation of Kiev into a city of beauty and culture.

The fifty-nine years following his death (1054–1113) were years of appallingly complex internecine wars between his numerous sons and grandsons and of rare moments of peace. The chaos caused by the in-fighting and the squabbling of the 'princes',[26] as *all* the male descendants of Ryurik were designated, was complicated by the irruption of a new enemy, the Turkic Polovtsians (*Polovtsy*),[27] who replaced the Pechenegs in the southern steppes and who harassed the Kievan State for a century and a half after their first raid in 1061.

But why and how did the chaos start in the first place? The main cause was undoubtedly the vexed question of succession. Prior to 1054 it looks as though the law of the jungle prevailed, ruler succeeding ruler by brute force. Before his death, so the Primary Chronicle tells us, Yaroslav admonished his sons to live in peace, 'brother heeding brother', and to maintain his distribution of territories: the eldest surviving son (Izyaslav) being given Kiev; the second eldest (Svyatoslav) Chernigov; the third (Vsevolod) Pereyaslavl' and so on. What exactly this meant as far as succession to the throne of Kiev as well as to the other lesser thrones was concerned, Yaroslav – or the chronicler, more likely – forbore to mention. It seems probable, however, that the 'system', if it can so be called, ideally envisaged *lateral* succession to the supreme throne (brother succeeding brother until all the brothers died,

---

26. *knyaz'*, plur. in Old Russian '*knyazi*', in modern Russian *knyaz'ya* – probably derived from the Nordic kuning/king.

27. Their Russian name. The Byzantines called them Cumans; they called themselves Kipchaks.

then the sons of the eldest brother followed by the sons of the second eldest brother and so on), while all the surviving sons of Yaroslav, including the eldest, were given *patrimonies* which were to be their permanent possessions – i.e. which could be disposed of within each branch of the family. It did not of course mean that each time a prince died the other members of the family all moved up a peg. It just meant that Kiev and all that went with it – the principality itself, the headship of the clan and perhaps some claim on Novgorod such as the right to place a son as ruler there – fell to whoever was senior in this lateral or horizontal system, but that each prince also had his own patrimonial nest which, ideally again, should remain in perpetuity in his particular branch of the family.

Of course it didn't work. There were too many members of the family – Yaroslav had had six sons – too many dispossessed and therefore rebellious princes whose fathers had died early or whose lands had been appropriated by stronger relatives, too many squabbles over territory and power, and, above all, too few princes of the calibre and the toughness of a Yaroslav or a Vladimir to command the respect and the obedience of their relatives. So Yaroslav's descendants fought one another, displaced one another, called in outside help for their fratricidal wars, tried – usually in vain – to resist the Polovtsians. At the same time local town populations were beginning to show that they too had a voice, that they too could influence affairs. In 1068, for example, after a meeting of the city assembly (*veche*) of Kiev, the populace deposed the senior prince, Izyaslav, and replaced him with a captive relative of his whom they freed from the dungeons. It was not the last time that the people of Kiev were to play a decisive role in the history not only of the city itself but also of the whole of Kievan Rus'.

In 1113 the political situation in Russia changed suddenly and dramatically. An energetic, intelligent and statesmanlike grandson of Yaroslav, Vladimir Monomakh (thus named probably in honour of his maternal grandfather Constantine IX Monomachus[28]), became prince of Kiev – not through observing the 'rules' of lateral succession (according to this 'system', a first cousin of his should have succeeded to the throne), but because rioting broke out in Kiev on the death of his predecessor. The long-suffering populace, after decades of misrule and governmental inefficiency, its anger exacerbated by the money-lenders' exorbitant interest rates, set about plundering those who were

---

28. Obolensky, *Six Byzantine Portraits*, pp. 84–5.

considered responsible for the chaotic state of affairs. Knowing Vladimir Monomakh to be the only man capable of averting what threatened to become a social revolution, the *veche* begged him to come and rule.

Both Vladimir Monomakh (1113–25) and his son Mstislav 'the Great' (1125–32) managed somehow to restore a semblance of unity in Russia. The two decades of their rule were the period of the greatest strength and solidarity of the Kievan State from Yaroslav's death to the capture of Kiev by the Mongols in 1240. Their authority was undisputed. Both were able to ensure unconditional obedience from all the princes. The power of the Polovtsians was broken largely by their energetic and skilful military activity: as a result the Polovtsy were pushed away from the traditional trade routes and many of the numerous khanates were rendered innocuous by intermarriage with Russians and by conversion to Christianity; many too were dispersed, some to Georgia, some to Hungary. They were no longer the menace they had been in the last decades of the eleventh century.

The unity achieved by Vladimir and his son, however, was only temporary. From 1132 onwards the Kievan State entered into a period of steady political decline. It was not that there were no strong and intelligent princes in the family. There were: Yury Dolgorukiy, Andrey Bogolyubskiy (the son and grandson of Vladimir Monomakh) and Yury's son Vsevolod III. But their spheres of influence were not Kiev but north-east Russia.

Within Kievan Rus' — that is to say, the district of Kiev itself, Volynia in West Russia, Turov, Smolensk, Chernigov and Pereyaslavl' — fragmentation of the individual principalities and a bitter three-cornered struggle between two branches of Vladimir Monomakh's descendants and the princes of Chernigov (the descendants of Yaroslav's second eldest son) were, in all probability, the main causes of Kiev's decline, rather than lack of Byzantine commercial interest or Polovtsian danger in the south. Separate branches of the Ryurikovichi concentrated more and more on areas which came to be recognized as their inalienable heritages: one branch of Mstislav's descendants, for example, built up their patrimonies in West Russia (Volynia and Galicia), another in Smolensk; while the old principality of Chernigov split into two major sectors: Chernigov and Novgorod-Severskiy, which in their turn split into yet smaller principalities.

Of course, in the hundred years between Mstislav's death and the Mongol invasion of 1237 there were periods of stability in Kiev, and the stability depended largely on the power and the intelligence of whoever happened to be prince of Kiev. And Kiev was still 'the mother of the Russian cities'; it was still the great lure and prize of the warring princes, who struggled to assume the prestigious title of 'prince of Kiev'.

Real power, however, shifted to the north-east, to the 'land beyond the forests' (or Suzdalia as it is often called) centred in the earliest period on the towns of Rostov and Suzdal', *and later on Vladimir-on-the-Klyaz'ma* river, founded by Vladimir Monomakh in 1108. The first of the memorable builders of north-east Rus' was Yury Dolgorukiy, prince of Suzdal' (died 1157), aptly called by an imaginative historian 'the Christopher Columbus of the Povolzh'e [the upper-Volga district]'.[29] During his rule the Rostov-Suzdal' State took shape: frontiers in the south with Chernigov and in the west with Novgorod became fixed; new towns, including Moscow, were built, some with names borrowed from the south (for example, Pereyaslavl' Zalesskiy – 'beyond the forests' again); colonization was vigorously fostered; links with the south were strengthened (Yury himself was twice prince of Kiev); and his many sons were set to rule the major towns, some even controlling districts in the south at the same time. His son Andrey Bogolyubskiy (1157–74: so named from the palace he built at Bogolyubovo near Vladimir) did still more to strengthen Suzdalia by extending his frontiers eastwards along the Klyaz'ma in an attempt to secure the Volga and Oka rivers from attacks by the Volga Bulgars; while in the far north, in the lands watered by the Northern Dvina – and nominally controlled by Novgorod – his influence was beginning to be felt. At the same time he showed few aspirations for power in Kiev: a son of his seized Kiev in 1163 and that same son put Andrey's brother on the throne. Andrey preferred to concentrate his energies in the north-east, where he made Vladimir his capital. As will be seen later,[30] he even attempted to establish ecclesiastical independence of Suzdalia from Kiev.

Two years after Andrey's death in 1174, the throne of Vladimir was taken over by his youngest brother Vsevolod III (1176–1212), the first ruler officially to assume the title of 'grand prince' (*velikiy knyaz'*), and not of Kiev but of his capital, Vladimir. Like his brother, he strengthened the power and authority of Vladimir-Suzdalia by shifting the frontiers west and east and by penetrating still further north into Novgorod territory. Not only supreme ruler of north-east Russia, where his many sons treated him with the utmost respect and obedi-

29. Presnyakov, *Obrazovanie*, p. 27.
30. See below, p. 54.

ence, but also recognized in the south by all the descendants of Vladimir Monomakh and the princes of Chernigov as *primus inter pares*, indeed as overlord in all Russia, he somehow managed to control – at times, it seems, to mastermind – the wayward and capricious behaviour of his hot-headed cousins in what had once been Kievan Rus'. As the great-grandson of Vladimir Monomakh, the tough and resilient Ryurik Rostislavich, admitted to his son-in-law Roman Mstislavich in 1195: 'We cannot exist without Vsevolod: we have placed in him the seniority amongst all [our] cousins in the tribe of Vladimir [Monomakh]';[31] and in 1203 we find Roman, then all-powerful ruler of Galicia and Volynia and recent master of Kiev, known to Western chroniclers as 'Rex Russiae' and 'Rex Ruthenorum',[32] talking of Vsevolod as 'father and master'.[33] Vsevolod seemed to treat southern Rus' as his own: he placed princes on thrones (including that of Kiev); he distributed towns, now to one now to another; he threatened armed intervention to keep the fragile peace or, when necessary, used diplomacy to avert war. In the major struggle for mastery over Kiev between Vsevolod Chermnyy ('the Red') of Chernigov and Ryurik Rostislavich, which lasted from 1205 to 1212 and in which Kiev changed hands no less than five times, Vsevolod wisely refrained from intervening, letting his squabbling cousins fight it out for themselves. He died in 1212, having ruled north-east Russia with skill, tact and patience and having manipulated political power in the south for much of his reign as grand prince of Vladimir.

The days of the supremacy of the grand prince of Vladimir were over, at least for the time being. The eleven years before the first exploratory invasion of the Mongols in 1223 saw fierce in-fighting amongst Vsevolod's sons, and it was only in 1218 that his second eldest surviving son, Yury, managed to establish himself firmly on the throne of Vladimir. By contrast, the south of Russia was relatively stable, that is to say was largely in the hands of the Rostislavichi once more. For from the death of Vsevolod's namesake, Vsevolod Chermnyy of Chernigov, also in 1212, the Chernigov princes kept themselves to themselves and did not intrude into the Kievan scene until long after 1223. With little or no interference from Chernigov the Rostislavichi were able to extend their influence over most of southern Russia, and by 1223 Kiev, Galicia (after a period of turmoil and

31. *PSRL*, vol. 2, cols. 685–6.
32. Fennell, *The Crisis*, p. 24.
33. *PSRL*, vol. 1, col. 419.

occupation by Poles and Hungarians), Smolensk and probably Pere-yaslavl' and Turov were in their hands, while most of Volynia was held by 'King' Roman Mstislavich's son Daniil.

In early 1223 a Mongol[34] army, or perhaps a probing reconnoitring force, from the empire of Chinghis Khan appeared in the southern steppes. After various skirmishes with the Mongol outposts, the Russian army, consisting of troops from Galicia, Smolensk, Kiev, Turov-Pinsk and Chernigov and stiffened by Polovtsians who had first brought the news of the invasion to the Russians, met, and was defeated by, the Mongols on the river Kalka (a tributary of the Kalmius which flows into the Sea of Azov west of the river Don?). Although the Mongols chased the remnants of the Russian army to the Dnepr, they went no further than a small town on the west bank of the river, which they sacked. They then withdrew.

The various chronicles which report the invasion and the fighting give no reliable clues as to the dimensions of the Russian defeat. All we know is that nine princes were killed, which is half the number of those that took part; perhaps, then, about half of the Russian troops were casualties. As for the Polovtsians, they were no longer a force to be reckoned with after 1223. The north of Russia escaped scot-free. No troops from Suzdal' or Novgorod took any part in the fighting.

Most curious of all is the total lack of concern shown by the contemporary chroniclers. They had no idea who these new invaders were: 'They returned from the river Dnepr, and we know not whence they came and whither they went. Only God knows...'[35] Just another steppe invasion perhaps? The Russians had not long to wait before they found out.

They had just fourteen years of respite, years in which nothing whatsoever seems to have been done to prepare for the return of the enemy. In Suzdalia, although internecine war had virtually ceased, no attempts were made to establish a central command which might

34. The Mongols were originally one of the tribes inhabiting present-day Mongolia. In the twelfth century they were defeated by their neighbours the Tatars. The term 'Mongol' has survived because Chinghis Khan was of Mongol stock. However, contemporary Russian sources invariably used 'Tatar' to denote the Mongols in Russia, and there is considerable conflict in the use of 'Mongol' and 'Tatar' in Russian historiography. In this book the term 'Mongol' will be used instead of 'Tatar-Mongol' and 'Tatar'. Note that the basic ethnic substratum of the 'Tatar-Mongols' who subsequently controlled the Russian lands from the Kipchak Horde were Turkic steppe-nomads – in the main Kipchaks/Polovtsians. See Khoroshkevich and Pliguzov, in Fennel (*sic*), *Krizis*, p. 20.
35. *NPL*, pp. 63, 267. For a detailed account in English of the events of 1223 (as well as of the subsequent major invasion), see Fennell, *The Crisis*, pp. 63–8, 76–83.

facilitate resistance in case of a repeat invasion. In the south the relative stability of the eleven years from the two Vsevolods' deaths to 1223 continued for a few more years. But it was too good to last. In 1235 civil war broke out and we find the principalities of Galicia, Smolensk and Chernigov – the latter resuscitated under the vigorous leadership of Vsevolod Chermnyy's son Mikhail – at each other's throats, all fighting for control over the south. In the five years before the eventual fall of Kiev to the Mongols in 1240, the city changed hands no less than seven times. By 1237 the southern princes had exhausted their resources. Totally disorganized, disorientated and disunited, they were to prove no match for the Mongols. And the northerners, for all their political equilibrium and lack of inter-princely friction, seemed to be living in a dream world of false security, utterly oblivious of the menace on their borders.

The great invasion of the Tatar-Mongol armies under Chinghis Khan's grandson, Khan Baty, began in the winter of 1237 with the capture of Ryazan', followed by that of Vladimir-on-the-Klyaz'ma (February 1238), the defeat of the main Suzdalian army under Grand Prince Yury on the river Sit' north-west of Uglich (March 1238) and the nearly simultaneous capture of the south-easternmost town in Novgorod territory, Torzhok (also in March 1238). Novgorod was left untouched, and, after taking Kozel'sk in the north of the district of Chernigov, the Mongols left for the southern steppes to rest and regroup. In the spring of 1239 the final phase began: Pereyaslavl' fell in March, Chernigov in the autumn. With the capture of Kiev on 6 December 1240 the Russian campaign was virtually over. After taking Vladimir and Galich in the west, the Mongols moved into Hungary and Poland and began their attempt to conquer the rest of Europe.

3

Before leaving our historical outline of the period, a word must be said about Novgorod. Much of the prosperity and strength of whoever controlled Kiev, Suzdal' or Vladimir depended on Novgorod, the second largest city of medieval Russia, whose wealth came from trade – especially western trade – and from its huge northern colonies stretching in the twelfth century to the Arctic in the north and from the borders of Finland to the Urals.

From the earliest times the great city-state had been unable to defend itself from its enemies and had depended upon an extraneous prince (together with his army, of course) to fight its wars and defend its frontiers. What exactly the prince's functions in Novgorod were in the early days we do not know: no treaties, no contracts have survived. But presumably it was more than just being the city's military defender: no doubt he had other administrative and judicial functions to perform and presumably he was granted land and money as a reward for his services. It was irksome of course for the Novgorodians to have to rely on an outsider for their defence, to have to *ask* for a prince; and by the early twelfth century, as Novgorod's urge for independence grew, so little by little the power of its mercenary prince eroded: the office of *posadnik* (roughly the city's chief executive) became elective, chosen annually from Novgorodian boyars by the *veche* or town assembly; furthermore, the *veche* acquired the right to elect the city's bishop (archbishop from 1165). And from 1136, when a former prince of Kiev's son was arrested with his family and ignominiously ousted, Novgorod was able, in principle though by no means always in practice, to select its own prince from any dynastic line.

But it must not be imagined that Novgorod in the twelfth century and the first forty years of the thirteenth was in any way close to becoming a republic. Strong rulers could always oblige the city to accept their nominees and the really tough princes were able to impose their own terms on Novgorod. The fact is that Novgorod was always militarily vulnerable and whatever troops it could itself provide were never sufficient or competent enough to defend it. To make matters worse for Novgorod, the boyar groupings were as often as not divided in their allegiance to the purveyors of princely rulers and were rarely able to form a consolidated opposition to whoever was appointed their prince.

CHAPTER TWO

The Beginnings of Kievan Christianity

Although Russia became a Christian State only at the end of the tenth century, when the ruling prince was baptized and when the vast task of Christianizing the largely pagan population began, Christianity seems to have taken root still earlier amongst those living in the territory known as Kievan Rus'. I say 'seems to have taken root' because much of our knowledge of this earlier Russian Christianity is based on shaky sources: legend and myth, fragmentary and often contradictory evidence, hypotheses based on unsupported textual fragments, and so on. However, there can be no doubt that before 988, the date conventionally accepted nowadays for the 'baptism of Russia', there *were* Christians at the court of the prince of Kiev and elsewhere in his realm.

We need spend little time on considering the two earliest accounts of Christian penetration into Russia – the tales of the Apostle Andrew's visit to Russia and the conversion of Bravlin, both of which bear all the hallmarks of pure mythology. According to one of the first entries in the earliest Russian chronicle compilation, the *Tale of Bygone Years* or the Primary Chronicle, the Apostle Andrew, while preaching in the Greek colony of Sinope on the south shore of the Black Sea, decided to journey to Rome by the extraordinarily circuitous route via Cherson in the Crimea, the Dnepr river, the land of the Slovenians and Scandinavia. On the way he stopped first at the site of the future city of Kiev, where, predictably, he prophesied the founding of a great town with many churches; then 'he came to the [land of the] Slovenians where Novgorod now [stands]'. Here he observed the locals' peculiar ablutions. On his eventual arrival in Rome he told how he 'saw their wooden bath-houses which they heat to extremes. They strip, and, naked, pour a tannic decoction over themselves; they then take sapling switches and beat themselves to such an extent that they barely come out alive. They pour cold water over themselves and thus revive themselves.' This purely anecdotal and colourful description ends with a playful piece of rhyming punning, rare indeed for the Russian chronicler: 'tormented by no one, they torment themselves – ablution but not affliction (*moven'e, a ne muchen'e*).'¹ The sheer implausibility of the narrative is enhanced by the fact that a scribe writing in the same chronicle under the year 983 (perhaps even the same one who penned the Andrew tale) denies that any of the apostles had ever set foot in Russia.² Still, the story of Andrew's visit seems to have left its mark: Vsevolod, Vladimir I's grandson, not only founded the first Russian church dedicated to St Andrew (Kiev, 1086³), but had his son, Vladimir Monomakh, given the baptismal Christian name of Andrew; furthermore, one of his grandsons and one of his great-grandsons were the first Russian princes to be known by the name of Andrew.⁴ Indeed, the legend still remained firm in men's minds as late as the sixteenth century. Ivan the Terrible in 1582 told the papal envoy Antonio Possevino: 'We received our Christian faith from the early Church, when Andrew, the brother of the Apostle Peter, visited these lands on his way to Rome. We in Moscow [!] received the Christian Faith here in Muscovy [!] at the same time as you received it in Italy . . .'⁵

The story of the 'conversion of Prince Bravlin' is just as unlikely to have been based on fact as is the Andrew tale. The sources are even flimsier. In the fifteenth- or sixteenth-century Russian translation of the Greek *Life* of the eighth-century St Stephen, archbishop of Surozh (modern Sudak in the Crimea), one of the miracles describes the invasion of the Crimea by 'Prince Bravlin' from Novgorod, who captured Surozh, entered the church of St Sofia and plundered gold and silver vessels on the tomb of the saint. He was immediately punished by having his head twisted back to front. Realizing that the

---

1. *PVL*, vol. 1, p. 12; *PSRL*, vol. 2, cols. 6–7.

2. *PVL*, vol. 1, p. 59. Cf. Nestor's 'Lection' on the 'Life and Death of the Blessed Martyrs Boris and Gleb' (*AHE*, p. 3).

3. *PSRL*, vol. 2, col. 197. In 1089 a church of St Andrey was built in Southern Pereyaslavl' (*PVL*, vol. 1, p. 137).

4. Andrey Dobryy (d. 1142) and Andrey Bogolyubskiy (d. 1174). Note that after the conversion princes were given *additional* Christian names at baptism, but continued to be known by their secular names (e.g. Vladimir, Oleg, etc.). From the mid-eleventh century, however, they tend to be known by their *Christian* names, while still retaining their secular names.

5. Graham, *The Moscovia*, p. 69. On the possible dating of the Andrew legend, see Poppe, 'Two Concepts', pp. 497–501; Chichurov, '"Khozhdenie"', p. 14.

punishment had been inflicted by St Stephen, he ordered his boyars to replace the stolen goods and was rewarded by a vision of St Stephen who told him to accept baptism on the spot. Bravlin and his boyars were christened in the church they had just vandalized by Archbishop Philaret (St Stephen's immediate successor to the see of Surozh) and returned home after releasing all prisoners. Needless to say, no 'Bravlins'[6] are known to have existed at the end of the eighth or the ninth centuries, or at any other time for that matter, and no other sources mention him or his invasion of the Crimea. The whole episode looks all too much like the fruit of a later Russian scribe's fertile imagination.[7]

It was not until the second half of the ninth century that Christianity seems to have put out some tentative, but still credible, roots in the nascent Russian State. As we saw in the previous chapter, in approximately 857 or 858 two Varangian chieftains named Askol'd and Dir, 'not members of [Ryurik's] kin but boyars' according to the Primary Chronicle, moved south, seized and settled in what was to become the city of Kiev, and eventually, in 860, sailed down the Dnepr to the Black Sea with a flotilla of two hundred boats. On 18 June they laid siege to Constantinople. The horrors of the siege and the violence of the invaders were vividly illustrated in two homilies addressed to the inhabitants by the patriarch Photius. Yet when the siege was eventually lifted, clearly some sort of agreement was reached with the marauders: seven years later Patriarch Photius announced in an encyclical to the Patriarchs of the East that the people of Rus' had 'exchanged their heathen teaching . . . for the pure faith, having made themselves our subjects and friends . . . and had accepted a bishop and a pastor and were embracing the religious observances of the Christians with much zeal and fervour'.[8] It is perhaps worth remembering that in 864, three years before Photius's letter, the Bulgarians had accepted baptism from Byzantium.

Photius's encyclical is not the only source to talk of the treaty and the dispatch of a bishop to the heathen Rhos/Rus', but it is the closest to the events. The emperor Constantine Porphyrogenitus, writing in

6. Indeed, in one version of the translated miracle he is called *knyaz' branliv i silen zelo* ('a warlike and very strong prince').

7. On the 'Bravlin' episode, see Golubinsky, *IRTs*, vol. 1, I, pp. 53–62; Vernadsky, *Ancient Russia*, pp. 280–1; Vasil'evsky, *Trudy*, vol. III, pp. 95–6; Kartashev, *Ocherki*, pp. 64–8; Pritsak, 'At the Dawn', pp. 102 ff.

8. Photius, *PG*, vol. 102, col. 737. For a translation of and notes on Photius's two homilies (III and IV), see Mango, *The Homilies*, pp. 74–110.

the following century, also mentions a pact, baptism and a bishop, attributing the initiative to the emperor Basil I (867–86);[9] while Photius's successor and rival, Patriarch Ignatius, is said to have ordained an archbishop whom he sent to the 'people of Rhos' in 874 after the conclusion of a treaty.[10] From all this evidence it would appear that the invasion of 860 did lead to some form of agreement between Byzantium and its barbarian northern neighbours and that, although the Russian sources are silent on the outcome of the raid, nevertheless some form of tentative proselytizing clearly did take place. And might not Askol′d and Dir themselves, the rulers of Kiev at the time, have accepted baptism?

All we learn from the meagre information contained in the Russian chronicles is that they stayed in Kiev until 882, when they were killed by the soldiers of Ryurik's kinsman Oleg. However, the chronicler adds that 'they [the slayers of Askol′d and Dir] carried [Askol′d] to the hill and buried him on the hill which is now called the Hungarian Hill where Ol″ma's mansion is now situated; and on that grave Ol″ma built the church of St Nicholas; and Dir's grave is behind [the church of] St Irina'.[11] Who Ol″ma was is not known,[12] but the fact that a church was built on the site of Askol′d's grave and that the chronicler, writing at least a century and a half later, took the trouble to note that Dir's grave was close to the church (and monastery) of St Irina (built in 1037) might well indicate that both Varangians were believed in the eleventh century to have accepted baptism after their raid on Constantinople.

But even if this were true and even if Kiev in the 860s did become the see of a bishop or an archbishop sent by the patriarch, this, the first phase of Christianity in the Russian lands, lasted for only a short time, for Askol′d's and Dir's successor to the throne of Kiev, Oleg (882–912), seems to have been a resolute pagan.

The sparse chronicle entries devoted to his reign record only his military exploits: his subjugation of the neighbouring tribes and his attack on Constantinople in 907, which ended in a treaty highly favourable to the Russo-Varangians. The chronicler or chroniclers, again writing probably in the eleventh or the early twelfth century,

9. Kartashev, *Ocherki*, pp. 74–5; Litavrin and Florya, 'Obshchee i osobennoe', p. 237.

10. *Theophanes Continuatus*, pp. 342–3.

11. *PVL*, vol. 1, p. 20.

12. Though see Vernadsky (*Ancient Russia*, pp. 332, 341–2), who considers him to have been a Magyar *voevoda* and that *Ol″ma* = Olom.

clearly knew precious little about his reign: twenty years are left blank and much of the information given is remarkably fragmentary and unrevealing. But there are no mentions of Christianity in Rus', and when the Varangians conclude their treaty with the Greeks, they swear 'according to the law of Rus' by their weapons and by Perun their god and by Volos god of cattle'.[13] Furthermore, the description of the campaign of 907 against Constantinople ends with the words: 'Oleg was called the knowing one (*veshchiy*), for they were heathen and ignorant people.'[14] Evidently there were no traces left of Christianity in the State of Rus' – or else its practitioners were keeping a very low profile indeed. At the end of the description of the treaty between the Russians and the Greeks (dated 911 in the chronicle, but presumably referring to the treaty immediately following the campaign of 907), the chronicler adds: 'the emperor Leo honoured the Russian envoys with gifts . . . and attached his men to them to show them the beauty of the churches . . . instructing them in their faith and showing them the true faith'[15] – perhaps a later addition influenced by the entries under the year 988?[16]

Not until the last year of the reign of Igor' (913–14), Oleg's successor, do we learn again of the existence of Christians among the Russo-Varangians. The eleventh-century annalists clearly knew practically nothing about the events of Igor''s rule – indeed, twenty-two of the thirty-two years are left blank in the Primary Chronicle. However, after the description of his two raids on Byzantium in 941 and 944, we find some quite unequivocal references to Christianity recorded in the Primary Chronicle in the text of the treaty concluded with the Greeks in 944/945. After the introductory clause naming Igor''s envoys at the peace negotiations, merchants and military alike, we read in clause 2:

> Should anyone on the Russian side contemplate breaking this covenant, then let those of them who have accepted baptism incur retribution from Almighty God . . . and let those who have not been baptized receive no help either from God or from Perun, and may they not be protected by their own shields, but may they perish by their swords, by their arrows and by their other weapons . . .[17]

No less unambiguous are the details of oath-taking in Constantinople contained in the text of the treaty itself:

13. *PVL*, vol. 1, p. 25.
14. Ibid.
15. Ibid, p. 29.
16. See *PVL*, vol. 2, p. 280.
17. *PVL*, vol. 1, p. 35.

We, those of us who have been baptized, swore in the cathedral [of St Sophia in Constantinople] by the church of St Elias [Elijah] and upon the holy Cross and upon this charter, to observe everything that is written in it and not to violate any of it[s clauses]; and should anyone on our side violate them, whether he be prince or any other person, whether he be baptized or not baptized, may he have no help from God . . .[18]

Finally, the chronicler records the equivalent oath-taking ceremony in Kiev:

in the morning Igor' called the envoys and went to the hill where [the statue of] Perun stood and they laid down their arms and their gold[en accoutrements], and Igor' and whosoever of his men were pagan Russians took the oath, while the Christian Russians were led to the oath in the church of St Elias . . . this was the assembly church,[19] for there were many Christian Varangians and Khazarians.[20]

And so by the end of Igor''s reign Christianity had at last clearly begun to take root in the Kievan State: Christians in the army, Christians amongst the merchants, Christians amongst the neighbouring Khazarians living in Kiev, and all with their church. Of course we cannot tell how numerous they were, how influential, how close to the prince's court, nor can we tell how much of the above information was simply invented by monk-chroniclers of a different age attempting to show a few glimpses of light in the murk of pre-conversion paganism. But still, Christianity was there. It was a base on which future baptizers could build.

Yet two princes in a row show no signs of being infected by the new faith. Igor''s son Svyatoslav betrayed not the slightest willingness to consider conversion – quite the opposite in fact. When his mother Ol'ga, already a Christian, attempted to persuade him to accept baptism, she was rebuffed: 'he ignored what she said and did not listen to her'. He countered her frequent exhortations with the somewhat implausible argument that his retinue (*druzhina*) would laugh at him if he accepted Christianity, to which she replied: 'If you are baptized, then everyone will do the same', an explanation which, the chronicler tells us, made him exceedingly angry with his mother.[21]

---

18. Ibid., p. 38.
19. *Sbornaya tserkov'* – *not* cathedral church, which would have little meaning in early ninth-century Kiev, but 'the church where people gathered'. See Vodoff, *Naissance*, pp. 49, 380 n. 1. See also Golubinsky, *IRTs*, vol. 1, I, p. 497. There is, incidentally, no further mention of the church of St Elias in the chronicles.
20. *PVL*, vol. 1, p. 39.
21. *PVL*, vol. 1, p. 46, *s.a.* 955. If the date (955) is correct, then Svyatoslav was only 13 at the time. See below, p. 28, n. 25.

Although Svyatoslav, who was to become the great warrior, the victorious general, the archetypal fighter-prince, was only a boy at the time of this verbal brush with his mother, he appears to have remained totally indifferent towards Christianity for the rest of his reign. However, there is no evidence of active hostility to, or persecution of, the faith, nor are there any hints of a pagan revival during this period. We cannot say whether this was due to Svyatoslav's extreme preoccupation with military conquests and his seeming lack of interest in home affairs (he is reported to have said to his mother and his boyars in 969: 'it is not pleasing to me to stay in Kiev; I wish to live in Pereyaslavets on the Danube [in Bulgaria], for that is the centre of my land'). But it is not improbable that Christianity was allowed to grow in Kiev after one of the great turning points in the history of the early Russian Church – the baptism of Ol'ga.

Few events in the early history of the Russian Church have engendered quite so much controversy among scholars – and often quite bitter controversy – as Ol'ga's conversion to Christianity. Not that anyone doubts that she *was* baptized. All are agreed on that. But when, where and under what circumstances? These are the questions that divide the academics. The solution of the problem, as one of them has noted,[22] could contribute to our understanding of Russia's relations with Byzantium and its western neighbours in the mid-tenth century. But as far as the history of the Russian Church is concerned, just when and where the act took place is of somewhat less interest or importance.

Scholars' dates differ widely: 946, 954, 955, 957, 959, 960 have all been conjectured. As for place, Constantinople is the most favoured, though some serious scholars plump for Kiev. Of all the theories propounded, I prefer to accept 946 as the date of Ol'ga's baptism and Constantinople as the place.[23]

Of the main sources – two Russian (the Primary Chronicle and the monk Iakov's Eulogy to Vladimir), two Byzantine (the Book of Ceremonies and the Chronicle of John Scylitzes) and one Latin (Adalbert's Continuation of the Chronicle of Regino of Prüm) – all

22. Obolensky, 'The Baptism of Princess Olga', p. 159.
23. 946 as the date of Ol'ga's trip to Constantinople is convincingly argued by Litavrin ('O datirovke' and 'Puteshestvie'); however, he considers that Ol'ga was baptized later in Constantinople 954/955 ('K voprosu'). See also Vodoff (*Naissance*, pp. 52–4), Nazarenko ('Kogda zhe knyaginya Ol'ga') and Tinnefeld ('Die russische Fürstin Olga'). Müller considers 946 the date of Ol'ga's trip to Constantinople but that she was baptized earlier in Kiev (*Die Taufe*, pp. 72–82). Obolensky ('The Baptism of Princess Olga') puts the date of her baptism at 960 and the place – Constantinople. Featherstone ('Olga's Visit', pp. 293–7) considers that she was baptized in Constantinople in 957.

but one (the Book of Ceremonies) agree that Ol′ga was baptized in Constantinople. The Book of Ceremonies, compiled by Emperor Constantine VII Porphyrogenitus, Ol′ga's contemporary, while describing in detail her reception in Constantinople, makes no mention of her baptism.

When Igor′ died in 944, slain by the neighbouring Drevlyane, his wife became regent for the duration of their son Svyatoslav's minority. As we read in the previous chapter, her first recorded act was to avenge her husband's death, which she did by slaughtering large numbers of Drevlyane. The Primary Chronicle excels itself in a highly entertaining and equally implausible passage redolent of legend and saga which portrays Ol′ga as a monster of trickery and cruelty. But the chronicler's voice changes abruptly for the next expisode in her career – her voyage to Constantinople – only to show that in these early entries one can rarely trust the tone and the content of the Primary Chronicle. The narrative begins:

> Ol′ga went to the Greeks and arrived at Constantinople. At that time Constantine, the son of Leo, was emperor, and she came to him. And seeing that she was extremely fair of face and intelligent, he was amazed at her wisdom. And he conversed with her saying: 'You are worthy to rule with me in my city.' But she understood and said to the emperor: 'I am a heathen. If you wish me to be baptized, then baptize me yourself. If not I shall not be baptized.' And the emperor and the patriarch baptized her.

After describing the patriarch's religious instructions, which Ol′ga drank in 'like a sponge absorbing water', the chronicler tells us that she was given the name of Helen ('like the ancient empress, the mother of Constantine the Great' – as well, he might have added, as the wife of Constantine VII). Her baptism is followed by the beguiling anecdote of her battle of wits with the emperor and her predictable victory:

> After her baptism the emperor summoned her and said: 'I wish to take you for my wife.' And she said: 'How can you take me for your wife? For you baptized me yourself and have called me your [god]daughter. Now that is not permitted amongst Christians [i.e. a man may not marry his goddaughter]. And this you know full well.' And the emperor said: 'You have outwitted me, Ol′ga.'[24]

---

24. *PVL*, vol. 1, p. 44. In all probability the bare facts of the chronicle story come from the 'Eulogy of Princess Ol′ga' contained in *The Memory and Eulogy of Vladimir*, written by the monk Iakov in the third quarter of the eleventh century (see Zimin, 'Pamyat′ i pokhvala', p. 69). Note that Iakov writes that Ol′ga went to Constantinople 'after the death of her husband Igor′', i.e. close to 944.

No doubt the chronicler, writing up his tale of Ol'ga's baptism a century and a half after the event, was carried away by the desire to be one up on the Greeks in cunning and guile – perhaps out of a feeling of resentment at Greek overlordship in the early Russian Church? Whatever the reason for this entertaining piece of fiction, one can only extract from it confirmation of the fact that Ol'ga came to Constantinople, was baptized by the patriarch and that her baptismal sponsor was either the emperor or, more likely, his wife Elena, whose name she was given in lieu of the pagan Ol'ga. As for Constantine's desire to marry Ol'ga, we need only bear in mind that his wife was present at the reception of Ol'ga's retinue and that she was Ol'ga's sponsor at her baptism. Furthermore, Ol'ga was probably not exactly of an age to stimulate marital desires in the emperor.[25]

What happened? In the late summer of 946,[26] still a pagan, Ol'ga set off to Constantinople with a suite of about a hundred. The aim of her mission was twofold: first, to accept Christianity and thus strengthen the links with Byzantium; with this intention she brought with her a priest, Grigory,[27] no doubt from the church of St Elias in Kiev. The second aim was presumably to renew or reinforce the trade agreement contained in the treaty of 944 – no less than forty-three merchants were included in her suite – and perhaps to enquire about a royal bride for her son. Ol'ga was baptized – when and by whom is not known, but probably in the early days of her stay in Constantinople, by the patriarch and in the presence of her sponsor the empress.

How successful Ol'ga's mission was as far as the reinforcement of the terms of the treaty of 944 was concerned we cannot say. The very detailed account of her ceremonial reception at the court, provided by the emperor himself in the Book of Ceremonies,[28] gives us no hint

25. The Primary Chronicle affirms that she was married off to Igor' in 903, while the later Arkhangel'skiy Chronicle (PSRL, vol. 37, p. 58) adds that she was 10 at the time. However, the Ipat'evskiy Chronicle gives 6450/942 as the date of Svyatoslav's birth (ibid., vol. 2, col. 34). This might mean that she was *born* in 903, and that she was 39 when she gave birth to Svyatoslav and 43 when she went to Constantinople. See also Vlasto, The Entry, p. 249, n.(c).

26. Both the monk Iakov and John Scylitzes say that Ol'ga journeyed to Constantinople *after Igor''s death* (944). See Obolensky, 'The Baptism of Princess Olga', p. 162.

27. Mentioned in Constantine Porphyrogenitus, De caeremoniis, p. 597. See Müller, Die Taufe, pp. 77, 79.

28. For a translation into English of most of the fifteenth chapter in which Ol'ga's visit is described, as well as an exhaustive commentary, see Featherstone, 'Olga's Visit', pp. 298–305.

whatsoever as to what discussions were carried out by her ambassadors and her commercial representatives ('merchants'). All we hear of are the receptions, the banquets and the sophisticated trappings (organ music, mechanical twittering birds and roaring gilt lions, etc.) used to impress foreign ambassadors. As for the results of Ol'ga's baptism – alas, still less is known. As Ludolf Müller points out, Ol'ga could have had her sights set on a bishopric (under a Greek metropolitan, say of Cherson), an independent metropolitanate under the patriarch of Constantinople, an autocephalous archbishopric or even a patriarchate. For Ol'ga must have been aware that the head of the Bulgarian Church had recently received the title of Patriarch from Constantinople.[29]

But none of this came true. Ol'ga returned with her suite and the priest Grigory, by now no doubt her father-confessor, to Kiev, disappointed and disillusioned. Nor, as we have seen, was she to get any satisfaction from her son, who remained adamantly pagan and refused to listen to her pleas to convert to Christianity. During the next thirteen years the only evidence of the growth of Christianity in Kiev is the fact that a second church, this time dedicated to St Sofia, was consecrated in 952,[30] doubtless to commemorate Ol'ga's baptism in the great cathedral of St Sophia in Constantinople. During these thirteen years we hear of no moves by the Church in Byzantium to send any priests, let alone bishops, to Kiev. Then, in 959, according to a Western chronicle written by one Adalbert,[31] later the first arch-bishop of Magdeburg, envoys from 'Helen [i.e. Ol'ga], Queen of the Russians (Regina Rugorum)', turned up at the court of King Otto of Germany in Frankfurt-am-Main asking for a bishop and priests to be sent to Russia.[32]

Was this just a desperate act of Ol'ga's after thirteen frustrating years of waiting in vain for clergy from Byzantium? Or was it an attempt to achieve some sort of political alignment with the Ottonian kingdom? Both, perhaps. This time, however, Ol'ga's envoys met with some success. According to Adalbert's Chronicle, one Libertius was consecrated shortly afterwards as 'bishop for the Russian people'.

29. Müller, *Die Taufe*, pp. 80–1.

30. This evidence comes from an inscription in an early fourteenth-century parchment Apostle: 'on that day [11 May] there took place the consecration (*svyashchenic*) of St Sofia in Kiev in the year 6460 [= 952]'. See Kartashev, *Ocherki*, p. 104; Rybakov, *Yazychestvo*, p. 390.

31. Adalbert was in all probability the anonymous author of the continuation of Abbot Regino of Prüm's Chronicle.

32. Regino of Prüm, *Chronicon*, p. 170; Lampert of Hersfeld, *Annales*, p. 38.

Libertius, however, never set off for his eastern diocese, but died in early 961, whereupon Adalbert himself was appointed in his place. His mission to Russia ended in failure, and in 962 he returned home with difficulty, some of the members of his suite being killed *en route*. Alas, he gives no details of his stay in Russia, nor does he say why he abandoned his see after so short a time. It seems unlikely, though, that he encountered dogmatic difficulties when dealing with the members of his Russian flock: it was nearly a hundred years before the so-called Catholic–Orthodox 'schism' of 1054 occurred, and anyhow it was improbable that he or any of the newly converted Christians in Kiev had much idea of the theological differences between the Churches of Rome and Constantinople, such as they were at the time. More likely he encountered opposition from the adherents of the resolutely pagan Svyatoslav – by now 19 or 20 years old and emerging from under his mother's tutelage. And could it not be that linguistic problems made his office unacceptable in Kiev? After all, Church Slavonic, intelligible to both the Bulgarians and the Russo-Varangian Christians, must have been the accepted liturgical language in the early days of Kievan Christianity. And Adalbert would surely have had great difficulty in persuading the Kievans to accept a Latin liturgy.[33]

Whatever the reasons for the failure of Adalbert's mission, one thing is certain: Latin Christianity had suffered the first of its many setbacks on Russian soil.

Nothing more is known of Ol'ga's endeavours to build up her Church or even to try to put it on a more acceptable footing with what was later to become the patriarchal mother Church of Byzantium. There were no more recorded missions either to Constantinople or, not surprisingly, to the West. She died on 11 July 969, having requested that there be no pagan festivities (*trizna*[34]) celebrated at her grave and, presumably, no pagan burial mound, 'for', as the chronicle adds, 'she had her priest [and] he buried the blessed Ol'ga'.[35]

What was Ol'ga's contribution to the building and fostering of Christianity in Russia? The eleventh-century eulogists were not sparing in their paeans: Ol'ga, 'illuminated by God's grace', 'enlightened by the Holy Spirit', was for them 'the forerunner of the Christian land', 'the morning star before the sun', 'the pearl in the dung'.[36] But such

---

33. See Müller, *Die Taufe*, p. 85.

34. The *trizna* usually consisted of military contests and/or a wake.

35. *PVL*, vol. 1, p. 49.

36. See ibid. for the encomium which follows the brief account of her death and burial in the Primary Chronicle, and the monk Iakov's Eulogy to Princess Ol'ga (Zimin, 'Pamyat' i pokhvala', pp. 69–70).

expressions were merely part of an attempt to promote her eventual canonization. Alas, as we have seen, the miserably inadequate sources only point to her failure – or her inability – to do more than support the fragile foundations of the Russian Church in the predominantly pagan atmosphere of the first half of the tenth century.

In the period between the death of Ol'ga (969) and the baptism of her grandson Vladimir (988) there is very little information on Christianity in Russia in the sources, Russian, Greek or Latin – indeed, in the Russian chronicles paganism plays the biggest role. There are, however, some hints in both the Latin and the Russian sources which lead one to believe that Svyatoslav's eldest son Yaropolk may have been if not a baptized Christian then at least a sympathizer with Christianity. As we saw in the previous chapter, the known facts of his life according to the Primary Chronicle are sadly thin on the ground. However, other sources throw a little more light on the question of his religious convictions.

According to the Latin chronicle of Lampert of Hersfeld, amongst the envoys to the moribund emperor Otto I in Quedlingburg in March 973 were Russians ('legati plurimarum gentium . . . Bulgariorum atque *Ruscorum*'.[37] In the recent opinion of the Soviet historian A. V. Nazarenko, the aim of the mission was not only to bear gifts to Otto, but also to test the ground for a political and dynastic alliance which would have necessitated Yaropolk's baptism.[38]

But was the embassy of 973 a genuine attempt on the part of Otto and Yaropolk to secure a bride for the latter and a military ally for the former? We should not forget that Yaropolk already had a wife, and what is more a Christian, an ex-nun brought as a prisoner from the Bulgarian wars by Svyatoslav and married to Yaropolk because of the 'beauty of her countenance'.[39] Or was it simply a reduplication of Ol'ga's embassy to Otto in 959, yet another request for clergy? And did not emissaries – admittedly reported only in the sixteenth-century Nikon Chronicle – come some four years later from the pope to Yaropolk, maybe as a result of Yaropolk's own embassy of 973?[40] After all, the silence of the Primary Chronicle – perhaps its unwillingness to admit that Yaropolk either favoured Christianity or even was baptized – may simply have been due to a desire on the part of the

37. Lampert of Hersfeld, *Annales*, p. 42; Nazarenko, 'Rus' i Germaniya', pp. 69–70.
38. Ibid., pp. 74 ff.
39. *PVL*, vol. 1, p. 53.
40. *PSRL*, vol. 9, p. 39, *s.a.* 979/980 (6487), but presumably in 977 or 978, assuming that Vladimir had Yaropolk murdered in 978; see above, p. 9, n. 18.

eleventh-century scribe not to minimize the glory of Vladimir's great exploit of 988.[41]

One small item, however, mentioned in the Primary Chronicle hints that Yaropolk, and perhaps his brother Oleg as well, were indeed either Christians or close to accepting their grandmother's faith. Under the year 1044 (6552) we read: 'the two princes Yaropolk and Oleg, the sons of Svyatoslav, were disinterred and their bones were baptized and they were laid to rest in the [tithe] church of the Holy Mother of God.'[42] Surely this could only mean that their nephew Yaroslav 'the Wise' had no actual record of their baptism, but knowing of his uncle's Christian proclivities decided to have them posthumously baptized? And surely it matters little whether Yaropolk, still less Oleg, was baptized in his lifetime or not? What is of importance is that for a brief spell the Christian tradition of Ol'ga and her followers in Kiev was kept alive or at any rate was not quenched by her eldest grandson.

Her youngest grandson, Vladimir, however, had quite different ideas about the role religion should play in the State. He began his reign with all the savagery of a Viking marauder. In 978 he suddenly appeared in Novgorod from Scandinavia with a Varangian army, removed Yaropolk's governors and established his own authority there. In the same year he attacked neighbouring Polotsk, killed the local chieftain Rogvolod, whose daughter Rogneda haughtily declined to marry him, and 'took his daughter for his wife'. He then moved south to Kiev, had his half-brother Yaropolk murdered, seized and raped his pregnant wife and sat upon his throne.[43]

The early years of his rule in Kiev were marked by an unprecedented resurgence of paganism. It was as though Vladimir was determined to undo the work of his grandmother. One of his first recorded actions after seizing power was to build a pantheon in Kiev dedicated to the main pagan gods known to the Russians:

> Vladimir began to rule alone in Kiev and he set up idols on the hill outside the palace: Perun, made of wood with a silver head and a golden moustache, and Khors, Dazhd'bog and Stribog and Simargl and Mokosh'. And the people sacrificed to them calling them gods; and they brought their sons and daughters and sacrificed them to the[se] devils, and they defiled the earth with their offerings. And the land of Russia and that hill were defiled with blood . . .[44]

41. See Vlasto, *The Entry*, p. 253.
42. *PVL*, vol. 1, p. 104.
43. Ibid., p. 54, *s.a.* 980. For the dating, see above, p. 9, n. 18.
44. *PVL*, vol. 1, p. 56.

Five of these were anthropomorphic: Perun, god of thunder and lightning, the protector of warriors; Khors and Dazhd'bog, gods of the sun; Stribog, god of the sky and perhaps of the winds; and Mokosh' or Makosh', goddess of fertility. The sixth, the winged dog-god Simargl, was god of seeds and crops.[45] They were by no means all of the pagan gods known to the Russians: in earlier treaties with the Greeks (907 and 971) those of the Russians who were pagan had sworn by Volos, the god of cattle, as well as by Perun. But there was no statue to Volos, nor were many others of the pagan divinities known to the eastern Slavs – Rod and Rozhanitsy (Lada and Lelya: fertility, harvest, spring), Svarog (fire), Pereplut (plenty) – included in Vladimir's pantheon.[46]

Vladimir's pantheon was not simply a place of worship for the pagan Kievans. It was also a place of human sacrifices. The Primary Chronicle under the year 983[47] describes with much gusto the martyrdom of two Varangian Christians, father and son, 'from the Greeks' – that is, *émigrés* from Constantinople. The story begins with the vague statement that 'Vladimir and his people made sacrifices to the idols'. Somewhat illogically we are then told that the 'elders and boyars' suggested casting lots for a boy and girl to be sacrificed. The lot for the boy fell on the Varangian's son. But when the father refused to surrender the boy, the 'people' came and killed them both. Unfortunately the narrative is flawed and inconsequential. Furthermore it has some suspicious textual similarities with the tale of the baptism of Russia found later in the same chronicle.[48] All of this leads one to suspect that the story was an attempt by a subsequent editor or chronicler to emphasize the horror of Vladimir's paganism and the miracle of his conversion. The same goes for an earlier passage (*s.a.* 980) describing his pre-conversion sexual prowess: after some of Vladimir's offspring by four of his many wives have been mentioned, we are told that he had 800 concubines, for 'he was insatiable in his lust for women, violating married women and maidens; for he was a lover of women like Solomon'.[49]

---

45. Only five pedestals were found in the excavations of 1975 – presumably the bases of the anthropomorphic gods. Where, if anywhere, Simargl's effigy stood is not known. See Rybakov, *Yazychestvo*, pp. 415–16. In Rybakov's view Mokosh'/Makosh' was a goddess; in Likhachev's (*PVL*, vol. 2, p. 324) a god.

46. Rybakov, *Yazychestvo*, p. 418.

47. *PVL*, vol. 1, pp. 58–9.

48. Ibid., vol. 2, pp. 326–7.

49. Ibid., vol. 1, pp. 56–7. Note that Bishop Thietmar of Merseburg in his chronicle called him a 'fornicator immensus et crudelis' (*Die Chronik*, p. 486).

However exaggerated all this may seem, it is quite evident that the first ten years of Vladimir's reign were remarkable for the propagation of paganism. What was his purpose? Did he simply act in resentment, or pique, to spite the memory of his grandmother and his half-brother? That he was attempting to counter Christianity there can be little doubt. The Soviet scholar B. A. Rybakov even goes so far as to posit a deliberate system of contrasts between the pagan and the Christian deities and maintains that Stribog, Dazhd'bog and Makosh' are the popular pagan equivalents of God the Father, God the Son and the Mother of God; in other words, he envisages three of the deities in Vladimir's pantheon as confronting and challenging Christianity.[50] Yet while it is clear that many pagan festivals, practices and even gods coalesced with and influenced popular Christian beliefs in Russia even long after the official 'conversion' of 988, Rybakov's imputation to Vladimir of such a deliberate confrontation seems fanciful, to say the least. More likely, the setting up of the pantheon, the deliberately anti-Christian attitude to monogamy and perhaps even the hint of human sacrifices were part of an attempt to weld together the variegated ethnic elements of his huge realm by reinforcing a religion acceptable to the vast majority.

---

50. Rybakov, *Yazychestvo*, p. 454.

CHAPTER THREE

The Baptism of Vladimir and his Subjects

Some ten years after his seizure of power in Kiev, Vladimir accepted Christian baptism and set about Christianizing his country. Let us first of all consider what probably happened in the fateful years from 987 to 990, before trying to analyse the reasons for Vladimir's abrupt and astonishing conversion.

As 988 was decreed by the Moscow Patriarchate as the date of the Christianization of Russia, 1988, the date of the millennium, was also the year of proliferation of conferences and of articles and books devoted to various aspects of it. Not that there were not innumerable similar works in the century preceding the millennium. There were. The result is that one is swamped by a large number of diverse scholarly views on practically every aspect of Russia's 'entry into Christendom'. Before choosing a path through the cluttered scholarship on the subject, we must first have a look at the primary sources themselves.

By far the most, but not always the most reliable, information is to be found, as one might expect, in the Russian Primary Chronicle.[1] This consists of: first, a lengthy description of the arrival in Kiev of Moslem, Roman, Jewish and Greek missionaries (s.a. 986) who outline the basic tenets of their faiths to Vladimir, the first three with great brevity, the fourth at extreme length; secondly (s.a. 987), Vladimir's decision to send envoys to investigate the Moslem, 'German' (i.e. Catholic) and Greek faiths (but not, curiously, the Jewish) and the envoys' glowing report of what they saw in Constantinople – it was

---

1. *PVL*, vol. 1, pp. 59–83. For an exhaustive review of the sources for this conversion, see Shepard, 'Some Remarks'.

this that finally brought Vladimir round to accepting baptism; and thirdly (*s.a.* 988), Vladimir's attack on and capture of Cherson in the Crimea, his wedding to Basil II's sister Anna whom he demanded in marriage, his baptism in Cherson and his return to Kiev where the baptism of the Russian people began. This vast narrative, compiled clearly by divers hands – authors and editors at a later date – contains, as is so often the case with the Primary Chronicle, much that is unbelievable, much that is pure fiction and at the same time a certain amount of credible fact.

The only other Russian source to contribute to our knowledge of the conversion is the monk Iakov's *Memory and Eulogy of Vladimir*,[2] but only in so far as it helps us with some of the problems of chronology. Of all the non-Russian sources, the most useful are the chronicle of the near-contemporary Christian Arab, Yahia of Antioch,[3] and the *Universal History* of the contemporary Armenian Asoghik (Stephen of Taron).[4] Other Arab writers are too late to be of any interest, while the Byzantine sources are either strangely non-committal or silent. However, Psellus and Leo the Deacon add a certain amount of information on the Russians' military activities in 988 and 989.[5]

What probably happened? I say 'probably' because, given the sometimes bewilderingly contradictory evidence of the sources, to say nothing of the quirks and vagaries of certain historians, no one can be certain of the facts. It is hard even to say what triggered off the events leading up to the conversion. Did the initiative come from Vladimir? Did it come from his advisers, many of whom may have been Christians? Or was it the Moslems – Bulgars from the middle Volga area – the 'Germans' from Rome, Judaic Khazars or the Greeks from Constantinople who took the first step? What is clear is that investigation undoubtedly took place on both sides, that is to say between the Russians and the Greeks. Whether the Bulgars, Khazars and Latins also scrutinized the Russians or were scrutinized by them is hard to say. Probably not; it may well be that the chronicler could not resist the opportunity of showing off his wit by giving Vladimir a few smart rejoinders to their declarations of faith.[6] But it is more than

2. See above, p. 27, n. 24.

3. Yahia-ibn Said of Antioch, *Histoire*. On Yahia as a source, see especially Shepard, 'Some Remarks', pp. 71–4.

4. See Poppe, 'The Political Background', p. 202, n. 22; Shepard, 'Some Remarks', pp. 69 ff.

5. Poppe, 'The Political Background', p. 202.

6. e.g. Vladimir's oft-quoted retort when the Bulgarian 'missionary' informed him that Moslems were forbidden to drink wine: 'Drinking is the joy of the Russians; we cannot do without it.' *PVL*, vol. 1, p. 60.

likely that Vladimir, once he had determined to abandon paganism and to opt for Christianity, made some stringent enquiries, sent his investigators to the patriarch and listened to what the representatives from Constantinople had to say about the faith.

The hardest questions to answer are: where and when was Vladimir baptized, what were his relations with the Greeks at the time, when and why did he attack and capture Cherson? The Primary Chronicle version, it will be remembered, switches abruptly and illogically from the Russian envoys' report on what they saw in Constantinople (987) to Vladimir's Cherson campaign (988), his demand that the emperor's sister be sent to Cherson, his baptism there and his marriage to Anna, and finally his return to Kiev and the eventual mass baptism of the Russian people. Clearly this is not what happened. But what did?

Now, we know in fact that in 988 and 989 (as well as in 990, 991 and 995[7]) Vladimir lent considerable military support to Emperor Basil II and was instrumental in quelling the dangerous rebellion of Bardas Phocas, who, having proclaimed himself emperor of Cappadocia in 987, marched to the gates of Constantinople in 988 and threatened the city. Why then should Vladimir attack Cherson, assuming that Cherson was loyal to Basil? The most likely answer, provided by the Polish historian Andrzej Poppe, is that Cherson in fact had sided with the rebellious Bardas Phocas and was besieged and captured by the army of Vladimir, who still supported the rightful emperor.[8]

According to Poppe's plausible argument, in the summer of 987 Basil dispatched his envoys to Kiev to ask for urgent military help against the usurper and at the same time to discuss the recompense, which turned out to be marriage to the 'born in purple' Anna, sister of two emperors, Basil and Constantine, which would of course have necessitated Vladimir's baptism. The Russian troops, some 6,000 strong according to the Armenian historian Asoghik,[9] arrived in Constantinople in the summer of 988. Vladimir's baptism, in all probability, took place at the beginning of 988[10] and that of the Russian people shortly afterwards. Some time in the same year Vladimir set off to the Dnepr

7. Poppe, 'The Political Background', p. 211.

8. Ibid. On the separatist tendencies of Cherson, see especially pp. 221–33. According to Tatishchev's, admittedly unreliable, eighteenth-century *History*, in 1076 the emperor Michael VII Ducas asked Svyatoslav and Vsevolod Yaroslavichi to aid him against the Bulgarians and Cherson. *Istoriya*, pp. 91–2; Kuz'min, '"Kreshchenie"', p. 50.

9. See above, p. 36, n. 4.

10. Poppe thinks that Vladimir was christened (oglashen) on St Basil's Day (1 January 988), received the Christian name of this saint after his godfather, the Emperor Basil, and was baptized at Epiphany, 6 January; cf. 'The Political Background', pp. 240–1.

rapids,[11] in all probability to meet his bride and bring her back to be wedded in Kiev.

The Russian troops arrived in Constantinople some time before the end of 988. Early in 989 Basil II's army, reinforced by the Russians, attacked, surprised and defeated Bardas Phocas on the eastern side of the Bosporus at the battle of Chrysopolis (modern Scutari). On 13 April 989 the final battle of the war with Bardas Phocas took place at Abydus on the south bank of the Dardanelles. Perhaps with the assistance of Russian boats and Russian soldiers, Basil defeated Bardas Phocas. Bardas himself was killed.[12] The insurrection was virtually over.

While the Russian expeditionary force was defending Constantinople and assisting the emperor to overthrow the usurper, Vladimir was besieging Cherson, which, in Poppe's view, was still holding out against Basil II. When the news of Bardas Phocas's death (13 April 989) eventually reached Cherson – probably in the summer of 989 – the city capitulated and was sacked. Having informed his new brother-in-law the emperor of his success, Vladimir returned to Kiev with Chersonite priests, relics, church vessels and ikons.[13]

These the bare bones of the story of Vladimir's baptism and the Christianization of Russia leave many questions to be answered. And the first is: did the main thrust come from the Greeks? In other words, was Emperor Basil's main aim simply to incorporate the Kievan State into the Byzantine Commonwealth as a newly baptized people under the jurisdiction of the patriarch of Constantinople? Or was the Greeks' demand that Vladimir accept baptism nothing more than the admittedly essential condition of his marriage to a purple-born princess, which in its turn was the reward for agreeing to protect the Empire in its hour of political crisis? Surely the second question must be answered yes, and the corollary must be that the initiative came from Vladimir, or rather that Vladimir, when faced with Basil's initial request, himself

---

11. *k porogom" khodi*. See Zimin, 'Pamyat" i pokhvala', p. 72.

12. For the dates of the battles of Chrysopolis and Abydus, see Poppe, 'The Political Background', pp. 236–7.

13. Both Müller (*Die Taufe*, pp. 111–13) and Vodoff (*Naissance*, pp. 74–81) follow Poppe's reconstruction of events. Rapov ('0 date') rejects Poppe's view largely on the question of dating and because his concept of Cherson's anti-Basil stance runs counter to the Russian versions and to that of Leo the Deacon. Obolensky ('Cherson') also rejects Poppe, mainly on the grounds of chronology and on the question of Cherson's disloyalty.

decided on the terms – the emperor's sister as his bride – which meant obligatory baptism. But obligatory baptism only for himself. The decision to baptize the Russian people must have come only from Vladimir and cannot have been an additional condition of Anna's marriage.

That the demand for a bride 'born in purple' was an exceptional one there can be little doubt. 'Purple-born' princesses were the daughters of 'purple-born' reigning emperors of Byzantium and born in the palace; and it was virtually unknown for one to be married off to a pagan 'barbarian'.[14] Vladimir must have been aware of this: the Christians amongst his courtiers would certainly have known all about the matrimonial customs of the Byzantine ruling family, and it may well be that Ol'ga herself had investigated the possibility of a royal bride for her son Svyatoslav. There was a risk of course that the Byzantine envoys would reject out of hand Vladimir's demand for a royal bride. But the situation was clearly a desperate one and they could only agree. Vladimir and his advisers on their side must have been anxious to win the most prestigious international prize available, the prize which would convert the prince of Kiev from a powerful pagan barbarian into the brother-in-law of the emperor of Byzantium, able to match himself in international diplomacy with the rulers of the Christian world as the master of a Christian State.

The decision, then, to accept Christianity from the Greeks was clearly Vladimir's. But were there alternatives to the Byzantine brand of Christianity open to Vladimir? In view of the sequence of events narrated above it seems highly improbable, if not impossible. Some historians in the past have, however, even doubted that Byzantium was the fount of Vladimir's Christianity, largely on the grounds, first, that the Russian and Greek sources are virtually silent concerning the Russian Church for the first half-century of its existence; secondly, that the Primary Chronicle's statement that in 1037 'Yaroslav founded the Church of St Sofia [in Kiev], [and] the metropolitanate' indicates that the office of metropolitan as head of the Russian Church was *first* established only in 1037 by Vladimir's son Yaroslav – in actual fact it simply meant that Yaroslav laid the foundations of the metropolitan (i.e. senior) church of St Sofia; and, thirdly, that Vladimir was not canonized before the thirteenth century – evidence of 'antagonism' between him and Byzantium. These and other arguments have led these historians to suggest that Vladimir accepted baptism from Bul-

14. See Obolensky, *The Byzantine Commonwealth*, pp. 196–7.

garia, or from Rome, or from Tmutorakan' (on the east of the straits of Kerch) or from Cherson; or that the Russian Church was autonomous up to 1037; or that the earliest bishops were foreign missionaries. But none of these arguments hold water, and few if any are the scholars who nowadays consider them to have any interest beyond the little light they throw on the mentality of those who dreamed them up and adhered to them in the past.[15]

Unfortunately, the available sources give us deplorably scanty information on how Vladimir was baptized, who baptized him, how the mass conversion of the Russian people took place, how Vladimir's Church was organized, what its links were with the patriarchate in Constantinople, and so forth. The first step, however, was undoubtedly the dispatch of a senior hierarch – a metropolitan or an archbishop – to Kiev together with a considerable number of priests; for before 988 Kiev could probably boast of two or three priests at the most for the two known churches in the city. But who was sent? Who was the first head of the recognized Church in Russia?

The answer is to be found in Nicephorus Callistus's *Church History* written at the beginning of the fourteenth century. In a digression on bishops who were transferred from one see to another he writes that during Basil II's reign 'Feofilakt is promoted from [the metropolitan see] of the Sebastians to Russia' ($\Theta\epsilon o\phi\acute{u}\lambda\alpha\kappa\tau o\varsigma$ $\acute{\epsilon}\kappa$ $\tau\tilde{\eta}\varsigma$ $\Sigma\epsilon\beta\alpha\sigma\tau\eta\nu\tilde{\omega}\nu$ $\epsilon\acute{\iota}\varsigma$ '$P\omega\sigma\acute{\iota}\alpha\nu$ $\acute{\alpha}\nu\acute{\alpha}\gamma\epsilon\tau\alpha\iota$).[16] Now, the Armenian historian Asoghik (Stephen of Taron) talks of an anonymous metropolitan of Sebaste (the capital of the Byzantine province of Armenia II), who, accused of harassing Armenian priests in his diocese, was removed from his see in 986/987 by the emperor, who sent him not to Kiev but to Bulgaria. There he was eventually put to death for deceiving the Bulgars – they had asked the emperor to send his sister as a bride for their ruler, but Basil had sent another woman in her place, and the metropolitan was suspected of complicity.[17] Clearly this anonymous metropolitan was Feofilakt. Asoghik's story, apart from locating his second see in Bulgaria and concluding with his murder there, fits in perfectly with Nicephorus. Feofilakt, then, was the first metropolitan of Russia sent by Basil to Kiev with the Greek embassy in 987 to discuss the Russo-Greek military alliance, the marriage of Basil's sister to Vladimir and

15. For a masterly discussion of the problem, see Müller, *Zum Problem*.
16. See Honigmann, 'Studies', p. 148. Honigmann finds no reason to doubt Nicephorus's evidence.
17. See Poppe, 'The Political Background', pp. 203–5.

the baptism of Vladimir and the Russians.[18]

How many bishops and priests Feofilakt brought with him – or sent for from Constantinople once Vladimir's marriage and baptism had been agreed upon – we do not know. Nor do we know how many priests Vladimir took with him homeward-bound from Cherson. Also we know very little about how the mass baptism took place or how Christianity took root in the State. As mentioned above, both Greek and Russian sources are singularly reticent about the Russian Church in the half-century following the events of 988 and 989.

The Primary Chronicle's version of Vladimir's first actions on returning to Kiev after the Cherson campaign in 989 is what one would expect after reading its account of the preliminaries to the conversion: destruction of pagan idols followed by mass baptism of rapturous neophytes. It could have been written a hundred or more years later by any intelligent and gifted scribe with no records, no memories handed down by previous generations – in fact with no knowledge of what actually happened. But still the story, like so many of the stories in the Primary Chronicle, is entertaining and highly readable. Needless to say, it gives us no real idea as to how Vladimir and his metropolitan set about the seemingly insuperable task of baptizing the entire population. First comes a vivid little vignette in which we are shown how Vladimir dealt with the statues of the pagan gods he had erected in his pantheon some ten years earlier. Some he ordered to be cast down, some hacked to pieces, some burned. Perun, however, he had tied to a horse's tail and dragged down to the river Dnepr, being flogged on the way by twelve men armed with staves – not, adds the chronicler, 'because he thought the wood[en idol] could feel the blows, but in order to confound the devil who had deceived men in this fashion'. Many were the unbelievers who wept for their old idol, for 'they had not yet received holy baptism'. The episode ends in a manner reminiscent of many a tale found in the Primary Chronicle. After Perun had been thrown into the river, Vladimir ordered his men to follow the statue's progress downstream and not to let it get stuck in the shallows, but to push it on until it passed through the rapids (present-day Dnepropetro-vsk); then it was to be allowed to float to the Black Sea. But the wind

18. Yahia of Antioch (*Histoire*, p. 423) says that Basil II sent Vladimir 'metropolitan(s) and bishops' (Shchapov, *Gosudarstvo*, pp. 26–7). Cf. the monk Iakov's words describing Vladimir's feasting: '[Vladimir] set up three tables, the first for the metropolitan, bishops, monks and priests' (Zimin, 'Pamyat' i pokhvala', p. 70). But see Shepard, 'Some Remarks', pp. 81–5.

blew it on to a sandbank, 'and from that day to this very day the place has been called "Perun's Sandbank"'.[19]

Having disposed of the embarrassing statues, Vladimir issued an edict commanding all unchristened inhabitants of Kiev to be baptized in the Dnepr, warning that anyone who refused would be his enemy. This, the chronicler writes, made the people go to the river 'with joy'. 'If this were not good,' they said, 'the prince and [his] boyars would not have accepted it.' Immersion in the river followed.[20] We are left to imagine how many of those of the still pagan population of Kiev (numbering probably not far off 30,000[21]) Vladimir's clergy managed to baptize – and, indeed, how much intimidation and force was required. It is hard to believe in the 'joy' of all or even most of the people. As will be seen later, paganism would retain a firm grip on the population of Russia for centuries to come. Furthermore, the Primary Chronicle itself gives us a hint of the difficulties encountered in the business of proselytizing. Still under the year 988 we are told that Vladimir began to have the children of 'the best people' – members of his court and officers of his army, presumably – educated in book-learning, and that their mothers 'wept for them, for they had *not yet become strengthened by the faith*, but they wept for them as though they were dead'.[22]

The only real indication we have of the progress of Christianization during Vladimir's reign (980–1015) is the record of church-building. But again, especially in the early days, it is thin. Apart from the vague and not very illuminating statement of the Primary Chronicle that 'he [Vladimir] began to found churches and to appoint priests to them throughout the towns',[23] all we have notice of (and not always entirely reliable notice) are four new churches in the capital city of Kiev: St Basil's (988) on the site of the old pantheon;[24] the stone Tithe church of the Mother of God (built by Greek architects and masons from 989 to 996);[25] the first wooden cathedral of St Sofia (built probably soon after 988);[26] and the stone church of St Peter and St

19. *PVL*, vol. 1, p. 80.

20. Ibid., pp. 80–1.

21. A recent estimate for the population of Kiev in the mid-eleventh century gives 36,000 to 40,000. See Mezentsev, 'The Territorial and Demographic Development', p. 169.

22. *PVL*, vol. 1, p. 81. Vlasto (*The Entry*, p. 283) thinks that the children of the 'best people' were being trained for service in the Church.

23. *PVL*, vol. 1, p. 81.

24. Ibid., pp. 56, 81.

25. Ibid., pp. 83, 85.

26. Poppe, 'The Building'.

Paul (1008).[27] As for the 'towns', only two are on record: the church of the Transfiguration in Vasil'ev just south of Kiev (996)[28] and the church of the Elevation of the Cross in Pereyaslavl' (1008).[29] However, the metropolitan was clearly not the only prelate[30] in Russia in the thirty-five years following Vladimir's baptism: there were at least four sees before 1025: Belgorod, in close proximity to Kiev, whose bishop was probably the metropolitan's suffragan;[31] Novgorod, whose founder-bishop Ioakim (Joachim) is said to have come from Cherson in 989;[32] probably Chernigov;[33] and perhaps Polotsk in the north-west.[34]

So the total number of churches built on the vast expanse of Vladimir's realm during the first twenty-seven years after the conversion was not much more than a dozen.[35] As for monasteries, there is no *written* record of any during this period.[36] All of this simply goes to show that the process of converting the population was a slow and laborious business – not surprising, in so far as there can have been few home-trained local priests, few Greek bishops or priests who could serve in a tongue intelligible for the neophytes, few people able to explain even the elementary principles of the faith and the canons of ethical behaviour, few Russians capable of acting as readers, choristers or acolytes. Vladimir and his metropolitan had their hands full. The task must have appeared to them a heavy one indeed.

And yet in spite of all these near-insuperable difficulties and in spite of the resistance of many of the people, the Christianization did go

27. *PSRL*, vol. 9, p. 69.
28. *PVL*, vol. 1, p. 85.
29. *PSRL*, vol. 9, p. 69.
30. See above, p. 41, n. 18.
31. Shchapov, *Gosudarstvo*, pp. 36–7.
32. *NPL*, pp. 159–60. Here (wrongly) called 'archbishop'.
33. Poppe, 'L'Organisation', p. 177; cf. Shchapov (who thinks the see was established between 1024 and 1036), *Gosudarstvo*, p. 38.
34. Poppe, 'L'Organisation', p. 184; Kartashev, *Ocherki*, p. 150; Shchapov, *Goysudarstvo*, p. 39. Cf. Arrignon, 'La Création', *passim*.
35. There are some gross exaggerations of the number of churches: Bishop Thietmar of Merseburg, who wrote his Chronicle from the tale of a German knight who was in Kiev in 1015, says that there were more than 400 churches in the city ('plusquam quadringenta habentur ecclesie', *Die Chronik*, p. 531); while according to the Nikon Chronicle, up to 750 churches in Kiev burned down in the fire of 1017 (*PSRL*, vol. 9, p. 75). Sapunov ('Nekotorye soobrazheniya', p. 316) estimates the number of churches in the tenth century to have been 25. However, his estimates are from both written and archaeological sources.
36. Sapunov, however, says there were seven in the tenth century (ibid., p. 322).

ahead and the future rulers of Kiev did have a firm base on which to build.

How did Vladimir and Feofilakt succeed in their task? First, it must not be forgotten that there were at least two churches in existence in Kiev before 988 as well as a number of practising Christians at the prince's court and perhaps elsewhere. And, secondly, it is not impossible that the Greeks imported from neighbouring Bulgaria priests – perhaps even a bishop or two – who at least were able to serve the Liturgy and preach to their congregations, in an artificial language which, though by no means identical with the various vernaculars, was at least comprehensible to all the Slavonic races in the tenth and eleventh centuries. For the Bulgarians by 988 had already a century and a quarter of Christian tradition behind them – they had accepted Christianity from Byzantium in 864 – and many of the Russians had close connections with Bulgaria as a result of Svyatoslav's Balkan campaigns of 967–72.[37]

37. See, however, Arrignon, 'La Rus' entre la Bulgarie . . .', p. 711.

CHAPTER FOUR

The Organization of the Russian Church

THE METROPOLITANS

Let us now consider the position of the new Russian Church *vis-à-vis* the mother Church of Byzantium. Metropolitan Feofilakt, there can be little doubt, acted as the direct appointee of the emperor and the patriarch of Constantinople, and his function initially was to baptize Vladimir and to assist him in the conversion of as many of his subjects as could be urged or compelled to accept Christianity. But what of his successors as primates of the Russian Church in the two-and-a-half centuries before the Mongol invasion? What was the relation of the twenty-one metropolitans of Kiev (or, in the second half of the twelfth century, 'of Kiev and all Russia', $\tau\tilde{\eta}s$ $\pi\acute{a}\sigma\eta s$ '$P\omega\sigma\acute{\iota}as$) to Byzantium? How were they elected? And by whom? How were they consecrated? What were their functions as leaders of the Russian Church? What were their relations to the bishops of the dioceses?

The 28th canon of the 4th Oecumenical Council (451) laid down that the actual selection of a candidate for metropolitan – i.e. the senior bishop of a province – be carried out by a council of bishops of the province concerned. In the appointment the sole function of the patriarch of Constantinople as supreme head of the Greek Church consisted in the consecration of whoever the local bishops chose. However, from the tenth century onwards, in practice the patriarch not only consecrated the bishop as metropolitan but also elected him: that is to say, he chose the best of three candidates who were presented to him at a special patriarchal synod.[1] This certainly seems to have

---

1. Golubinsky, *IRTs*, 1, I, pp. 272–3; Poppe, 'La Tentative', pp. 10 ff.; Obolensky, 'Byzantium', pp. 51–2.

been the case with the election and consecration of nearly all of the twenty-two metropolitans of Russia before 1240. There were, however, two notable exceptions, both Russians and probably the only Russians[2] among the sea of Greeks: Ilarion (1051–?54) and Klim or Kliment (1147–55).

As for the appointment of the first of these, all we know is what the Primary Chronicle tells us: 'Yaroslav [the Wise] appointed Larion the Russian as metropolitan in [the cathedral of] St Sofia having summoned the bishops.'[3] In other words, Yaroslav convoked a synod of local bishops who elected Ilarion, thus harking back to the 28th canon of the 4th Oecumenical Council. There is, however, no mention anywhere of Ilarion's *consecration* as metropolitan by the patriarch. Even if we assume that in fact Ilarion may have gone to Constantinople for his consecration, his election seems to have been a breach with what was current practice, i.e. the election of one of three candidates by the patriarch. Still, Ilarion's appointment was certainly not evidence of an attempt on the part of Yaroslav and his bishops to make the Russian Church *independent* of Constantinople. Nor was it a political act. More likely than not it was simply the result of poor communications between Kiev and Constantinople.[4] An interesting, though by no means conclusive, footnote to Ilarion's appointment is contained in the sixteenth-century Nikon Chronicle: 'the Russian bishops [i.e. the Greek bishops in Russian sees] met together and appointed Ilarion, a Russian, metropolitan of Kiev and all the Russian land, neither severing themselves from the Orthodox patriarchs and the piety of the Greek faith, nor declining to be appointed by them . . .'[5]

Klim's appointment took place under very different circumstances. In 1145 his predecessor, Metropolitan Mikhail (1130–45), left Kiev and went to Constantinople. He had long acted as a referee in the bitter political struggle between the Monomashichi (the descendants of Vladimir Monomakh) and the Ol'govichi (the descendants of Oleg, the son of Svyatoslav of Chernigov), and not always as an impartial referee in that he tended to urge the Monomashichi to yield to the Ol'govichi in their various clashes.[6] In 1147 Vladimir Monomakh's

2. Obolensky, however, thinks – or thought in 1957 – that some of the other metropolitans may also have been Russians, although there is no evidence to support this view ('Byzantium', pp. 25–33, 45–7).

3. *PVL*, vol. 1, p. 104.

4. See, however, Poppe's view in 'La Tentative'.

5. *PSRL*, vol. 9, p. 83.

6. See below, p. 115.

grandson Izyaslav Mstislavich, who, on a wave of anti-Ol'govichi feeling, had become prince of Kiev in the previous year, set about filling the empty see. He clearly had no intention of reinstating Mikhail, who in any case may have been dead by then. In his place he appointed a Russian monk, Klim or Kliment, metropolitan of Kiev. Once again the election was carried out by a synod of local bishops. The wording of the earliest and most detailed chronicle account – that of the southern Hypatian Chronicle – shows precisely what happened:

> In that same year [1147] Izyaslav appointed Klim metropolitan . . . The bishop of Chernigov said: 'I know that it is right for bishops to meet in council and to appoint a metropolitan.' And the bishop of Chernigov and [the names of four others follow] met in council. But the bishops of Novgorod . . . and Smolensk . . . said [to Klim]: 'It is not according to the law to appoint a metropolitan without the patriarch; the patriarch appoints the metropolitan. And we shall not revere you, nor shall we serve with you, for you have not received blessing either from St Sophia [in Constantinople] or from the patriarch. If you make amends and are blessed [i.e. consecrated] by the patriarch, then we shall revere you . . .'[7]

And so for the second time a Russian bishop was appointed metropolitan according to the old practice of selection by a synod of local bishops and without consecration by the patriarch. It is striking too that the two dissident bishops protested against this revival of Yaroslav's method of electing the head of the Russian Church. This time, however, it is clear that Klim was made metropolitan for purely political reasons. The fact that the appointment was carried out without the patriarch's blessing did not in any way signify a break away from the Greek Church. In fact Klim could not have been consecrated by the patriarch as the patriarchal throne was vacant at the time. His position as metropolitan depended on, and was the result of, Izyaslav's ascendancy in the struggle for Kiev.

All the remaining pre-Mongol metropolitans – all of them probably of Greek origin – appear to have been both elected and consecrated in Constantinople (and from 1204 in Nicaea), and there is little reason to believe that the majority of them were anything but loyal servants of the patriarch and emperor. That is not to say, however, that the Russian civil authorities were not able on occasion to influence the choice of candidate or did not try to do so.[8] From time to time no doubt the rulers of Kiev objected to this or that metropolitan sent to them, or put forward their own candidates; and indeed there are

---

7. *PSRL*, vol. 2, col. 339.
8. See Hannick, 'Kirchenrechtliche Aspekte'.

instances when attempts were made to urge the Greeks to conform with the wishes of their local bishops. Izyaslav's brother, Rostislav Mstislavich, for example, during his reign as prince of Kiev (1159–67), on one occasion is said to have 'sent for' Bishop Feodor who was then consecrated in Constantinople and dispatched as metropolitan to Kiev;[9] and when Metropolitan Feodor died in 1163, Rostislav attempted to have his brother's old protégé Klim reinstated. When this failed, he grudgingly agreed to accept the candidate of Constantinople (Metropolitan Ioann IV, 1164–66), but only after the emperor's envoy had liberally presented him 'with many gifts'.[10] Seventy-five years earlier Vladimir Monomakh's father, Vsevolod Yaroslavich, may well have been instrumental in the appointment of the successor to Metropolitan Ioann II. The Primary Chronicle tells us that in 1089 his daughter Anna 'went to the Greeks [i.e. to Constantinople] . . . and brought back Metropolitan Ioann [III] the Eunuch'.[11]

All in all, the evidence seems to show that in the pre-Mongol period the patriarchal throne exercised relatively little control over, and indeed barely interfered with, the Russian metropolitanate. And as a result the metropolitans themselves enjoyed a generous degree of independence from Constantinople which few of their numerous fellow-metropolitans in Byzantium could have dreamed of. The formal obligations of the Kievan metropolitans *vis-à-vis* the patriarchate were probably more honoured in the breach than the observance. Unlike the metropolitans in Byzantium, they never seem to have paid any formal dues or taxes to the patriarch.[12] Although they were members of a standing patriarchal synod, there is little to show that they attended regularly, indeed, probably most of them never attended at all; the trip from Kiev to Constantinople was a lengthy and onerous one, and they can have had little time left over from looking after their huge Russian province.

Their functions as metropolitans of Kiev (and later of all Rus'), apart from such purely routine duties as the consecration of churches

---

9. According to the Hypatian Chronicle: 'In that year [1161] Metropolitan Feodor arrived from Constantinople in the month of August, for Prince Rostislav had sent for him' (*byashet' bo posylal po n' knyaz' Rostislav*), *PSRL*, vol. 2, cols. 514–15.

10. Ibid., col. 522. According to this version Rostislav decided to send a mission to Constantinople urging the emperor to reappoint Klim. However, before the mission had even had time to leave Russia, Metropolitan Ioann had arrived accompanied by the emperor's envoy.

11. *PVL*, vol. 1, p. 137. Note that the verb 'brought back' (*privede*) implies that Anna (who had been a nun for two years – see *PSRL*, vol. 2, col. 197) was not merely accompanying him back.

12. See Shchapov, *Gosudarstvo*, pp. 166–7.

or the enthronement of princes, concentrated on the bishoprics under their aegis. Theirs was of course the ultimate responsibility for the smooth running of the bishoprics within the metropolitanate. It was their duty, and right, not only to create sees where necessary but also to appoint bishops either to new sees or to vacant old ones; to close sees if necessary and to remove erring or unsatisfactory bishops. Consequently, it was also their prerogative to pass judgement on any of their bishops.[13] In theory metropolitans also summoned annual synods of all the bishops in the province; but since the province was so vast, it was rarely practicable for such synods to take place. For a bishop to be summoned from Novgorod, say, or Suzdal′ and to travel to the metroplitan's seat in Kiev to attend a synod was more often than not difficult or impossible, just as it was virtually impossible for the metropolitan regularly to visit all the bishops in his province.

Much of the functioning of the metropolitans depended of course on their personalities and capabilities, but also on the determination of the princes – not just of Kiev but also of the dependent principalities and districts – to interfere in the management of the dioceses. As the number of principalities increased – as well as the number of dioceses – so the State in the shape of the princes themselves began gradually to encroach on the prerogatives of the metropolitans. It would be naïve to assume, as the chroniclers would often have us believe, that the Ryurikovichi automatically and invariably respected the authority of the hierarchs. They didn't. Nor were they prepared always to accept their decisions implicitly. But it is not until the second half of the twelfth century that there is any real evidence of actual interference by a prince in what had hitherto been traditionally accepted as the statutory duties and privileges of the metropolitans.

The first such case is reported in the 1160s, the troubled age following Klim's metropolitanate. The bishop of Chernigov, Antony, joined Metropolitan Konstantin II in condemning the abbot of the Kievan Monastery of the Caves for not fasting on those of the nine 'Great Festivals' (*Gospodskie prazdniki*)[14] which fell on a Wednesday or a

13. An early example was Metropolitan Efrem's handling of the case of Bishop Luka of Novgorod, who was 'slandered' by his 'serf' in 1055. Luka spent three years in Kiev while the case was heard by the metropolitan. He was acquitted in 1058. His serf was punished by having his nose and both hands cut off. *NPL*, pp. 182–3.
14. i.e. the Nativity of the Mother of God, the Presentation, the Annunciation, Christmas, the Purification, the Epiphany, the Transfiguration, the Dormition of the Mother of God and the Exaltation of the Cross.

Friday. Unfortunately for Bishop Antony, he also 'many times forbade the prince of Chernigov to eat meat on [Wednesdays and Fridays of] the Great Festivals, and Prince Svyatoslav, having no desire [to obey him], threw him out of his episcopate'.[15]

If Konstantin was unable to prevent the totally unjustifiable expulsion of one of his bishops or to reinstate him, still less twenty years later was Metropolitan Nikifor II able to cope with an opponent altogether tougher and more experienced than Svyatoslav. Shortly after his consecration Nikifor appointed a Greek, one Nikolay, as bishop of Rostov. However, the grand prince of Vladimir-Suzdal', Vsevolod III, refused to accept him. 'The people of our land did not choose this one [Nikolay],' he told Nikifor. 'But you appointed him. Let him go wherever you wish. But for me appoint Luka . . . abbot of St Saviour' – evidence, perhaps, that the local *veche* may have had a hand in nominating candidates? The southern Hypatian Chronicle goes on to describe the metropolitan's humiliating climbdown: 'But Metropolitan Nikifor did not want to appoint him. But owing to the great coercion of Vsevolod and Svyatoslav, he appointed Luka . . .'[16] The scribe of the Suzdalian Lavrent'evskiy Chronicle, who could scarcely mention Vsevolod III without a dose of unctuous praise, hints at simony in Nikolay's appointment and goes on to moralize on the wickedness and 'unpleasingness to God' of 'jumping on to the rank of bishop for payment'; the wish of 'the priest and the people' is the 'one called by God and the holy Mother of God [i.e. Luka]'. The entry concludes with a hymn to the virtues of Vsevolod's candidate.

It was not until the second quarter of the thirteenth century, significantly a time when there was no ruler of the calibre of Vsevolod III on the throne of Vladimir or Kiev, that a serious attempt was made to rectify matters by putting a stop to princely meddling in the affairs of the bishops. In 1224 Kirill I (1224–33), the last but one and perhaps the most far-sighted of all the pre-Mongol metropolitans, appeared on the scene. Not only did he enjoy the friendship and respect of the Kievan Monastery of the Caves[17] – Konstantin II's criticism of the abbot's fasting practices, it will be remembered, had soured relations between the metropolitan and the monastery – but he also saw to it

15. *PSRL*, vol. 1, cols. 354–5. The Nikon Chronicle, embroidering as usual on the theme, adds that 'Antony went to Kiev and stayed with Metropolitan Konstantin'. He evidently never returned to his see. Ibid., vol. 9, p. 236.

16. Ibid., vol. 2, cols. 629–30. The Svyatoslav mentioned here is the same Svyatoslav who had ousted Bishop Antony. He was now prince of Kiev.

17. See Podskalsky, *Christentum*, pp. 296–8.

that there was no question of princely interference in the affairs of the diocese. Indeed, as Poppe remarks, he strove to strengthen and consolidate the Russian Church and to make it independent of princely power.[18] In an epistle – probably prompted by Kirill himself – from Patriarch Germanus II to the metropolitan,

> all the pious princes and other senior people are ordered on pain of excommunication utterly to refrain from [laying hands on] the [landed] possessions of the churches and the monasteries . . . and to refrain from [tampering with] episcopal jurisdiction concerning divorces, ravishment, abduction; for the divine and holy canons and Christian law order only bishops to judge and correct these misdeeds. Thus I order [the princes] to refrain from these things.[19]

Although the patriarch only mentions here a small section of what lay at that time in the jurisdiction of the metropolitan and bishops (i.e. elements of family and marriage law), nevertheless his missive clearly spells out the determination of the head of the Russian Church to stamp out lay interference.

THE BISHOPS AND THEIR SEES

Bishops were as a rule appointed and consecrated by the metropolitan of Kiev, although from time to time, as we have seen, princes had a say in promoting their own candidates; perhaps, too, even local town assemblies may have participated in their selection.[20] Available sources unfortunately say very little about the appointment of the earliest bishops and nothing about the size or the boundaries of their sees, although in some cases these probably coincided with the boundaries of the principalities themselves. Of the fifteen dioceses known to have existed in the pre-Mongol period, for example, the only tenth-century diocese whose bishop is actually named is that of Novgorod (Bishop Akim or Ioakim (Joachim)[21]). However, as has been mentioned above (see p. 43), as well as Novgorod, both Belgorod and Chernigov

18. Ibid., p. 203.
19. *RIB*, vol. 6, cols. 82–4.
20. See the words attributed to Vsevolod III concerning Nikifor II's appointment of Bishop Nikolay in Rostov (see above, p. 50). See also below (pp. 52–3), the case of Novgorod in the second half of the twelfth century.
21. See above, p. 43. Note that the sixteenth-century Nikon Chronicle mentions the appointment in 992 of no less than four named bishops in Chernigov, Rostov, Vladimir in Volynia and Belgorod (*PSRL*, vol. 9, p. 65), all of whom are mentioned in earlier and more reliable chronicles as flourising in only the second half of the eleventh century.

probably also had bishops during Vladimir's reign, and perhaps Polotsk too.[22]

The real growth seems to have taken place in the eleventh century with the addition of the sees of Turov, Pereyaslavl', Yur'ev (on the river Ros'), Rostov and Vladimir in Volynia, bringing the total of Russian bishoprics up to nine. The bishops themselves, most of them Greek, must have been appalled on arrival in Russia when they realized the immensity of their dioceses; for the total area of the metropolitanate at the end of the eleventh century was some 1,400,000 square kilometres, while Byzantium, with much the same area, was served by about 750 sees in the middle of the same century.[23] During the twelfth century and the first two decades of the thirteenth, another six dioceses were created.[24]

By no means all these fifteen dioceses were equal in importance and size. The bishop of Belgorod, for example, as the suffragen or vicar of the metropolitan, probably had no diocese at all, but nevertheless seems to have enjoyed a senior position amongst most of the other bishops in so far as when the metropolitan was absent he deputized for him. Perhaps too he was even responsible for the ecclesiastical administration of the principality of Kiev.[25]

The largest of all the sees was that of Novgorod. Up to the middle of the twelfth century, as far as we know, all, or at any rate the majority of, the bishops of Novgorod were elected and consecrated in Kiev by the metropolitan and then sent to Novgorod. In early 1156, however, one Arkady was elected locally by 'all the city' – including the prince and the clergy. It may only have been because at the time there was no metropolitan in Kiev and in the confusing years following Klim's divisive metropolitanate it was essential for Novgorod to have a bishop *in situ*. Indeed, Arkady was warned that it was only 'until a metropolitan arrives, and then you will go [to Kiev] to be appointed',[26] which he did two years later. As for his successor Il'ya, there is nothing to show that he was not both elected and consecrated in Kiev (1165), although the chronicle merely mentions that he was 'appointed' (*postavlen*), the standard expression for 'consecrated', by Metropolitan

22. For a recent review of Russian bishoprics up to the twelfth century, see Arrignon, 'La Création'.

23. See Poppe, 'L'Organisation', p. 217.

24. Smolensk, Ryazan', Vladimir-on-the-Klyaz'ma in the south-east and north-east; Peremyshl', Galich and Ugrovsk in the south-west.

25. See Shchapov, *Gosudarstvo*, pp. 36–7; Arrignon, 'La Création', pp. 28–9.

26. *NPL*, pp. 29–30, 216.

Ioann.[27] In 1186, however, his brother Gavriil was elected, as Arkady had been, by 'the Novgorodians and Prince Mstislav and the abbots and the priests',[28] and then sent to Metropolitan Nikifor II for consecration. It seems, then, that the process of electing Novgorod's bishop in the city itself, and by what was probably a *veche* together with the prince and the local clergy, began either in 1156 or in 1186. Whichever it was, it was a sure indication of Novgorod's urge for independence, just as was the election of the city's *posadnik* by the *veche* and the gradual assumption of the right to choose its own princes.

It is difficult to say just when the bishopric of Novgorod was elevated to an archbishopric. Just as the early Kievan sources sometimes hesitate between the titles 'metropolitan' and 'archbishop', so the earliest Novgorod chronicle tends to use 'archbishop' and 'bishop' indiscriminately, preference being given to the former. But in fact it was not until 1165 that the metropolitan formally conferred the title on Bishop Il'ya.[29] It did not make the Church of Novgorod in any way autonomous and independent of the metropolitan. The archbishopric was purely titular, and an indication of the solidarity of the Novgorod see.

Just as Novgorod received a titular – but permanent – archiepiscopate, so two of the other bishoprics in Russia, those of Pereyaslavl' and Chernigov, were granted titular – but temporary – metropolitanates in the second half of the eleventh century. Why this happened is hard to say. Perhaps the most persuasive explanation is that the two metropolitanates were created soon after the death of Yaroslav the Wise when his three eldest surviving sons, the rulers of Kiev, Chernigov and Pereyaslavl', were attempting jointly to control the State as a triumvirate,[30] and that the deaths of the two eldest (Izyaslav of Kiev in 1078 and Svyatoslav of Chernigov in 1076) spelt the end of the metropolitanates of Chernigov and Pereyaslavl'. The trouble is that it is not quite certain who exactly the metropolitans in question were. In Pereyaslavl' it looks as though the first was Lev or Leon (in Greek sources known as 'Leon, metropolitan of Pereyaslavl' in Rus''[31]), author of a polemical treatise on the use of unleavened bread in the Latin rite, which places him shortly after the great 'schism' of the Orthodox and Catholic Churches in 1054.[32] But, alas, no more is

27. Ibid., pp. 31, 219.
28. Ibid., pp. 38, 228.
29. Ibid., pp. 32, 219.
30. See above, pp. 12–13.
31. 'Λέοντος μητροπολίτου τῆς ἐν Ῥωσίᾳ Πρεσθλάβας'.
32. See below, p. 91 ff., and Poppe, 'Le Traité'. For very different views, see Stokes, 'The Status', and Golubinsky, *IRTs*, vol. 1, I, pp. 328 ff.

known of him. There is a little more information, however, concerning Efrem, who in two Russian sources is mentioned as metropolitan of Pereyaslavl',[33] who became head of the see some time in the late 1070s and who probably died at the end of the century, not long before his successor Simeon was appointed *bishop* of the diocese in 1101.[34]

As for Chernigov, there is only evidence of *one* metropolitan, and that evidence is somewhat fragile. In the description of the translation of the relics of SS Boris and Gleb in 1072 which occurs in the anonymous *Tale of the Passion and Encomium of the Holy Martyrs Boris and Gleb* we read that amongst those present were 'Metropolitan Georgy of Kiev, the other [metropolitan] of Chernigov Neofit', as well as three bishops.[35]

So the two titular metropolitanates existed from approximately 1054 and faded out after the 'triumvirate' reverted to single rule in 1078.[36] In neither case was there any question of a move to split the metropolitanate of Kiev: there is no record of appeals either to the patriarch of Constantinople or to the metropolitan of Kiev. The only attempt in the pre-Mongol period to create a breakaway see was that of Andrey Bogolyubskiy, whose plans to found an independent metropolitanate in Vladimir-on-the Klyaz'ma in the 1160s were met with an adamant refusal from the patriarch.[37]

FINANCES AND JURISDICTION

How were the metropolitans and the bishops remunerated? Apart from fees paid by the 'white clergy'[38] and perhaps by certain of the monasteries to their bishops – a percentage of parishioners' contribu-

---

33. Nestor's Life of Feodosy, abbot of the Caves Monastery (in *Sbornik XII*, p. 54; *PLDR, XI–nachalo XII veka*, pp. 328–9) and *PSRL*, vol. 1, col. 208.

34. Shchapov, *Gosudarstvo*, p. 209.

35. *mitropolit'' Georgyy Kyyev'skyy, drugyy – Neofit'' Ch'rnigovskyy*. Later in the same passage 'metropolitans' is used in the dual number (*mitropolita*), *AHE*, pp. 55-6.

36. In that year Vsevolod became prince of Kiev and Pereyaslavl' and gave his son Chernigov. *PVL*, vol. 1, p. 135.

37. For a detailed exposition, see Barrick, Andrey Yur'evich Bogolyubsky, ch. 2.

38. In the Russian Church the priests and deacons are known as the 'white clergy' (*beloe dukhovenstvo*), while the monks are called the 'black clergy' (*chernoe dukhovenstvo, cherntsy*). 'White' priests and deacons must be married (although today there are, exceptionally, some celibate 'white' clergy), while the monks are celibate. Only a

tions, ordination fees and so forth about which relatively little is known – the major sources of income came from legal fines for a series of statutory offences within the jurisdiction of the Church and of course from such landed possessions that there were, i.e. taxation of the inhabitants of eparchial estates.

For the period we are talking about, the tenth century to 1240, a fair amount is known about the financial and juridical position of the Church thanks to two ecclesiastical legal Codes, the so-called Church Statute of Vladimir and the Church Statute of Yaroslav, neither of which exist in manuscripts earlier than the end of the thirteenth century but which can be, and have been admirably, reconstructed to their prototypes (end of the tenth/beginning of the eleventh centuries respectively). Both of these statutes changed and developed as they were edited and re-edited to suit changing circumstances and different areas of Russia throughout the pre-Mongol period. Furthermore, they can be corroborated and amplified by Svyatoslav Ol'govich's Statutory Charter of 1137 (Novgorod) as well as by Rostislav Mstislavich's Charter of 1136 (Smolensk).[39]

In 995 or 996 Vladimir's Kievan church of the Holy Mother of God, also known as the church of the Tithe (*Desyatinnaya tserkov'*), was completed and consecrated. According to the Primary Chronicle, Vladimir, after praying in his new church, pronounced the following words: 'I give this church of the holy Mother of God the tenth part of my possessions and of my towns.'[40] This somewhat vague statement probably meant that Vladimir bestowed on the church a tithe from the income of his treasury, that is to say a tenth of all the tribute received from his subjects as well as a tenth of all legal fines imposed by the prince in his judicial capacity. It was a beginning, but no more. There was no mention of the metropolitan or of the other churches in the State.

At the beginning of the eleventh century it appears that the tithe was spread to apply to all the bishops in the metropolitanate. It was not, however, until the twelfth century, or so it seems from a

---

monk can be ordained bishop, although a widowed priest, or a priest whose wife has taken the veil, can become a monk and then a bishop.

39. For a thorough and scholarly investigation of the eleventh- to fourteenth-century statutes, see Shchapov, *Knyazheskie ustavy*.

40. *PVL*, vol. 1, p. 85; Zimin, 'Pamyat' i pokhvala', p. 68.

textological investigation of Vladimir's Church Statute, that the Church's income was increased by granting bishops the right to judge not only 'Church People' – i.e. relatives of the clergy, those employed by the bishops or the churches, or those living on church premises – but also, for cases of family and marriage law, sorcery, magic and heresy, those *outside* the bishop's immediate jurisdiction, but within his eparchy. In Novgorod, for example, Prince Svyatoslav Ol'govich in 1137 attempted to increase the bishop's income by ensuring that he received a guaranteed fixed sum from the princely income (taxes from freshly colonized acquisitions in the Northern Dvina river district).[41] Although in Svyatoslav's Charter there is no word of the Church in Novgorod owning or being given landed possessions, in Rostislav Mstislavich of Smolensk's Charter we read: 'The village of Drosenskoe . . . with its land to the [church of the] Holy Mother of God and to the bishop [Manuil], and the village of Yasenskoe with its honey-farmer and land . . . to the Holy Mother of God; and I have given the Monshinskiy land in Pogonovichi to the Holy Mother of God and the bishop . . .'[42] – clear evidence of land grants bestowed by the prince on the bishop and his cathedral church for their upkeep. Rostislav's Charter also lays down the juridical division of labour between the bishop and the prince: the bishop has the right to judge 'Church People' in cases of divorce, bigamy and forbidden marriages (i.e. kindred and affinity), poisoning and murder, while abduction is shared with the prince's court.[43]

By the end of the twelfth century and the first forty years of the thirteenth, the main strength and wealth of the Church in Russia came from its landed property. At the same time we find a general broadening of the Church's jurisdiction – that is to say, the *bishops'* jurisdiction, for the white clergy and the monks had no right to act as judges. As well as 'Church People' we now find, in the category of those subject to Church law, physicians (*lechtsy*), *proshcheniki* (peasants given by the prince to the Church), monasteries, monastic hospitals, monastic guest-houses and almshouses; while together with family and marriage law, sorcery, magic and heresy, bishops are given the exclusive right to judge crimes committed against the Church: thefts from churches, corpse-robbing, sacrilege (carving wooden crosses; graffiti on church walls; bringing cattle, dogs or birds into church) – in other

41. *PRP*, vol. 2, pp. 117–18.
42. Ibid., p. 41, clause 4.
43. Ibid., clause 6.

words, crimes committed specifically against the Church which now are to be dealt with by the courts of the bishops.

While Vladimir's Church Statute and the charters of Svyatoslav and Rostislav deal mainly with the limits of the bishops' legal functions, in particular with the question of who could be tried in the Church courts, the Church Statute of Yaroslav, as a codex of Church law, is more concerned with the details of the cases within the bishops' jurisdiction – types of offences and penalties awardable.

The earliest version of Yaroslav's Statute, dating to the mid-eleventh century (1051–53), stresses in its introductory clause the exclusion of the lay judiciary in the jurisdiction of the Church: 'it is not right for these cases to be judged by the prince or his boyars'.[44] Punishment too was mainly in the purview of the metropolitan or the bishops, although in some cases such as abduction and adultery there is a rider to the effect that 'the prince may punish' (*a knyaz' kaznit'*) – maybe an indication that in the early days the Church lacked punitive officials and therefore was obliged to rely on civic organs of punishment.[45]

By far the biggest group of offences lies within the realm of family law (marriage break-ups, pagan marriages, adultery, fornication within the family, incest, contumely, assault and battery, abduction). As for the 'black' and 'white' clergy themselves and church officers (readers, sub-deacons, etc.), Yaroslav's Statute gives the bishop the right to pass judgement in cases of drunkenness, breach of monastic celibacy, fornication and unfrocking of priests and monks.

In the second half of the twelfth century and the beginning of the thirteenth several additions were made to the earliest version of the Statute. Again these are mostly complexities of marriage law – breach of pre-marriage contract, remarriage without legal divorce, validity of marriage outside the Church (i.e. 'pagan' marriages').[46] Of considerable interest are those articles which outline grounds for divorce which were valid at the time. Not surprisingly, most of these concern the guilt of the wife: adultery (whether caught *in flagrante* or confirmed by witnesses); attempt to murder her husband or failure to report a plan to kill him; relations with people outside the marital home which might constitute a threat to her honour; disposal of his goods after

---

44. Ibid., 1, p. 259.

45. Shchapov, *Knyazheskie ustavy*, p. 298.

46. According to Metropolitan Ioann II's 'Canonical Answers', it appears that even in the 1080s 'only boyars and princes' were married in church. 'Common people' dispensed with 'blessing and crowning' (i.e. church ceremony) and limited their marriages to 'dancing, music and clapping'. *RIB*, vol. 6, col. 18 (No. 30).

robbery; and – somewhat unexpectedly – failure to report the planned burglary of a church.[47] Finally, there are some interesting sidelights on contacts with Jews and Moslems: for example, fornication with a Russian woman incurs heavy penalties, but there is no mention of any form of intercourse, social or sexual, with Latins being forbidden or discouraged.

As for the penalties laid down in the Statutes, needless to say they varied from period to period and still more – and often still more surprisingly – from offence to offence. The basic punishments were fines payable to the metropolitan or the local bishop, often with compensation to the victim. Occasionally the court would leave the determination and infliction of the punishment to the husband of the erring wife – for example, in cases of her practising pagan cults (magic, witchcraft) or of theft from her husband or father-in-law. For a wife who quits her husband without divorce and marries another man, the punishment was tonsure for the wife and a fine paid by the second husband to the metropolitan or the bishop. In minor infringements of family law the judge was able simply to prescribe penance.

Much of the ecclesiastical legal system in early Russia was, as one might expect, inherited from Byzantium. But there were considerable differences. As Shchapov points out, most of the misdemeanours dealt with by the Church authorities in Russia – rape, abduction, divorce, bastardy, fornication, incest, bigamy, bestiality, insult, theft and arson – were within the jurisdiction of the civil courts in Byzantium and were punished by the Greek Church only with ecclesiastic disciplinary measures: admonition, penance or excommunication.[48] But whereas the senior Greek hierarchs enjoyed wealth from landed estates, annual taxation of the parish clergy and tribute,[49] the Russian metropolitans and bishops compensated for their relative landlessness by means of their harmonious sharing of the legal procedure with the State.

THE CREATION OF SAINTS

Side by side with the establishment of the Church in Russia – the organization of its hierarchy and its priesthood – went the creation of

47. Shchapov, *Knyazheskie ustavy*, pp. 247 ff.
48. Ibid., pp. 304–5.
49. Kartashev, *Ocherki*, pp. 203–4.

a whole communion of Russian saints. From the death of Vladimir's grandmother Ol'ga in 969 to the end of the twelfth century, one hundred and forty-eight Russians or others living in Russia are known to have been venerated as saints,[50] although in fact very few were canonized until later, mostly at the time of the 'official' canonizations instituted by Metropolitan Makary in the middle of the sixteenth century.

Not surprisingly, just over half of this number of saints were monks. They are followed by some thirty-three prelates (bishops, archbishops and metropolitans), thirty princes and princesses, twelve Greek architects, builders and painters who in the eleventh century constructed the Church of the Dormition in the Monastery of the Caves, two 'Varangian' martyrs (see above, p. 33), one nun (Evfrosy-nya of Polotsk) and Boris's servant Georgy (see below, p. 108). A number of these were recognized as martyrs, though not so often as martyrs for refusing to renounce Christianity as 'passion-sufferers' (*strastoterptsy*) or sometimes non-resistant victims of political assassination. And two, Vladimir and his grandmother Ol'ga, were designated 'equal to the Apostles' (*ravnoapostol'nye*).[51]

One of the great difficulties facing anyone investigating the history of saintship in Russia, particularly saintship in the pre-Mongol period, is the problem of establishing what the process of canonization was in the early Orthodox Church. What conditions were necessary for a person to be numbered among the saints? Who could authorize the process – local bishop, metropolitan, patriarch? And what precisely *was* the process? It would seem that in all probability miracles, such as healings performed at the grave, incorruptibility of remains, odours of sanctity exhaled by the corpse and so forth, were a *sine qua non*, or at least that any form of canonization was extremely difficult without them. It is also likely that in most cases *local* veneration – in the diocese, or even in the church where the burial took place or to which the relics may have been translated – preceded *universal* recognition of sanctity, in other words full canonization, with the concomitant writing of the saint's *Life*, composition of a service to the saint, recognition by the metropolitan and ultimately the patriarch, and the inscription of the saint's name and date of death in the diptychs.

Most perplexing of all is the silence of the sources concerning the canonization of Vladimir and Ol'ga. True, the early chronicles appear

---

50. Lilienfeld, *Der Himmel*, p. 11.
51. For a complete list, see ibid., pp. 124–36.

to lavish on them misleading epithets – 'blessed', 'pious', 'divine', 'Christ-loving', 'holy' – but most of these are probably no more than interpolations made in a later age when their sanctity was officially and universally recognized; true, the Primary Chronicle and the monk Iakov praise them to the skies ('thrice-blessed among princes' for Vladimir, and 'forerunner of the Christian land . . . dawn before light', etc. for Ol'ga); and, true, Metropolitan Ilarion compares Vladimir with Constantine the Great ('equal in wisdom, equal in the love of Christ, equal in honouring the servants of God'[52]), but there is no mention of a church or monastery dedicated to either before the fourteenth century;[53] their names were clearly regarded as pagan in the pre-Mongol period (in the princely dynasty 'Vladimir' was not used as a Christian name[54] and only four women are known to have been given the name of Ol'ga throughout the twelfth and thirteenth centuries); no icons of either were painted, as far as is known, before the fifteenth century;[55] no early *Life of Vladimir* was written, while the earliest brief *Life* of Ol'ga only exists in a South Slavonic version datable to the end of the thirteenth/beginning of the fourteenth century, and it gives no indication as to when or why Ol'ga was canonized. And yet, of course, both *were* canonized.

Much work on the question has been done by scholars from Golubinsky to the present day, and nearly all agree that neither was formally canonized in the tenth, eleventh or even the twelfth centuries. This writer's views are that the only possible *termini a quo* and *ad quem* for the years of the canonization – at any rate of Vladimir – are 1283 and 1311[56] respectively, and that the canonization of both Vladimir and Ol'ga in fact took place in 1284, the date of the only Council of all the Russian bishops convened by Metropolitan Maksim in Kiev. Although the sole source to mention this Council, the Nikon Chronicle, says nothing about its deliberations, it reports that in the following year Maksim visited 'all the Russian land, teaching, instructing and

---

52. Ilarion's one fleeting mention of Ol'ga (Müller, *MIL*, pp. 118–19) is probably a later interpolation, but see Müller's view: ibid., p. 23.

53. Indeed, no churches or nunneries dedicated to Ol'ga are recorded before the end of the seventeenth century.

54. Vodoff, 'Pourquoi', pp. 448–9.

55. But see Fennell, 'When was Ol'ga Canonized?', p. 78.

56. The *Life* of Aleksandr Nevskiy, written *c.*1283 (*PLDR, XIII vek*, pp. 426–39) in what was probably its prototype, has no mention of *Saint* Vladimir (the date of his death, 15 July, being the same as that of the Neva battle), but *later* versions have; 1311 is the date of the building of the stone church in Novgorod dedicated to *Saint* Vladimir. See Fennell, 'The Canonization', pp. 322–3.

administering' – and doubtless spreading the news of Vladimir's and Ol'ga's canonization: both Novgorod, where Vladimir ruled before Kiev and where the first church to him was soon to be built, and Pskov, where Ol'ga was born, being specifically mentioned.

Why the canonization of Vladimir was so long delayed cannot be plausibly explained away by any political disagreements or misunderstandings between Kiev and Constantinople or by any opposition on the part of the patriarch to the glorification of Vladimir. The reason was more likely the absence of miracles following his death: there were no healings at his grave, indeed no possibility of odours of sanctity or incorruptibility, as his body was not exhumed before the seventeenth century. As for Ol'ga, the monk Iakov contrasts her grandson with her by stressing the imperishableness of her body ('her holy body remained incorruptible in the grave . . . Thus God glorified His servant Ol'ga'[57]). However, these words ascribed to Iakov may well have been added at a later date and cannot be considered as evidence of her early canonization. Both Vladimir and Ol'ga were no doubt the objects of local veneration in Kiev, Novgorod and, for Ol'ga, Pskov before their ultimate canonization at the end of the thirteenth century.

57. Zimin, 'Pamyat' i pokhvala', pp. 69, 70.

CHAPTER FIVE
Religious Activity and Monasticism

1

While we have a certain amount of information concerning the election, functions and emoluments of the senior echelons of the Russian Church in the two hundred and fifty years before the Mongol invasion, unfortunately we know very little about the workforce itself – the parish priests, the 'white clergy' of the towns and villages. We have, alas, no idea as to how in the early days they were recruited, how they were trained, how, indeed, they learned the basic principles of the Orthodox faith and how they were taught to run their parishes. We hear of no schools, no spiritual academies for the training of the clergy, unless of course Vladmir's scheme to educate the children of the 'best people' in 988 (see above, p. 42) involved the foundation of a seminary. We can only assume that just as in the eleventh century Metropolitan Georgy brought with him a specialist to initiate the monks of the Kievan Monastry of the Caves into the complexities of the Studite Rule (see below, p. 67), so the early metropolitans brought with them from Constantinople – or perhaps sent for from slavophone Bulgaria – instructors capable of drumming into the heads of the neophyte deacons and priests the basic essentials of their profession. After a generation or two the supply met the demand, as priests trained members of their parishes or indeed their own sons to succeed them in the ministry.

That the demand was indeed met there can be no doubt, for the two-and-a-half centuries after the conversion witnessed an extraordinary growth in the number of churches in Russia. We mentioned above (see pp. 42–3) that the written records show only about twelve churches built during the first twenty-seven years after the baptism of

Vladimir. Other estimates, however, indicate that more than double
that number were in existence in the tenth century alone, although
this figure includes archaeological as well as written evidence, to say
nothing of churches which probably existed before 988. Obviously it
is impossible to estimate with anything approaching accuracy the total
number of churches, parishes and priests in the eleventh, twelfth or
early thirteenth centuries. However, according to the reckoning of
one Soviet medievalist, B. V. Sapunov, of the churches to whose
construction a date can be assigned there were 25 in the tenth century,
37 in the eleventh, 138 in the twelfth and 46 in the first forty years of
the thirteenth century – a total of 247. To these can be added another
76, the building of which cannot be dated.[1] But the total of 323, says
Sapunov, is only a tiny fraction of the *probable* total of *all* churches
built in Russia in the period. His general conclusions are that in the
two-and-a-half centuries between Vladimir's conversion and the
Mongol invasion some 2,000 town churches were built or rebuilt. To
these must be added, first, 20,000–30,000 *private* chapels – churches or
chapels in the houses of individual laymen[2] – and seemingly some
6,000 village or country churches.[3] Even if these calculations are
exaggerated – though Sapunov considers them 'conservative' – there
can be no doubt that church-building increased enormously in the 250
years we are talking about and that the number of parishes and priests
multiplied correspondingly.

2

The growth of monasteries was no less striking. Sapunov's figures
show a steady increase comparable to that of the number of town
churches: according to his reckoning the number of monasteries
founded (988–1240), the dates of which can be established from the
sources, is 71 (tenth century – 7; eleventh – 18; twelfth – 30; 1200–40
– 16), to which must be added another 56 whose dates cannot be
fixed: a total of 127, or, allowing for underestimation, 200.

It is hard to say which and where was the earliest monastery in
Russia. In his Sermon on Law and Grace (between 1037 and 1051)

1. Sapunov, 'Nekotorye soobrazheniya', p. 320.
2. Ibid., pp. 320–1. On private chapels in Byzantium and Russia, see Golubinsky,
IRTs, vol. 1, I, pp. 471–3; Froyanov, 'Nachalo', pp. 290 ff.
3. Sapunov, 'Nekotorye soobrazheniya', p. 320.

Metropolitan Ilarion talks of 'monasteries arising in the hills' and 'monks appearing' as the result of Vladimir's decision to Christianize all Rus';[4] and the Primary Chronicle under the year 1037, after mentioning Yaroslav's founding of the monasteries of St George and St Irina, extols the growth of Christianity: 'the Christian faith began to bear fruit and to multiply, and monasteries began to be [founded].'[5]

The earliest Kievan monasteries about which we have any firm information all date from the middle of the eleventh century. By far the most distinguished, powerful and enduring is the great Kiev Monastry of the Caves (*Kievo-pecherskiy monastyr'*). According to the confused and muddled story of its origins which found its way into the Primary Chronicle under the year 1051, a layman by the name of Antip,[6] from the town of Lyubech near Chernigov, set off on a pilgrimage to the great centre of Orthodox monasticism, Mount Athos (the eastern promontory of the peninsula of Chalcidice). There he was tonsured and given the name of Antony. The abbot of the monastery – maybe the Russian monastery of Ksilourgou[7] – who instructed him in the monkish way of life, said to him: 'Go back to Rus' and may the blessing of the Holy Mountain be [with you], for there will be many monks because of you.' On his return Antony, after wandering from monastery to monastery, none of which was to his liking, came across a cave overlooking the river Dnepr where Ilarion himself had once lived as a hermit. He settled either in or near Ilarion's cave. His renown as a hermit spread, and, after Yaroslav's death (1054), he was joined by the apostolic number of twelve followers whom he tonsured and with whom he dug 'a great cave and a church and cells'. He then bade them 'live by themselves', appointed their first abbot, one Varlaam, and set off to a nearby hill where he dug himself a cave and resumed his eremitical existence. Eventually the number of monks increased to such an extent that they came to Antony and asked his permission 'to found a monastery'. Antony asked Izyaslav of Kiev, Yaroslav's eldest surviving son, for land, and the monks were given 'the hill which is above the cave'. There Abbot Varlaam and the monks 'laid the foundations of a great church and

4. Müller, *MIL*, p. 106.

5. *PVL*, vol. 1, p. 102.

6. *LPS*, p. 45. He was canonized (unknown where) under his monastic name Antony. No *Vita* has survived.

7. Or perhaps in the monasteries of Esphigmenou or Iviron. See Prosvirin, 'Afon i russkaya Tserkov'', p. 12. About Antony and the first Russian monasteries on Mount Athos, see Moshin, 'Russkie na Afone', pp. 58–67.

surrounded the monastery with a palisade, built many cells, completed the church and adorned it with ikons'. 'Such', the chronicler concludes, 'was the origin of the Monastery of the Caves'; and he adds: 'This is the Monastery of the Caves [which] issued from the Holy Mountain.'[8]

The monastery flourished throughout the pre-Mongol period under a number of intelligent, distinguished and often saintly abbots. The first of these, Varlaam, whom Izyaslav transferred to his new monastery of St Dmitry in 1062, was replaced by the first of all Russian abbots to be canonized, St Feodosy (died 1074).[9] His *Life*, written by a fellow-monk, Nestor, author of one of the accounts of the murder of SS Boris and Gleb and perhaps the first redactor of the Primary Chronicle, is remarkable not only for its exhilarating portrayal of the dramatic conflict between Feodosy and his formidable mother, who does all she can to restrain him from becoming a monk, but also for the wonderfully vivid pictures of his life in the monastery. Nestor describes in detail his ascetic practices, his temptations, his humility and gentleness, his 'wretched garments' unbefitting his rank as abbot, his concern with the economic welfare of the monastery, his insistence on strict discipline, his concern for beggars and the sick, his building of almshouses and his dealings with the outside world.

Feodosy's abbacy marked the beginning of the growth and prosperity of the monastery. The pattern of his rule was to have a profound influence on the future of Russian monasticism. It must be remembered that the Caves Monastery was not a 'princely' monastery, neither founded by a prince nor dependent on a princely line. Nor was it directly dependent on the metropolitan, and indeed in the course of its early history it was frequently in conflict both with the princes and with the metropolitans – and even at times with Constantinople. And yet it must not be imagined that it remained aloof from the political life of the country. It did not, and, what is more, it made its voice heard. In 1068, for example, when Prince Izyaslav of Kiev had fled the country after the Triumvirate's defeat at the hands of the Polovtsy, the Kievans released the rebellious Prince Vseslav of Polotsk whom Izyaslav, having broken his solemn oath on the Cross, had gaoled in Kiev. The monastery, in the person of the chronicler, voiced its deep disapproval of Izyaslav: 'And Vseslav sat upon the throne in Kiev. Thus God revealed the power of the Cross. For Izyaslav had

8. *PVL*, vol. 1, pp. 104–7.
9. There is no evidence to show that St Antony was ever abbot of the Caves Monastery.

broken his oath on the Cross by seizing him.'[10] And it was not just Izyaslav towards whom the monastery's hostility was directed; for in 1073, when his two brothers, Svyatoslav and Vsevolod, quarrelled with him and drove him out of Kiev, the monastery condemned their action in no uncertain terms:

> The devil stirred up strife among the brothers . . . Svyatoslav and Vsevolod joined together against Izyaslav. And Izyaslav quit Kiev . . . Svyatoslav was the cause of his brother's expulsion, because he desired more power . . . And Svyatoslav sat upon the throne in Kiev, having chased his brother out, thus transgressing the commandment of his father[11] and still more that of God.[12]

In his *Life* of St Feodosy Nestor is even more condemnatory:

> There was at that time a certain disarray amongst the three princes caused by the all-cunning devil: two of them stirred up trouble against the eldest, Izyaslav, the lover of Christ, indeed the lover of God. When he was driven out of the capital city, the two of them came into that city and sent for our blessed Father Feodosy, urging him to come and dine with them . . . And the venerable Feodosy, knowing that [Izyaslav's] expulsion was unjust, told the messenger: 'I shall not come to the table of Beelzebub and partake of food soaked in blood and murder . . .'[13]

The political independence of the Kievan Monastery of the Caves, which enabled its first abbot to refer to the prince of Kiev as seated at the table of Beelzebub and to rebuke him for his behaviour, was due to two things: first, to the fact that it was not founded by a prince and thus was not tied to any one branch of the Ryurikovich dynasty; and, secondly, to the social origins of many of the monks themselves, at any rate in the early days. Antony may have been of well-to-do if not boyar stock – he certainly enjoyed easy access to the prince of Kiev – while of the early monks Feodosy was the son of one of Izyaslav's senior officials, a boyar perhaps; Varlaam, the first abbot, was the son of a boyar and clearly a favourite of Izyaslav; and Efrem, later metropolitan of Pereyaslavl' (see above, p. 54), had held high rank at Izyaslav's court. It was not surprising that the monastery was able to treat with a prince of Kiev on equal terms, to hold its own in the political conflicts of the age and, later in the twelfth century, to allow its premises to be used as a neutral, Geneva-type centre, where princes could thrash out their differences.[14]

10. *PVL*, vol. 1, p. 115.
11. See above, pp. 12–13.
12. *PVL*, vol. 1, pp. 121–2.
13. *Sbornik XII*, p. 85; *PLDR, XI–nachalo XII veka*, p. 376.
14. In 1150 and 1169. See Shchapov, *Gosudarstvo*, p. 156.

The preeminence of the Caves Monastery becomes only too clear if we look at the activities of many of its monks. At least five of them, in the period we are talking about, founded their own monasteries closely linked with the mother foundation, and many of its alumni became bishops.[15] For, indeed, it was a nursery of future prelates as well as being a centre of culture and learning, with its chronicle-writers, its hagiographers, its historians. There was no question but that the Monastery of the Caves was the leading monastery in the whole country; indeed, it was the first whose abbot was raised to the rank of archimandrite in the second half of the twelfth century.[16]

Much of the monastery's success was due to its organization and its strict discipline. However much Antony may have learned from the monastery on the Holy Mountain where he was professed, it was Feodosy who first began to 'seek a monastic Rule'. According to one version, one Mikhail, a monk of the great Studite Monastery in Constantinople, renowned in the past for the strictness of its Rule, came from Constantinople together with Metropolitan Georgy (metropolitan from *c.*1065 to 1078). Evidently the metropolitan either knew of Feodosy's quest or planned himself to introduce the Studite Rule to Russian monastic life. Whatever the reason, Feodosy managed to obtain a copy of the Rule from Mikhail and

> established how in his monastery singing should be carried out, how prostrations should be performed, how readings should be read, and how monks should stand [i.e. behave] in church, and all the church ritual, and how monks should sit in the refectory and what they should eat on what days, all in accordance with the Rule. Having obtained all this, Feodosy transmitted it to his monastery. And all the monasteries imitated the Rule of this monastery, for the Caves Monastery is honoured as the oldest of them all.[17]

Apart from introducing the strict Studite Rule, according to which the monks lived a communal life under the authority of the abbot and owned no personal possessions, Feodosy added a totally new dimension to the life of the State: he created a charitable welfare service.

15. Tikhomirov, *Drevnerusskie goroda*, p. 179.
16. *c.*1171 Abbot Polikarp was first given the title of archimandrite. The rank, in the Greek Church, signified the head of a group of monasteries and was bestowed by the patriarch. In the Russian Church it meant little more than the head of a large monastery. See Shchapov, *Gosudarstvo*, pp. 159–60.
17. *PVL*, vol. 1, p. 107. See Tachiaos, 'The Greek Metropolitans'. A slightly different version is found in the *Life* of St Feodosy included in the Paterikon of the Caves Monastery. See *Kyyevo-Pechers'kyy pateryk*, p. 39.

Hitherto, as far as we can tell, there had been no attempt on the part
of the State to provide for the poor, the hungry, the prisoners and the
sick. But Feodosy changed all this. In Nestor's *Life*, after a touching
little tale of some robbers whom Feodosy had pitied – he fed them,
taught them 'to offend no one and to do no harm', and then set them
at liberty – Nestor reflects on Feodosy's compassion and his charitable
deeds:

> For such was the mercy of our great Father Feodosy that if he saw a
> beggar or a suffering or ill-clad pauper, he had great mercy on him and
> grieved deeply for him . . . And for this reason he had a building
> constructed near the monastery . . . where he bade the beggars, the blind,
> the lame and the sick to dwell, and he gave them what they needed from
> the monastery['s resources], and he gave them a tenth part of all that the
> monastery possessed. And to the prisoners he sent every Saturday a
> cartload of bread.[18]

In a later age, when the State was all too anxious to secularize the vast
lands of the monasteries, the Church was quick to defend its property
by repeating what might have been Feodosy's dictum: 'the wealth of
the Church is the wealth of the poor.'

By creating an institution which was anything but closed to the
outside world, by showing a readiness to criticize the conduct of the
rulers of Kiev if it was felt to be unjust, by making the monastery not
only a centre for cultural activities but also a venue for inter-princely
political exchanges and a nursery for the episcopate and above all by
providing accommodation for the poor, a hospital for the sick and a
soup-kitchen for the starving, the great abbot of the Kievan Monastery
of the Caves was setting the tone, and providing a model, for Russian
coenobitic monasticism in the centuries to come.

Far less is known of the so-called 'princely' monasteries of the age,
for there are practically no records of their pattern of life or of the
activities of their superiors. All were closely linked to their lay
founders and their descendants. The only houses founded by Vladimir's
son Yaroslav were the Kievan monasteries of St Georgy and St Irina,[19]
about which virtually nothing is known except that they were consecrated in the middle of the eleventh century and that they were
funded exclusively by Yaroslav's treasury.[20] A little more information
is available about the monasteries inaugurated by the 'triumvirate' of

18. *Sbornik XII*, pp. 75–6; *PLDR, XI–nachalo XII veka*, p. 362.
19. Georgy was Yaroslav's baptismal name; Irina – that of his wife, Ingigerd.
20. Shchapov, *Gosudarstvo*, pp. 132–3.

Yaroslav's sons, Izyaslav, Svyatoslav and Vsevolod. Izyaslav's monastery of St Dmitry (Izyaslav's baptismal name), to which, as we have
seen, he transferred Varlaam of the Caves Monastery as its first abbot
in 1062, was certainly the family monastery of Izyaslav and his
descendants. In 1086 or 1087 his eldest son Yaropolk was buried in its
church of St Petr which Yaropolk himself had built; while the second
church of the monastery, that of St Mikhail, built by Izyaslav's second
son Svyatopolk in the beginning of the twelfth century, was used as
Svyatopolk's burial place in 1113, as well as that of two of his great-
grandsons in 1190 and 1195. Svyatoslav's family had two monasteries:
one, St Simeon's, founded by Svyatoslav in Kiev and the other, St
Kirill's, founded by Svyatoslav's grandson Vsevolod (prince of Kiev
1139–46) just outside Kiev. Both were used to house family burial
vaults. The youngest member of the triumvirate, Vsevolod, his son
Vladimir Monomakh and his grandson Mstislav Vladimirovich are
known to have founded four monasteries between them, all of them
closely connected with various branches of Vsevolod's many descendants. Of particular importance was the great Monastery of St Mikhail
in Vydubichi near Kiev, probably built in the 1060s, which vied with
the Kiev Monastery of the Caves both culturally and administratively,
especially as a centre of chronicle-writing from the beginning of the
twelfth century. All of these monasteries, as well as those founded by
other branches of the princely family – and these included the great
twelfth- and thirteenth-century monasteries and nunneries of
Vladimir-on-the Klyaz'ma – were quite distinct from the Kiev Caves
Monastery in so far as they seem to have owed their allegiance first
and foremost to the families of their founders and probably to have
depended to a large degree for their funding on princely generosity.

Of the Novgorodian monasteries, the most important, wealthy and
influential, the great Yur'ev Monastery, founded probably by Yaroslav
the Wise (baptismally Georgy; Yury = Georgy) could hardly be
called a 'princely' foundation proper, as Novgorod's princes came
from different branches of the Ryurikovich dynasty (see above, pp. 18–19).
Still, it appears to have been patronized in the early twelfth century by
Vladimir Monomakh's son Mstislav and grandson Vsevolod.[21]

At the end of the Primary Chronicle's account of the early years of
the Caves Monastery (*s.a.* 1051), the passage describing the introduction of the Studite Rule by Feodosy ends with the words: 'From this
same monastery all the monasteries adopted the [Studite] Rule.'[22]

21. Ibid., p. 148.
22. *PVL*, vol. 1, p. 107.

Alas, there is no information to substantiate this claim of Nestor's: there are no descriptive *Lives* of abbots like that of Feodosy, no *Lives of the Fathers* like the wonderful Paterikon of the Monastery of the Caves. Were the princely monasteries and the Novgorod monasteries truly coenobitic? And did the Caves Monastery itself continue strict observance of the Studite Rule? The great nineteenth-century historian of the Russian Church, E. Golubinsky, had serious doubts. True coenobitism (*obshchezhitie*) – the disciplined communal life in which the brethren had no personal possessions – in his view, gradually gave way to the idiorhythmic way of life (*osobnozhitie* – 'living apart'), according to which each monk lived his own life in his own cell, with his own possessions, his own food.[23] In his opinion, after the death of Feodosy 'only a small particle of true coenobitism introduced by him remained', while his view of Russian monasticism in general, from the end of the eleventh century to 1240, is even more pessimistic. But still the monasteries were there, and they survived. And however much the discipline may have slackened after the first flush of post-Conversion enthusiasm, it was only a question of time before the reformers reconstituted and overhauled Russian coenobitism in the fourteenth century.

3

In the fifteenth and sixteenth centuries all the ills of monasticism were time and again attributed to *styazhatel'stvo*, or acquisitiveness, which meant the acquisitiveness not only of individual monks but also of the monasteries themselves – in other words, landownership. To what extent did monastic landownership develop in pre-Mongol Russia? Did the monasteries depend for their survival and upkeep on the ownership and development of landed estates?

We know most about the Caves Monastery's landed possessions. This is not necessarily because the monastery was endowed with more land than any of the others, but simply because we know so much more about the place from the voluminous records of its life, especially its life in the eleventh century. In all the versions of Feodosy's

---

23. Golubinsky, *IRTs*, vol. 1, II, pp. 631 ff. See also Podskalsky, 'Der hl. Feodosij', p. 719.

stewardship there are frequent mentions of the monastery's villages (*sela*), in other words its lands. 'Princes and boyars' are mentioned as frequent visitors to the 'noble-minded Feodosy', to whom they confessed their sins and whom they rewarded by 'bringing him a small part of their possessions', while 'others gave even their lands [to the brethren] to be managed by them'.[24] Before his death we find Feodosy summoning all the monks, including 'those that were in the monastery's lands'.[25] Indeed, at the very beginning Izyaslav is said to have granted Antony 'the hill which is over the cave' – the first record of a land grant by a prince to a monastery in Russia. Curiously enough, the only other recorded land grants to the Caves Monastery – apart from 'a monastic hostel . . . with lands' in distant Suzdal'[26] – were all made by Izyaslav's descendants. His eldest son Yaropolk is known to have given the monastery at some time or other three 'districts' (*volosti*) in or near Volynia, as well as land 'near Kiev',[27] while his childless daughter Nastasia was not only buried in the monastery in 1158 but gave it 'five villages with serfs – all of them even to the [last] kerchief'.[28]

Of the other monasteries in Russia our only knowledge of landholdings is of those in Novgorod, and very little at that. The Yur'ev Monastery, as the leading monastery in Novgorod territory, probably owned most land. But only two of its land grants have survived for the pre-Mongol period. The land of Buytsi, some 200 kilometres south-south-east of Novgorod near the border with the principality of Smolensk, was given to the monastery by Vladimir Monomakh's son and grandson, Mstislav and Vsevolod Mstislavich, in 1130 together with various taxes and juridical fees, normally paid to the prince; and shortly afterwards Vsevolod gave the monastery yet another district, that of Lyakhovichi on the Lovat' river south of Novgorod.[29] Other Novgorod monasteries, for example the Panteleymonov and Khutynskiy, are also known to have owned land, but we have no idea of the size of their holdings.[30]

24. *na popechenie im* (*Sbornik XII*, p. 60; *PLDR, XI–nachalo XII veka*, p. 338). Whether this implies a loan or a grant is hard to say.

25. *Sbornik XII*, p. 90; *PLDR, XI–nachalo XII veka*, p. 384.

26. Mentioned *s.a.* 1097 (*PSRL*, vol. 2, col. 228; *PVL*, vol. 1, p. 169).

27. *PSRL*, vol. 2, col. 492. Two of the districts, 'Nebel'skaya' and 'Luch'skaya', were in Volynia, where Yaropolk had ruled from 1078 (*PVL*, vol. 1, p. 135). The third, 'Derevskaya', may have been in Turov, Izyaslav's and Yaropolk's patrimony.

28. *i vse da i do povoya* – i.e. every single one of them. *PSRL*, vol. 2, col. 493.

29. *GVNP*, No. 81, pp. 140–1 and No. 80, pp. 139–40.

30. Ibid., No. 82, p. 141 and No. 83, pp. 161–2. As for size, the approximate area of Buytsi and Lyakhovichi was 800 sq. km. each. See Shchapov, *Gosudarstvo*, p. 154.

So the answer to the question 'to what extent did monastic landownership develop in pre-Mongol Russia?' is, we don't know, because there are so few sources to tell us. Chronicle compilers and editors were by and large more concerned with the incessant squabbles, wars and alliances between the princes than with the domestic economy of the monasteries; and land contracts between donors and recipients simply have not survived. However, it would be rash to suggest, as some historians have done, that most monasteries in pre-Mongol Russia were indifferent to landownership and depended mainly on the generosity of their founders, patrons and benefactors.

CHAPTER SIX

The Process of Christianization

PASTORAL CARE: THE 'QUESTIONS OF KIRIK'

With the formidable increase in the number of churches and parishes from Vladimir's baptism to the Mongol invasion, there must have been vast problems for the clergy not only in acquiring the technical knowledge for performing the religious services and explaining Christianity, but also in looking after the moral lives of their flocks, most members of which in the eleventh and twelfth centuries, especially in country districts, had barely been weaned from their old pagan ways of life. This could of course be done by preaching. But how frequently, if at all, did priests deliver sermons? To go by the few surviving specimens of pre-Mongol homiletic literature – Metropolitan Ilarion's great monument of rhetoric, his Sermon on Law and Grace, the twelfth-century Bishop Kirill of Turov's oratorical extravaganzas and the primitive catalogue of the basic tenets of the faith in the only known sermon of Bishop Luka of Novgorod (1036–c.1059)[1] – it would seem that sermons were too florid for many to understand or too dry and simple to be of much use as guides for living the Christian life.

But if congregations were unlikely to understand, listen to or be inspired by sermons on how to conduct their lives, individuals were certainly made aware of what was right and wrong at the confessional. While we can learn a certain amount about the behavioural pattern of

---

1. See Fennell and Stokes, *Early Russian Literature*, pp. 40–54, for an evaluation of the style and contents of the above. Eight of the 'teachings' (*poucheniya*) of Abbot Feodosy of the Kiev Caves Monastery have survived. But these are mainly concerned with monastic discipline and behaviour. See also Podskalsky, *Christentum*, pp. 84–106.

73

the family in Kievan Rus' from the Church Statutes of Vladimir and Yaroslav as well as from the legal codices (for example, from the *Russkaya pravda*), we can get a far more vivid picture from the penitentials – those works which deal with the imposition of penance according to the canons of the Church. Without any doubt the most illuminating of these works as far as the pre-Mongol period is concerned is the remarkable so-called 'Questions of Kirik' (*Voproshanie Kirika*).[2]

It consists of a hundred and one questions put by Kirik, an otherwise unknown priest-monk, and twenty-four and twenty-eight questions put by equally unknown 'white' priests, Savva and Il'ya respectively; the answers to these questions are given by Bishop Nifont of Novgorod (1131–56). Although Kirik himself was a monk and a few of his questions refer to monastic affairs, many of the questions of all three are concerned with the public and private life of the clergy themselves – a sort of code of clerical behaviour – and also of course with the conduct of lay parishioners, particularly with their family relationships. It might be expected that such questions put to the bishop of Novgorod would refer mainly to urban communities, but a few of them are concerned with rural parishes as well.

The number of subjects treated in the questions is large, and many, not surprisingly, have to do with the Liturgy itself. Several of Kirik's questions are connected with the Eucharist: should Communion be given to a person having an epileptic fit or to a lunatic?[3] What penance should be given to a person who vomits after receiving Communion?[4] How should a priest give Communion to the sick?[5] May a person with a suppurating sore or a bleeding tooth receive Communion?[6] Most of these questions are answered by the bishop with common sense. 'If', for example, 'a person vomits having taken Communion from over-eating or drunkenness, then forty days of penance [the nature of the penance is not specified]; if from nausea – twenty days; if from a sudden onset of illness – then less.' As for whether someone with a suppurating sore is worthy of receiving Communion, Nifont leaves Kirik in no doubt whatsoever: 'He is indeed worthy. It is not the stench from pus that debars man from the Sacrament, nor that which comes from the mouth of others, but the

---

2. Printed in *RIB*, vol. 6, cols. 21–62. For a detailed investigation, see Giraudo, 'Voprošanie'.

3. *RIB*, vol. 6, cols. 28 (No. 16), 29 (No. 18).

4. Ibid., cols. 21–2 (No. 1).

5. Ibid., col. 37 (No. 56).

6. Ibid., cols. 39, 40 (Nos. 61, 62).

stench of sin.' These were clearly very actual matters for Kirik and the two priests, and the questions were not asked lightly.

Still more worrying were those questions connected with the priest's own sexual practices. May a priest serve who has had intercourse with his wife on the day before the Liturgy? And if a priest wishes to serve on a Sunday and a Tuesday, may he have intercourse with his wife on the Monday? Nifont replies: 'If he is young and unable to abstain, it should not be forbidden . . .'[7] He shows no less indulgence in his reply to questions as to whether a priest should be allowed to serve after a noctural emission: 'If your thoughts have been directed to some woman, then it is not fitting [to serve]; but if you have prepared yourself for the service and Satan tempts you, desiring to deprive you of the service, then, having performed your ablutions, serve.'[8]

The problems facing Kirik and his two colleagues at the confessional were no less burdensome, and again most of them were connected with the penitents' intimate relationships. For example, should a man who has had intercourse with his wife during Great Lent be given Communion? This question enraged the bishop; 'In anger he answered: "Is that what you teach? That men in Lent should refrain from [intercourse with] their wives? That is a sin on your part!"'[9] Nifont, however, shows no leniency to what may have been the widespread problem of concubinage. Kirik, somewhat naïvely, asks: 'Some people openly have concubines and have children by them as though by their wives, and others do this secretly with many of their serfs. What is better?' To which the bishop replies: 'Neither the one nor the other.'[10]

The three priests were by no means only concerned with the shortcomings of men: women's transgressions and problems also caused them to seek Nifont's advice. Some of these are linked with surviving pagan practices. Il'ya, for instance, asks Nifont what penance should be imposed on women who take their sick children to sorcerers (*volkhvy*) instead of to a priest or who attempt to rekindle flagging desire in their husbands by giving them the water to drink in which they have washed their bodies. In both cases the bishop's snap answers are clear-cut: seven weeks of (unspecified) penance (or three 'if they are young') for preferring sorcerers to priests; and seven weeks of

7. Ibid., cols. 30, 31, (Nos. 28, 29); col. 45 (No. 77).
8. Ibid., cols. 55–6 (No. 17).
9. Ibid., cols. 37–8 (No. 57).
10. Ibid., cols. 41–2 (No. 69).

penance or a year without Communion for attempting to stimulate a frigid husband.[11] Seven weeks of penance is also prescribed for women who 'take their children to be prayed for by a Varangian priest [a magician perhaps? or a priest of another faith?], for these women are like those of "double faith"'[12] – i.e. Christian and pagan (see below, pp. 86 ff.). Clearly too it is women whom Kirik refers to when he talks of 'preparing bread, cheese and mead for Rod and Rozhanitsy [pagan deities of fertility]': Nifont sternly tells him to 'forbid them strongly: somewhere it is said "Woe unto them that drink to Rozhanitsa!"'[13] The uprooting of pagan survivals was evidently high in Nifont's list of priorities.

The questions and the answers cover a multitude of other problems, some not unexpected: the baptism of adults, the 'conversion' of Latins, fasting, pilgrimages to Jerusalem – every effort made to discourage these in that they lead to 'idleness, drinking and feasting' – usury practised by priests and laymen, homosexuality in women (but, in men, only an obscure reference to 'the sin of sodomy'), 'uncleanliness' of women, accidental miscarriages ('no penance if not caused by potions'); some bizarre: 'is it right for a priest to serve in a robe into which a fragment of a woman's dress has been sewn?' asks Savva. 'It is,' answers the bishop, adding, 'Do you consider a woman is a pagan then?' But all of these show just how seriously priests took their pastoral duties, how they agonized over their own misdemeanours and those of their flocks.

Above all, the 'Questions of Kirik' shows what good fortune he and his confrères had to seek advice from so humane a bishop as Nifont. Again and again Nifont reveals his good sense, his moderation, even his humour. When told by the naïve Kirik, 'I read that if a man lies with his wife on a Sunday or a Saturday or a Friday and a child is conceived, then that child will be either a thief or a robber or a fornicator or a coward and that the parents should be given two years of penance', he merely responds: 'Books like that ought to be burned!'[14] In answer to Il'ya's question about what to do 'if a man wants to repent but realizes that he cannot refrain from fornication', he says: 'Take him, and when he has heard your instructions, he will refrain.'[15] And when Il'ya asks his opinion about two girls enjoying

11. Ibid., col. 60 (Nos. 18, 14).
12. Ibid., col. 60 (No. 16).
13. Ibid., col. 31 (No. 33).
14. Ibid., col. 44 (No. 74).
15. Ibid., cols. 59–60 (No. 13).

sexual relations with each other, he merely shrugs it off with, 'Better than doing it with a man.'[16]

No less humane and sensible was Il'ya, the first bishop of Novgorod to be given the title of archbishop in 1165.[17] During his episcopate he wrote a treatise (*pouchenie*) consisting of a number of precepts for the clergy of his diocese – mainly questions of confession and penance.[18] There is little that is different in tone and contents from the earlier penitential, and the moderation shown is reminiscent of Nifont's.[19] For example, when talking about penance for those confessing over-indulgence in food and drink, he advises priests 'to judge according to the person concerned: should he be robust, then give him a bigger penance (*bolshyu zapoved'*); but should he be weak, then a lighter (*l'zh'shyu*) one, lest he fall into despair'.[20] On another occasion he points out that he himself is no angel (*ne angel esm'*);[21] and in a section dealing with fornication , concubinage and abduction, he recommends that a certain amount of tolerance be shown.[22]

PAGAN SURVIVALS: WITCHCRAFT AND SORCERY

It is evident from the 'Questions of Kirik' that Bishop Nifont was more concerned with instructing priests on how to combat survivals of heathen practices than with pontificating on offences attributable to mere human frailty. This was where the danger to the Church lay. But just how serious was this danger? To what extent did paganism survive after the Conversion? What did it consist of and in what areas was it most deep-seated?

Thanks mainly to archaeology, a considerable amount is known about the pagan religion of the Eastern Slavs before the coming of Christianity; and, not surprisingly, much work has been done on the subject by Soviet scholars.[23] The first written record of pagan burial ceremonies is found in the early undated entries in the Primary

16. Ibid., col. 62 (No. 23).
17. See above, pp. 52-3.
18. Printed in *RIB*, vol. 6, cols. 347–76.
19. Indeed, he may have been the 'white' priest Il'ya who added 28 further questions to those of Kirik and Savva (see above, p. 74), in which case his wife either took the veil or died and he became a monk.
20. *RIB*, vol. 6, cols. 357–8 (No. 9).
21. Ibid., col. 362 (No. 15).
22. Ibid., col. 367 (No. 18).
23. Notably by B. A. Rybakov, *Yazychestvo*.

Chronicle where the chronicler is discussing the geography and cus-
toms of the various peoples inhabiting the future State of Kievan
Russia. After extolling the virtuous and peaceable customs of the
Polyane, the natives of the Kievan region itself, and condemning the
bestial and murderous life-style of the Drevlyane (north-west of
Kiev), he goes on to describe those tribes east of the Dnepr, the
Radimichi, the Vyatichi and the Severyane, who

> had one and the same custom: they lived in the forest like any wild
> animal, eating all that is unclean and speaking obscenely in front of their
> fathers and daughters-in-law. They had no marriages, but they had
> saturnalia (*igrishchi*) amongst the villages; they would gather for these
> games, for the dancing and for all the devilish songs, and the men would
> carry off wives for themselves . . . And if anyone died, they held a *trizna*[24]
> over the corpse. After this they build a large wood-pile, and they put the
> corpse on the pyre and burned it. They then collected the bones and put
> them in a little vessel which they placed in a small coffin on the road . . .[25]

What is of interest and value here is not the 'saturnalia', which is
probably just the chronicler's addition to make the pagans sound even
more unacceptable to his readers, but the description of the burial
customs. Examination of burial mounds in Smolensk and Pskov
shows that from the sixth century onwards the main form of disposal
of corpses was cremation, the ashes being placed in an urn or a hole in
the burial mound or else being scattered on the ground. In the ninth
century interment began gradually to replace cremation, and by the
end of the tenth century, under the influence of Christianity, it
became the accepted practice, especially in urban communities.[26]

More is known about the rites, mysteries and objects of worship
and sacrifice among pre-Christian Eastern Slavs. Apart from Vladimir's
heathen gods who represented the elements of nature – sun, sky,
winds, thunder, lightning, fire, as well as fertility and vegetation
(seeds, crops), we hear of sacrifices of animals and human beings to
devils, bogs, wells, lakes, springs, rivers, stones, trees, animals, birds.
The emperor Constantine VII Porphyrogenitus, writing in the middle
of the tenth century, describes in his *De Administrando Imperio* the
Russians' sacrificial habits on the island of St Gregory (present-day
Khortitsa), south of the rapids on the Dnepr river: 'they perform their

---

24. For *trizna*, see above, p. 30, n. 34.
25. *PVL*, vol. 1, p. 15. The passage ends with the words 'the Vyatichi still do this
today [i.e. in the second half of the eleventh century!]. This was the custom of the
Krivichi and other heathens who knew not God's law, but made a law for themselves.'
26. Rybakov, *Yazychestvo*, pp. 110–11; Froyanov, 'Nachalo', p. 303.

sacrifices because a gigantic oak-tree stands there; and they sacrifice live cocks. Arrows, too, they peg in round about, and others bread and meat . . . They also throw lots regarding the cocks, whether to slaughter them, and then whether to eat them, or whether to leave them alive.'[27]

Bishop Kirill of Turov in the second half of the twelfth century waxed lyrical in his sermon on the first Sunday after Easter (St Thomas's Sunday), rejoicing at the end of the deification of the elements: 'Creation has renewed itself, for no longer are the elements – sun, flowers, springs, trees – called gods.' He has still more to say in the same sermon on the cessation of human sacrifices: 'From now on hell no longer accepts its offerings: children sacrificed by their fathers; nor is death honoured; for idolatry has ceased and devilish violence has been destroyed by the mystery of the Cross, and not only has the human race been saved, but it has been sanctified by belief in Christ.'[28]

Much of this, of course, is the pure rhetoric which the bishop was so often carried away by, and may not necessarily imply that the land of Turov had been hitherto a hotbed of pagan practices. But the fact that other writers as well talk of veneration of the elements and sacrifice to them confirms that this particular aspect of paganism was a very real threat to the spread of Christianity in the centuries after the conversion of Russia. In no uncertain terms Metropolitan Ioann II (1076/7–89) in his series of answers to the monk Iakov's queries on various canonical points[29] links heathen sacrifices with pagan marriage and polygamy as an evil to be combated: 'As for those who sacrifice to devils and to bogs and to wells, and those who marry without [the Church's] blessing and who reject their wives . . . and those who cleave to other women . . . all these people are foreign to our faith and are cast out by the catholic Church.' And he exhorts Iakov in no uncertain terms:

> Try with all your strength to impede this and to direct [the perpetrators] to the true faith. Instruct them not once, not twice, but many times until they learn and understand . . . Those who do not submit and who do not relinquish their wickedness are to be excluded from the catholic Church: they are unworthy of our commandments and have no part in them.[30]

---

27. Constantine Porphyrogenitus, *De administrando imperio*, pp. 60–1.
28. Ed. by Eremin, *TODRL*, vol. 13, p. 415. All Kirill's works are published and edited by the same scholar in the series, see bibliography.
29. *Kanonicheskie otvety mitropolita Ioanna II*, printed in *RIB*, vol. 6, cols. 1–20.
30. *RIB*, vol. 6, cols. 7–8 (No. 15).

In many of the rural areas these sacrifices were linked with the fertility of the soil and with the harvest, as well as with child-bearing and male fecundity. Rybakov talks of sacrificial objects being cast into water to appease the deity of the underwater and underground world and of the widespread ritual of drowning dolls.[31]

The greatest danger of all to the nascent Russian Church, however, came from the practitioners themselves, from the professional sorcerers, wizards and witches. The abundant vocabulary used in the sources to designate these magicians and their arts — *volkhv, kudesnik, koldun, koldun'ya, vedun, ved'ma, veshchiy, veshchitsa, charodey, charodeystvo*, etc. — shows just how widespread and popular sorcery and wizardry were in early Russia. And, again, Metropolitan Ioann II's injunctions show just how much importance he and the Church attached to the problem:

> Those who perform sorcery and magic, whether men or women, must be exposed and deterred from their wicked deeds by words and instruction. If they do not refrain from their evil, then they must be fiercely punished in order to deter them from their wickedness. But they should not be killed, nor should their flesh be slashed, for this is not accepted by the Church's teaching and instruction.[32]

He might well have added too that such punishment would hardly have facilitated the Church's task, especially in the rural communities. For there can be no doubt about it: sorcerers were close to the heart of the people.

But why did magic have such a firm hold on the populace in the pre-Mongol period? Why was it so dear to the Russians? Perhaps we should first ask: what exactly did the sorcerers themselves do?

To answer this question we must look at the various accounts of sorcerers and their activities found in the chronicles. With one exception, these refer to the eleventh century and were probably written by Nestor later in the century. On occasion the author clearly had no idea what their 'sorcery' consisted of. In 1024, for example, he describes how an unspecified number of *volkhvy* (magicians, sorcerers) in Suzdal' 'rose up and slaughtered the well-to-do folk according to [or: by means of] their satanic incitement and devilry, saying that they were holding [stores of] grain'. It took the presence of Yaroslav himself to quell the resulting 'great uprising' by expelling some of the *volkhvy* and executing others.[33] Here obviously the chronicler did not know

31. Rybakov, *Yazychestvo*, pp. 154, 155.
32. *RIB*, vol. 6, col. 4 (No. 7).
33. *PVL*, vol. 1, pp. 99–100.

what the magicians in fact did – unless it was that they used some sort of 'satanic incitement and devilry' to kill the grain-hoarders. But, alas, the text is unclear.

In a long entry for the year 1071, written not long after, he throws considerable light on a number of incidents which occurred then or later in a variety of places. In Kiev, for example, he records a clear case of divination. A *volkhv*, 'possessed by a demon', arrived in the city and prophesied to the people that 'in fifty years time the Dnepr would flow backwards and countries would change places, so that Greece would take the place of Russia and Russia the place of Greece, and other lands would likewise change places'. What exactly the purpose of this divination was is not stated. The episode is rounded off with the remark that 'the ignorant listened to him, but the faithful laughed, saying, "A demon is playing with you and will lead you to your ruin." This in fact happened to him. One night he disappeared without trace.'[34]

A far more convincing case of divination, this time one that resulted in a major upheaval in Novgorod, is described under the same year, 1071. This soothsayer 'pretending to be a god' is described as 'deceiving many people, almost the whole city', by saying that he could foretell the future by reviling the Christian faith and by offering to 'walk across the Volkhov river' in front of everybody. So convincing was his rhetoric that there was an 'upheaval in the city, and all the people believed in him and were about to kill the bishop'. The bishop, in full regalia and armed with a Cross, managed to diminish the number of the *volkhv*'s supporters by saying: 'Let those who believe in the *volkhv* follow him; but let the [true] believers follow the Cross.' However, more radical methods were needed. The local prince asked him if he could prophesy what was going to happen to him that day, to which he replied: 'I shall perform great miracles', whereupon the prince took out an axe from under his cloak and chopped him in two.[35]

The most factual description of *volkhv* activity is the long story of two magicians operating in the Rostov-Yaroslavl'-Beloozero area, also related under the year 1071. This time it was again connected with grain-hoarding and harvest failure, and in spite of a stream of moralizing by the author of the tale, there is still enough factual detail

34. Ibid., pp. 116–17.
35. Ibid., pp. 120–1. *PVL*, vol. 1, pp. 117–19. There is one other mention of a *volkhv* in the Rostov area *s.a.* 1091, but nothing is known of him, except that he 'perished quickly'. *PSRL*, vol. 1, col. 214.

to lend it an air of authenticity. At a time of famine two *volkhvy* appeared in Rostov from Yaroslavl' claiming to know who was hoarding grain. From Rostov they evidently went back to Yaroslavl', for we next hear of them progressing westward along the Volga and up the Sheksna river *en route* to Beloozero. At every settlement (*pogost*) they came to, they accused 'the well-to-do women, saying, "This one is hoarding grain, this one fish, this one furs"'. Then 'they cut open their backs at the shoulder-blades and by magic extracted from their bodies corn or fish, and they killed many women [sacrifices perhaps?] and expropriated their possessions'. The remainder of the story concerns their initial success (they had attracted 300 followers by the time they reached Beloozero), their eventual arrest by, and confrontation with, Prince Svyatoslav's agent Yan Vyshatych, who interrogates them on their beliefs (their 'god' is 'Antichrist', who 'dwells in the abyss'), and their death at the hands of Yan's men by hanging from an oak-tree. Apart from a certain amount of foretelling the future (wrongly – 'Our gods tell us you can do no harm to us'), the story is of most interest in so far as it illustrates yet another facet of the weapons of the *volkhvy*, namely their magic arts, in this case clearly an example of sleight-of-hand skilful enough to bemuse the gullible dwellers on the Volga and Sheksna rivers.

Still under the year 1071 the chronicler tells one more tale of sorcery, this time involving psychomancy. The spirit-raiser is a magician (*kudesnik*) practising in the Chud' area (modern Estonia), west of Novgorod. A Novgorodian comes to him 'wishing for sorcery from him'. There follows a realistic description of the magician's technique: 'according to his habit he began to summon demons into his house, while the Novgorodian sat on the threshold. The magician lay in a trance[36] and a demon struck and seized him. But the magician stood up and said: "The gods do not dare come, for you have something on you which they fear."' Not surprisingly, the object feared by the demons is the cross the Novgorodian is wearing. After it has been removed, the magician again summons the demons, this time successfully: 'They tossed him [the *volkhv*] in the air and gave the reason why the Novgorodian had come.' At this stage the narrative inconclusively fizzles out and deteriorates into a tame description by the magician of his gods: 'They live in the abysses; they are black and have wings and tails . . .'[37]

36. *v mechte*, perhaps '[as if] in a trance'.
37. *PVL*, vol. 1, pp. 119–20.

The only other account of *volkhvy* is to be found in the Novgorod First Chronicle under the year 1227[38] and is of interest only in so far as it deals perhaps with their medical skills. Four sorcerers were burned in the centre of Novgorod for 'making potions (*potvory*)'. The only trouble is that the meaning of the word *potvory* is obscure: it may mean 'potions' or 'poison' or simply 'magic'.

There can be little doubt, however, that of all the skills of the sorcerers that which bound them closest to the people was their therapeutic art. As we have seen from the priest Il'ya's questions to Bishop Nifont of Novgorod about what penance should be given to women who take their sick children to the local *volkhv* for healing and to those who try to kindle their husbands' libido by means of a primitive sort of aphrodisiac (probably recommended by the local *volkhv*-healer),[39] sorcerers, one-and-a-half centuries after the Christianization of the country, still exercised considerable control over the population by means of their 'potions and draughts' – not surprising in a society where medical skills were available only in monastic institutions. Alas, we know no more of the therapeutic techniques of the *volkhvy*, except that as well as prescribing love-potions and cures for sick children their services were evidently in demand for procuring abortions. Il'ya, again, asks his bishop: 'What if women do some damage to themselves and cause a miscarriage?' to which Nifont replies: 'If they do not cause damage by means of a potion (*zel'em'*), then no penance.'[40]

Needless to say, not all *volkhvy* were men. There were also witches – female wizards, soothsayers. Nestor, or whoever wrote the long entry for the year 1071 in the Primary Chronicle, in one of his digressions on the wickedness of magic and magicians, writes:

> Such is the power, the beauty [i.e. attraction] and the weakness of demons. By these means they lead people astray, bidding them recount their visions which appear to those who are imperfect in the faith – to some in sleep, to some in dreams – and thus they perform their wizardry by devilish instigation. But still more is devilish sorcery brought about by women. For in the beginning the devil led woman astray and she led man astray. Thus in this generation women practise sorcery by means of magic charms, of poison and of other devilish intrigues.[41]

---

38. *NPL*, pp. 65, 270.
39. See above, pp. 75–6.
40. *RIB*, vol. 6, col. 58 (No. 5). Cf. Smirnov, *Materialy*, p. 47 (No. 61): (under 'and there are our sins') '. . . should a woman drink a potion (*zel'e*) and abort a child (*izverzet' otrocha*)'.
41. *PVL*, vol. 1, p. 120.

This must of course be taken with a pinch of salt. In medieval Russia women in general tended to be looked upon as a means of temptation, as vessels of sin; they were treated on the whole – especially in the lower echelons of society – as inferior beings in a world in which life for men was hard, but was made even harder for women by men. It is not surprising that the chronicler-monk inveighs against women-*volkhvy* and accuses them of more devilish sorcery than their male counterparts. But he gives no concrete examples of their evil-doings.

The only other source to mention female *volkhvy* is the Arab traveller in the mid-twelfth century, Abu Hamid al-Gharnati, who describes his impressions of witchcraft in the Oka district and the drastic wholesale methods to eliminate it:

> Every ten years there is a lot of witchcraft and the old witches cause a great deal of harm to the women. Then they seize all the old women in their land, bind their hands and legs and throw them into the river: the old women who drown they leave, for they know that they were not witches; but those who remain on the surface of the water they burn alive.[42]

Again we learn nothing about what exactly the witches did to deserve their punishment, but in all probability it was mainly concerned with the harvest: foretelling the future, prophesying abundance or crop-failure.

From all the above we can see, first, that sorcerers, male and female, were looked upon by the Church as a major hindrance to the spread and consolidation of Christianity in Russia, and that much was done, both in the confessional and in the literature of the day, to make people aware of the danger to their souls from their allurements and blandishments. The main theatre of the activity seems to have been the northern part of the country – in particular Rostov, Yaroslavl', Suzdal' and Beloozero, as well as Novgorod in the north-west. Was this because the people of Rostov, say, or Beloozero were more backward, more gullible than the perhaps more sophisticated Kievans? Or was it simply because the remoter the areas from the main centres of Christianity, the more likely pagan practices were to prevail? Probably the latter. It is also difficult to say whether sorcery and witchcraft were more prevalent in the eleventh than in the twelfth and early thirteenth centuries. This is simply because most information on *volkhvy* comes from authors or compilers of the Primary Chronicle writing at the end of the eleventh or the beginning of the twelfth century. The long, chatty and informative entry of 1071 shows just

42. Dubler, *Abū Ḥāmid*, pp. 24–5 (Arabic); p. 63 (Spanish).

how engrossed its author was with the problem. Indeed, he was probably responsible too for the folkloric little tale of Oleg's horse (under the year 912),[43] and for the curious entry (*s.a.* 1044) concerning the birth of Vladimir's great-grandson, Prince Vseslav of Polotsk, whom 'his mother bore from sorcery (*ot v"lkhvovan'ya*)'.[44]

Secondly, it is clear that above all their magical devices – clairvoyance, spirit-raising, illusionism (sleight-of-hand, walking on water) – it was their medicinal skills (philtres, potions, aphrodisiacs) that gave them their hold on so much of the populace.

Finally, we must ask ourselves: was this phenomenon of magicians and witches symptomatic of some sort of social unrest (as we have seen, much of their activity was linked with disturbances, often indicative of a large following), or does it suggest dissatisfaction with Christianity or with the Church? The answer is that we just cannot say for certain. On some occasions doubtless popular discontent spilled over into support for anyone who offered an alternative to authority, or to those who in the popular mind might be held responsible for disaster: famine, fire, flood or drought. On others, perhaps, the *volkhvy*, as representatives of an ancient way of life which was not circumscribed by hidebound rules of moral conduct, might have offered an attractive contrast to what seemed like the rigidity of the Church.

Whatever the answers to these questions are, there can be no doubt that the practitioners of paganism coexisted with the clergy and that the old beliefs, as we shall see, ran parallel to the new ideas of Christianity.

43. Several years before his death Oleg asked *volkhvy* what he would die from, to which one of them replied: 'You will die from the horse you love to ride.' Oleg never rode on it again, but five years later asked his groom where the horse was and was told that it was dead. He then went to where the horse's bones lay and put his foot on the skull, from which a serpent crawled out, bit him and killed him. See *PVL*, vol. 1, pp. 29–30.

44. *PVL*, vol. 1, p. 104. The entry continues: 'when his mother bore him he had a *yazveno* on his head; the *volkhvy* told his mother: "bind this *yazveno* on him so that he may carry it to the end of his life" ... Because of this he is merciless in shedding blood.' What exactly a *yazveno* is is unclear. Cross translates it as a caul, a foetal membrane (according to the *OED*, a caul 'or a portion of it enveloping the head of a child at birth [is] regarded as lucky, and supposed to be a preservative against drowning'). See *The Russian Primary Chronicle*, pp. 139, 261. In the *Tale of Igor's Campaign* (believed by many to have been written at the beginning of the thirteenth century) Vseslav is portrayed as a werewolf capable of transforming himself into a wild beast and a wolf (see *Slovo*, p. 26).

'DOUBLE FAITH'

However much the clergy may have realized that magicians and witches were part of the Russian scene, and a highly regrettable part too, they were no less painfully aware of pagan survivals in the very way of life of the Russian people, especially in the countryside, in their festivities, their merry-making, their revels – all elements which were as hard to combat as the activities of the *volkhvy*, if not harder.

The fight against this aspect of paganism could of course be conducted in the confessional. But it was difficult in this early stage of the development of Christianity in Russia to put a stop to saturnalia or mere high spirits simply by means of admonition and penance. This is perhaps why frustrated clerical chroniclers and the occasional preacher so often used natural or national disasters as a pretext for expatiating on 'God's punishment for our sins' in the hope that their words would put the populace to shame. For example, under the year 1068, when the Polovtsians attacked and defeated the triumvirate (Izyaslav, Svyatoslav and Vsevolod) on the Al'ta river near Kiev, the chronicler used the disaster to lambast the Russians for their transgressions.

Having described the encounter and its outcome ('Because of our sins God sent the heathens against us, the Russians fled and the Polovtsians defeated them'), he launches into an enumeration of these sins: first, those mainly ascribable to the princes themselves – 'internecine war ... murder, bloodshed, quarrels, envy, hatred between brothers, slander'; then, after a number of quotations from the Old Testament, he lists the Russians' 'pagan' offences, beginning with superstitions:

> If someone meets a monk, a hermit or a pig, he turns back home; is not this pagan? ... Others believe that sneezing is good for the health of one's head. By these and other means the devil deceives us, turning us away from God by all manner of trickery: trumpets and strolling players [or perhaps magicians? *skomorokhi*], *gusli* [stringed instruments] and *rusalii* [festivals of remembrance for dead ancestors – revels]. For we see the pleasure grounds trampled bare and vast crowds of people on them, jostling one another, mounting spectacles invented by the devil – while the churches stand [empty]. When it is time for prayer, few are found in church. For this reason we are punished by God.[45]

This juxtaposition of empty churches and riotous pagan living is echoed in a twelfth-century work entitled 'Discourse [or perhaps 'Sermon'] on things made by man [i.e. images of pagan gods]':

45. *PVL*, vol. 1, pp. 112,114.

Many people live lazily and evilly, being too idle to read divine books . . .
But if dancers or musicians or some actor summons them to a theatrical
spectacle or to some idolatrous gathering, they all run there rejoicing . . .
and they spend the whole day watching the spectacle there . . . [but when
we are summoned to a church] we yawn and scratch ourselves, stretch,
slumber and say: 'It's raining' or 'It's cold', or some other lazy thing . . .
But at the spectacles where there is no roof, no stillness but many a time
rain and wind and blizzard – this we all accept with joy, participating in
the spectacle to the destruction of our souls. But as for the church where
there is a roof and a wondrous stillness, people do not want to come into
it for instruction; they are lazy . . .[46]

As far as the history of the spread of Christianity in Russia is
concerned, perhaps the most insidious aspect of the old beliefs and
ways of life is the curious association of paganism with Christianity.
This so-called 'double faith' (*dvoeverie*) – the simultaneous adherence
to both Christianity and heathen relics – is evidenced by many of the
Church's writings, not only in the period under consideration, but
also deep into the seventeenth century, and even as late as the
nineteenth century. In a work attributed to the Abbot Feodosy of the
Caves Monastery, double faith is strongly condemned ('should anyone
constantly praise both his own and a foreign [faith], then such a
person is of double faith (*dvoeverets*). This is close to heresy'[47]); and we
have already mentioned Bishop Nifont's comparison of women who
take their children to a 'Varangian' priest rather than to an Orthodox
one with 'those of double faith' and his imposition of a seven-weeks'
penance on them.[48]

The main danger of course lay in the linkage between pagan and
Christian festivals – particularly the autumnal festivals of Rod and
Rozhanitsy (deities of fertility) and the Christian festival of the Nativity of the Mother of God (8 September), which were celebrated either
at the same time or on consecutive days. An anonymous author,
writing in the early twelfth century, bitterly condemned the pagan
feasts, just as Nifont was to do in the middle of the century:[49] 'You
who prepare a feast for Rod and the two Rozhanitsy and who fill
your beakers to please the demons – you I give over to the sword, and
you will all perish by the sword . . . When the faithful shall feast then
will you be tormented with hunger . . . you who pray to idols and
prepare feasts in honour of Rod and Rozhanitsy.'[50] There were also

46. Rybakov, *Yazychestvo*, p. 458.
47. Ed. by Eremin, in *TODRL*, vol. 5, pp. 171–2.
48. See above, p. 76.
49. Ibid.
50. Rybakov, *Yazychestvo*, pp. 747–8.

clear links between the saturnalia which took place on the eve of Epiphany (5 January) and on midsummer night with the festivals of Epiphany (6 January) and the Birth of St John the Baptist (24 June). Writing some thirty-five years after the Mongol invasion, but still referring to practices current during much of the pre-Mongol period, Metropolitan Kirill II described in no uncertain terms the devilish goings-on at the time of, and linked to, Church festivals:

> I have learned of the devilish doings, the habits of the accursed heathens which still go on: on the divine festivals [of the Church] they mount diabolical spectacles with whistling and shouting and yelling, summoning shameless drunkards, beating people to death with staves, and robbing those killed of their clothes. This is a reproach to the divine festivals and is vexatious to the Church of God. Still more do they vex our Saviour . . . who gladdened our hearts with His holy festivals . . .[51]

Yet more vividly he talks of revels which take place 'on Saturday evening . . . on the eve of the holy resurrection': 'Men and women gather together and play and dance shamelessly and do foul things . . . like the impious heathens celebrate the festival of Dionysus. Men and women together whinny and neigh like horses and do foul things . . .'[52]

What was the reason for the prevalence of 'double faith' in early Russia? Was *dvoeverie* just a natural reaction to a rigorist attitude of the Church to what had been for so long the simple pleasures of the people – dancing, singing, acting and music – as well as the less reputable aspects of popular recreation – fornication, promiscuity, bawdry and carousing? Probably not, for we have little evidence to show that the Church was in any way successful in coping effectively with the problem. After all, these 'pagan' activities were more in evidence in country districts, where not only was there less moral supervision of the populace by the clergy, but also where the pleasures of revelry were the only relaxation for those who eked out an often precarious and difficult living from the land. Indeed, it is not surprising that the Church appears to have made little headway in stamping out *dvoeverie* in the course of the first two-and-a-half centuries of Russian Christianity and that it was to remain for centuries to come a thorn in the flesh of so many would-be preachers and reformers out to cleanse

---

51. *RIB*, vol. 6, cols. 95–6.
52. Ibid., col. 100. Both quotations are from the 'rules' of Metropolitan Kirill II at the Council of Vladimir, 1274, convoked to appoint Serapion bishop of Vladimir. The 'rules' were to remind the five assembled bishops of what the metropolitan found amiss in the Church and the people of his time.

the land of what was considered to be a sign of moral degradation, shameful indulgence and even heresy.

The trouble was that there was little the Church *could* do, especially in the early years when the metropolitans and bishops were struggling to build up an efficient network of monasteries, churches and parishes which could make Christianity the predominant factor in the lives of the Russians. It must not be imagined that the hierarchs were in any way ruthless in their attempts to uproot paganism. They weren't. At least not all of them were. We have already seen the example of Bishop Nifont, who showed a certain amount of restraint and common sense in advising his clergy on how to deal with these matters; and there were others like him.[53]

There is not enough written evidence to show that paganism and 'double faith' either increased or decreased significantly in the pre-Mongol period. As we have seen, in the earliest days sacrifices to the elements probably only retained their hold in the remote country districts and for a short time after the acceptance of Christianity, while burial soon replaced cremation. Rybakov, in his capital work on paganism in Ancient Russia, is of the opinion that in the upper echelons of Russian society paganism showed a distinct increase in the second half of the twelfth century.[54] But he has little convincing material to back this up: dissatisfaction with the Church's interference in 'the traditional way of life' of the growing number of princes and their boyars; the fact that the heroic *Tale of Igor''s Campaign* (for the composition of which he hazards no date) only mentions the Christian God twice and is drenched in the spirit of the heathen gods; and archaeological finds of gold and silver objects of women's apparel – ritual bracelets, head-dresses, diadems, etc., representing water, vegetation, rain, birds, griffins and various symbols of fertility – evidence that 'high-born women in the twelfth/thirteenth centuries took part in pagan rituals and in all probability headed and opened with their dancing the public festivities of the *rusalii*'.[55] As these heathen symbols at the turn of the century tend to give way to Christian symbols, he concludes that this so-called 'pagan renaissance' came to an end at the beginning of the thirteenth century.[56]

But still the written sources do nothing to confirm either that there

---

53. See, for example, the Instructions of Archbishop Il'ya of Novgorod (1165–86), *RIB*, vol. 6, pp. 347–76.
54. *Yazychestvo*, pp. 775–82.
55. Ibid., p. 776.
56. Ibid., p. 775.

was a 'pagan renaissance' amongst the élite or that, if there was, it just faded away towards the end of our period. Amongst the vast majority of the Russian population paganism was alive and well. Furthermore, it showed little or no sign of abating by the time of the Mongol invasion, nor after it either. It was there to stay – and for a long time.

CHAPTER SEVEN

Orthodox and Latins

THE SCHISM OF 1054

Amongst the many questions put by Kirik to Bishop Nifont which we discussed earlier is one which touches on the relations between Orthodox and Latins: how to receive Latin Christians into the Russian Church. It might be expected that a century after the 'schism of 1054' between the Latin and Orthodox Churches rebaptism would be obligatory: indeed, in 1144 Bishop Mathew of Cracow in a letter to St Bernard of Clairvaux said that the Russians were in the habit of rebaptizing Latins.[1] Yet in answer to Kirik's question: 'What if a person baptized into the Latin faith wishes to join us?', Nifont merely recommends an eight-day period of preparation followed by chrismation ('anoint him with the holy chrism') and Communion ('give him a candle and at the Liturgy give him Communion').[2]

What exactly was this 'schism' between the two branches of Christianity? How did it affect the newly baptized Russian Church? Indeed, what was the attitude of the clergy in Russia, both Greek and Russian, to the Church of Rome throughout the pre-Mongol period?

As historians of the medieval Church hasten to point out, the breach between Rome and Constantinople did not begin suddenly in 1054, nor did the events of that year lead to an immediate rupture of ecclesiastical relations. It was a process which had been developing for centuries past and which was to continue for centuries to come. Again

---

1. 'Gens ille Ruthenica ... in conjugiis repudiandis et rebaptizandis ... turpiter claudicere cognoscitur.' *Codex diplomaticus*, No. 17, p. 44; Vodoff, *Naissance*, pp. 310–11; Golubinsky, *IRTs*, vol. 1, II, p. 807.
2. *RIB*, vol. 6, cols. 26–7 (No. 10).

and again conflicts between Rome and Constantinople were patched up or partially patched up, only to start up again, often at the least provocation. This is not the place to discuss in detail the history of relations between the Western and Eastern Churches – it has been done by numerous historians and theologians.[3] Suffice it briefly to outline the bare facts of the story of the theological, political and cultural differences and conflicts between the two.

In the early fourth century the splitting of the Roman Empire into two parts centred in Rome and Constantinople led, not surprisingly, to the gradual estrangement of the two faiths, an estrangement which now ebbed, now flowed, depending often on extraneous circumstances – the barbarian invasions of Europe, the rise of Islam, the iconoclast movement in Byzantium, the coronation of Charlemagne as Holy Roman Emperor in 800, and – from 1095 to 1204 – the Crusades.

But it was in 1054 that matters seemingly came to a head. Two years earlier John, bishop of the Greek town of Trani in Apulia (north-west of Bari), received a letter from the head of the Bulgarian Church (Archbishop Leo) sent at the instigation of Patriarch Michael Cerularius. It attacked various malpractices of the Latins. The reason for the letter was that the Normans, who were conducting an aggressive military campaign in those parts of southern Italy where the Greeks still enjoyed political and religious authority, were attempting to prohibit Orthodox practices in areas under their control. The letter, destined ultimately for the pope, contained among other things a strong attack on the Latin use of azymes (unleavened bread) in the Eucharist. When the pope (Leo IX) eventually received the letter, he instructed his papal secretary, Cardinal Humbert, to draft two letters containing a defence of the Latin practices condemned by the Archbishop of Bulgaria and a reaffirmation of papal supremacy; and then, after conciliatory messages had arrived from the emperor and the patriarch, two more, this time answering, letters were drafted and sent off with Humbert and two other legates to Constantinople.

In Constantinople all went awry. The legates were ill-received by the patriarch. He was enraged and stunned by what he took to be the pope's words. The letters had perhaps – but by no means certainly – been altered or tampered with by the intransigent and hot-headed Humbert. On both sides tempers were frayed. Attacks and counter-

3. See, for example, Southern, *Western Society*, pp. 53–90; Runciman, *The Eastern Schism*. For an admirably readable and concise exposition, see Ware, *The Orthodox Church*, pp. 51–81.

attacks were made. Only the emperor (Constantine IX Monomachus) seems to have exercised a certain amount of self-control and tact: not only did he grant the legates a dignified reception, but he also attempted to defuse the situation between Humbert and the equally hot-headed patriarch. Eventually, on 16 July 1054, Humbert lost all control. He placed a Bull on the altar of St Sophia, stormed out of the cathedral with the other legates and, when a deacon begged him to take it back, refused to retract and dropped it in the street.

The Bull, which excommunicated the patriarch and his close follow-ers as well as the head of the Bulgarian Church, was an astonishing document.[4] It would have horrified Pope Leo IX, who had in fact died three months earlier, just after the arrival of the legates in Constantinople. It was basically a condemnation of Michael Cerularius and all his associates, as well as a list of the shortcomings of the Greek faith, for which the patriarch and his 'heretical' supporters were held guilty. Many of the accusations had little or no foundation in fact: for example, the Greek Church – that is to say, Cerularius and his followers – was charged with insisting on the rebaptism of Latins, which it wasn't, with refusing Communion to beard-shavers, which it didn't, as well as with encouraging castration and simony. But the most perversely subversive were the charges concerning married priests and the Nicene Creed. The Greeks were accused of *allowing* priests to marry, whereas in fact the 'white' clergy in the Byzantine Church had never been permitted to be celibate. Still more grotesque were the accusations that the Greeks *omitted* (!) the word *filioque* in the Nicene Creed.

The most serious accusation was of course the last. And in fact it was to prove by far the most important and the most intractable of the theologically divisive elements in the relations between the two Churches. The original Creed which was drawn up at the First Oecumenical Council of Nicaea in 325 and which was expanded at the Second Oecumenical Council of Constantinople in 381 contained the words 'I believe . . . in the Holy Spirit . . . *who proceeds from the Father* and who with the Father and the Son together is worshipped and together is glorified'. The Creed was recognized by both the Western Church and the Eastern Church until eventually the words 'and from the Son (*filioque*)' were added to 'who proceeds from the Father', and were accepted by the Latin Church. When exactly this took place is a matter of dispute. But it was probably the Church of

4. For the contents of the Bull, see Runciman, *The Eastern Schism*, p. 48.

Spain, in the sixth or seventh century, that first inserted the *filioque*. It was by no means accepted by all the Western Church, although the *filioque* was added to the Creed used in the Liturgy sung in Charlemagne's chapel, and indeed Rome itself abided by the *original* Creed until, in the early eleventh century, the *filioque* was finally adopted by the papacy.

But what did it mean? How did the presence or absence of the one word *filioque* make any difference to the understanding of the essence of the Trinity? A distinguished theologian of the Eastern Church has summed up the differences in this 'technical and obscure dispute' as follows:

> But if each of the persons is distinct, what holds the Holy Trinity together? Here the Orthodox Church, following the Cappadocian Fathers, answers that there is one God because there is one Father. In the language of theology, the Father is the 'cause' or 'source' of Godhead, He is the principle (*arche*) of unity among the three; and it is in this sense that Orthodoxy talks of the 'monarchy' of the Father. The other two persons trace their origins to the Father and are defined in terms of their relation to Him. The Father is the source of Godhead, born of none and proceeding from none; the Son is born of the Father from all eternity ('before all ages', as the Creed says); the Spirit proceeds from the Father from all eternity.
>
> It is at this point that Roman Catholic theology begins to disagree. According to Roman theology, the Spirit proceeds eternally from the Father *and the Son*; and this means that the Father ceases to be the unique source of Godhead, since the Son also is a source. Since the principle of unity in the Godhead can no longer be the person of the Father, Rome finds its principle of unity in the substance or essence which all three persons share. In Orthodoxy the principle of God's unity is personal, in Roman Catholicism it is not.[5]

The hostility of the Greeks to the Latins' adoption of the *filioque* was exacerbated as well by the consideration that the addition of one word was tantamount to denying the validity of the Oecumenical Councils, for they had not only issued the Creed but forbade any changes in it. Denying the authority of the great Fathers of the Church was not to be tolerated.

Of course, the nicer theological distinctions between the West and the East on the question of the procession of the Holy Spirit were by no means the only, or even, for many, the principal, bones of contention between the two Churches, even though they sharply divided those theologians in Rome and Constantinople who were actually capable of understanding them.

5. Ware, *The Orthodox Church*, p. 219.

Of the other major causes of dispute which offended or upset the Greeks – the Latins' use of unleavened bread for the Eucharist, the celibacy of the priesthood, papal supremacy, the practice of fasting on Saturdays and the celebration of ordinary rather than pre-sanctified Liturgies on Wednesdays and Fridays in Great Lent – none aroused more resentment and alarm and none was to affect Latin–Orthodox relations more sharply than the question of the infallibility of the pope.

Of the five great patriarchs – of Rome, Constantinople, Alexandria, Antioch and Jerusalem – the pope of Rome had always enjoyed honorary primacy as *primus inter pares* in view of his succession to St Peter, the first bishop of Rome; while ever since the Second Oecumenical Council of Constantinople (381) the 'bishop of Constantinople' (then raised to the dignity of patriarch) had been declared 'next to the bishop of Rome'. But in the eyes of the Greeks 'honorary primacy' did not mean universal supremacy, and it certainly did not imply that the pope was infallible. The great dispute between Pope Nicholas I and Patriarch Photius in the ninth century, the so-called 'Photian Schism', clearly began as the result of the former's belief that his absolute power extended to Constantinople and was in fact, as he himself expressed it, 'power over all the earth, that is, over every Church'.[6]

Of course, the whole question of the authority of the pope was frequently misunderstood, and indeed in the past it had often been accepted and admitted by the patriarchs of Constantinople.[7] Cerularius, however, in his conciliatory letter to Pope Leo IX which the latter received before the dispatch of Humbert to Constantinople, addressed the pope not as the customary 'Father', but as 'Brother'.[8] At the same time the title of 'Oecumenical Patriarch', which had been accepted by the patriarchs of Constantinople since the end of the sixth century, was likewise frequently misinterpreted in the West as an act of aggression on the part of Constantinople, although it in no way implied control over all the Churches in the universe,[9] any more than over the Churches of the other patriarchs. But while the Eastern Church laid no claims to authority over the Holy See, the papacy consistently believed in, and expressed, its supremacy over all the patriarchates and the pope's infallibility.

6. Ibid., p. 62. See also Runciman, *The Eastern Schism*, pp. 22 ff.
7. See ibid., p. 18.
8. Ibid., p. 43.
9. Ibid., pp. 18, 43 n. 1.

In spite of the bitterness engendered on both sides by the impulsiveness and intolerance of the main actors in the drama of 1054, little really seems to have changed in the mutual relations between Rome and Constantinople. For the time being at least contact between the two was still maintained. In the 1070s and 1080s the conflict flared up again, culminating in Pope Gregory VII's excommunication of Emperor Alexius Comnenus and the closure of the Latin churches in Constantinople by the emperor. But under Gregory's successor, Urban II, peaceful relations were once again established. It was the Crusades, however, the first launched by Urban II in 1095, the fourth ending in the tragic and brutal sack of Constantinople by the Crusaders of 1204,[10] which were finally to lead to the irreparable schism – the *real* schism – between East and West. The installation of a Latin patriarch in Constantinople, the refusal of the Greeks to accept him and the election of an Orthodox patriarch in Nicaea, whither the majority of the Greek bishops had fled, marked the virtual breach which was only fragmentarily and momentarily to be healed at the Councils of Lyons in 1274 and Florence in 1439.

RUSSIANS AND THE LATIN CHURCH

It has often been pointed out that one of the reasons for the tragic breach between the two branches of Christendom was sheer misunderstanding: mutual ignorance of West and East, often sparked off simply by language problems – few Greeks knowing Latin and still fewer Latins knowing Greek – by mistranslations and misinterpretations. And it is evident that, at any rate in the age of the Crusades, the vast majority of Christians in both East and West were totally unaware of the differences of opinion which from time to time led to excommunications, mutual accusations of heresy and schisms. If this was so in Rome and Constantinople, how much more was it the case in Russia!

Of course, all but two of the metropolitans and the majority of bishops in the pre-Mongol age being Greeks, one might expect a certain amount of anti-Latin feeling to be spread amongst the predominantly native priests and monks in Russia. Metropolitan Ioann II, for example, advised the monk Iakov not to concelebrate with 'those who

10. For a concise account of the events leading up to the fall of Constantinople, see Angold, *The Byzantine Empire*, pp. 284–96.

serve [the Liturgy] with azymes (*opresnikom'*) and who eat meat in Shrovetide and eat strangled meat'; but he goes on to say that 'it is by no means forbidden to eat with them for the love of Christ should the need arise. But if anyone wishes to avoid this, using purity or physical debility as an excuse, then let him do so. But be careful,' he adds, 'not to fall into temptation because of this or to let this cause much ill-will and misunderstanding: it is better to prefer the lesser evil to the greater.'[11] In the penitential 'The Commandments of the Holy Fathers' (*Zapovedi svyatykh otets'*), often ascribed to Ioann II's predecessor, Metropolitan Georgy, the advice is more rigorous: 'it is not right to take Communion from the Latins, or to take a prayer from them, or to drink from one cup with them, or to eat with them, or to give them food.'[12] Metropolitan Ioann is somewhat stricter when he deals with the question of Orthodox princes marrying their daughters to Latins: 'should the daughter of a pious prince be given in marriage to another country where they serve with azymes and do not refrain from strangled meat – this is extremely unworthy and unbefitting for the Orthodox . . .'[13]

The little that we know about relations between the Russians and the Latins from 1054 to 1240 (or at any rate to 1204) shows a curious mixture of tolerance and moderation and an almost entire absence of hostile attitudes on either side.[14] Prior to 1054 there is no evidence of any antagonism or disagreement between the nascent Russian Church and Rome. The sixteenth-century Nikon Chronicle – but, alas, no earlier source – mentions exchanges of envoys between Vladimir I and Rome at the end of the tenth and the beginning of the eleventh centuries,[15] while the great missionary bishop St Bruno of Querfurt in his letter to the German king Henry II (1008) describes his extraordinarily amicable relations with Vladimir I: at the end of 1007, as *archiepiscopus gentium*, thus styled by Pope Silvester II, he set off from Hungary to convert the Pechenegs. On his way to the steppes he spent some days in Kiev with Vladimir ('sovereign of the Russians', *senior Ruzorum*, as Bruno calls him), who urged him not to risk his life in so dangerous a venture, accompanied him with troops and later gave

11. *RIB*, vol. 6, col. 3 (No. 4).

12. Smirnov, *Materialy*, p. 123 (No. 102). F. J. Thomson claims that Metropolitan Georgy was *not* the compiler of the *Zapovedi svyatykh otets'*. See 'The Ascription', pp. 14–15.

13. *RIB*, vol. 6, col. 7 (No. 13).

14. 991, 994, 1000 and 1001, *PSRL*, vol. 9, pp. 64, 65, 68.

15. See Vodoff, 'Aspects et limites', pp. 160 ff.

him his son – probably Svyatopolk – to use as a hostage with the Pechenegs. No mention is made of any disparities of beliefs; indeed, clearly Bruno and Vladimir treated each other as though there was no difference between Orthodox and Latins.[16] In his sermon on Law and Grace, written at least three years before 1054, Metropolitan Ilarion seems to go out of his way neither to magnify Byzantium at the expense of Rome, nor to belittle the orthodoxy of Rome. At the beginning of his eulogy to Vladimir he says: 'With laudatory voices the Roman land praises Peter and Paul by whom they believed in Jesus Christ, the Son of God; Asia, Ephesus and Patmos [praise] John the Theologian; India – Thomas; Egypt – Mark; all lands honour and glorify each their own teacher who taught them the orthodox [i.e. true] faith . . .'[17] The *real* contrast is between idolatrous gloom before the conversion of Russia and the dawn of piety following it.[18]

Metropolitan Ioann's strictures on the inadvisability of marriage between Latins and the daughters of princes seem to have been totally ignored by the House of Kiev. Three of Yaroslav's sisters were married to Western rulers (the kings of Hungary and Poland and the margrave of Nordmark), as were three of his daughters (one, Elizabeth, to two kings: the first of Norway and the second of Denmark). His granddaughter Evpraksia became Adelheid when she married the German emperor Henry IV, having been previously married to yet another margrave of Nordmark.[19] Some six Russian princes had German wives, while Vladimir Monomakh married the daughter of King Harold of England, Gita, who came to Kiev via Denmark in *c*.1074 with a number of Anglo-Saxon fugitives and a suite of Danes provided by King Sweyn of Denmark to accompany her.[20] Altogether amongst the first four generations of the descendants of Vladimir I there were no less than forty-five foreign marriages, of which at least thirty were marriages to Latins.[21] How many of these involved rebaptisms from Orthodox to Latin or vice versa it is impossible to say. But in view of the total silence of the sources on the question, as well as Bishop Nifont's recommendation of nothing more than chris-

16. *Monumenta Poloniae*, pp. 224–5.

17. Müller, *Die Werke*, pp. 99–100; Poppe, 'Two Concepts', pp. 491, 494–6.

18. Müller, *Die Werke*, p. 105.

19. For her dramatic story, which 'would need a Dostoevsky properly to describe and interpret', see Vernadsky, *Kievan Russia*, pp. 40–2.

20. Alekseev, 'Anglo-saksonskaya parallel'', p. 55.

21. Vodoff, *Naissance*, pp. 310–11.

mation for Latins wishing 'to join us',[22] it is probable that few or none of the brides and bridegrooms were obliged to change the faith they were born into, or indeed considered it expedient or necessary to do so.

The most interesting case of a 'mixed' princely marriage which, in spite of what several historians have written about it, provides little or no indication of anxiety over 'conversion', is that of Yaroslav's son Izyaslav. His wife was Gertrude, granddaughter of King Bolesław I of Poland and aunt of King Bolesław II. When after the crisis of 1068 Izyaslav fled from Kiev to Poland,[23] he was able to induce his wife's nephew Bolesław II to assist him to regain his throne in Kiev in the following year. But when he fled for the second time in 1073, driven out by his brothers Svyatoslav and Vsevolod,[24] Bolesław was either unwilling or, more likely, unable to help him, while the Poles relieved him of his 'much treasure' and saw him off the premises. He then applied to the king of Germany, and future emperor, Henry IV, for assistance. Henry received him (*Ruzenorum rex Demetrius* [Izyaslav's baptismal name] *nomine*, so Lampert of Hersfeld styled him) and dispatched an envoy to Svyatoslav. The envoy, heavily bribed by Svyatoslav, who happened to be a relative of his by marriage, had no difficulty in persuading Henry IV not to support Izyaslav.[25] Izyaslav then sent his son Yaropolk to Rome to try to get Pope Gregory VII to support him in his conflict with Svyatoslav and to help him recoup his confiscated 'treasure' from Poland. On 17 April 1075 Gregory wrote to Izyaslav, assuring him of the Holy See's support for every just cause, but of little else. However, Gregory also wrote to Bolesław ordering him to return to 'the king of the Russians' that which had been taken from him. Eventually the crisis was solved not in the West but in Kiev, for in 1076 Svyatoslav died and in the following year Izyaslav went back to Kiev, once again with Polish help, and regained his throne.[26]

Vernadsky in his history of Kievan Russia asserts that Izyaslav 'addressed himself . . . to Pope Gregory VII, expressing his willingness to make Russia "St Peter's fief"', and that the pope 'granted the principality of Kiev to Izyaslav and Iaropolk as fief'.[27] But the sources mentioned above – the Primary Chronicle, Lampert of Hersfeld's

22. See above, p. 91.
23. See above, pp. 13, 65–6.
24. See above, p. 66; and *PVL*, vol. 1, pp. 121–2.
25. Lampert of Hersfeld, *Annales*, p. 202.
26. *PVL*, vol. 1, p. 132. See also Ramm, *Papstvo i Rus'*.
27. Vernadsky, *Kievan Russia*, pp. 86, 344; Vlasto, *The Entry*, pp. 288 ff.; Ramm, *Papstvo i Rus'*, pp. 64–6. For a balanced view of the whole question, see Arrignon, 'A propos de la lettre'; Poppe, 'How the Conversion', p. 292.

Chronicle and Pope Gregory's letters to Izyaslav and Bolesław II – give no information whatsoever to support such a view. Gertrude was clearly a Latin by birth and upbringing, but there is nothing to show that this in any way inclined her husband towards Rome, or that either Izyaslav or Yaropolk or even the pope had any plans to convert Kiev into a 'papal fief' or to induce all the Yaroslavichi to renounce their Orthodox faith. Indeed, as we have seen,[28] Izyaslav was called by Nestor when commenting on his expulsion from Kiev in 1073 'the lover of Christ . . . the lover of God' – hardly terms that the rigidly Orthodox Nestor would have used for anyone flirting with the Holy See. The whole story merely illustrates the relaxed view of Latin–Orthodox relations taken by Izyaslav and his family, as well as by the pope.

Nothing is known about marriages between Latins and members of other social strata in Kievan Russia. Yet it is very probable that there were many such marriages, especially in the ranks of boyars, merchants and soldiers who were likely to have had contacts with their Western counterparts. And it is equally probable that the differences between the Churches were simply overlooked. There were of course numerous Westerners in Russia. Many cities had sizeable foreign colonies (merchants, architects, builders) and several – for example, Kiev, Novgorod, Pereyaslavl', Ladoga, Polotsk and Smolensk – had one or more Latin churches.[29] There is even evidence of the penetration of Irish monks from Regensburg into Kievan Russia. One Brother Maurice is said to have been given furs worth £100 silver by a prince (perhaps Vladimir Monomakh?), and indeed there was an Irish cloister in Kiev, fugitives from which fled to Ireland via Vil'na in 1242.[30] We know too that monks of the Dominican Order who had settled in Poland appeared in Kiev some time around 1228, only to be driven out five years later by the then prince of Kiev, Vladimir Ryurikovich.[31]

It was certainly not the 'schism' of 1054 that made the Russians truly aware of the dichotomy within the Christian Church. Indeed, how *could* they have been aware of the ebb and flow of the worsening relations between Byzantium and Rome in the eleventh and twelfth centuries? Did the Greek metropolitans seriously try to arouse in the

28. See above, p. 66.
29. See Udal'tsova *et al.*, 'Drevnyaya Rus'', pp. 42, 56; Kartashev, *Ocherki*, p. 265.
30. Alekseev, 'Anglo-saksonskaya parallel'', pp. 57–9.
31. Golubinsky, *IRTs*, vol. 1, II, pp. 808–9; Długosz, *Annales*, p. 266.

Russians a sense of aversion to Rome? Or to call to their attention the growth of popular animosity in Byzantium to the Holy See? To be sure, apart from the advice given in the penitentials (such as Ioann II's injunctions to the monk Iakov and the 'Commandments of the Holy Fathers' – see above, p. 79), there *was* a certain amount of anti-Latin propaganda, much of it unoriginal, repetitive and based on Greek treatises. Metropolitan Nikifor I (1104–21), for example, wrote two epistles: one to Vladimir Monomakh, probably in answer to a request for information about the Roman Church and containing a list of Latin 'errors' (twenty in number and including the use of azymes, the eating of unclean food, beard-shaving, bishops' ring-wearing, celibacy of the priesthood and, of course, the *filioque*); the other (nineteen 'errors' this time) to Svyatopolk Izyaslavich, Vladimir Monomakh's predecessor on the throne of Kiev.[32] Two works composed by Greek hierarchs in Russia were destined purely for foreign consumption: Metropolitan Lev's treatise on the azymes (which also dealt with the Presanctified Liturgy, strangled meat and the *filioque*) was in all probability never translated into Church Slavonic;[33] while the Metropolitan Ioann II's main attack on the Latins' divergences from the 'true faith' was written in his letter to the antipope Clement III (1080–1100).[34] Only one anti-Latin polemical work seems to have enjoyed a certain degree of popularity: the treatise 'on the beliefs of the Varangians'. This disquisition on the malpractices of the Latins, which was later (in the fourteenth or fifteenth centuries[35]) to be inserted into the Paterikon of the Kievan Monastery of the Caves as 'Questions of the pious prince Izyaslav [Yaroslavich] concerning the Latins',[36] contains Abbot Feodosy's exposition on their 'evil faith and their impure law'. But so lurid are the alleged evils which Feodosy outlines to Izyaslav ('they eat dogs and cats, they drink their own urine – this is wicked and accursed – and they eat tortoises and wild horses and asses and strangled meat and bears and beavers'[37]) that it is hard to believe that even the most naïve and ignorant of readers or listeners would have lent credence to his words. In any case, how much of this polemical

32. Podskalsky, *Christentum*, pp. 177–9.
33. *RIB*, vol. 36, pp. 73–101; Poppe, 'Le Traité'; Podskalsky, *Christentum*, pp. 171–2.
34. Ibid., pp. 176–7.
35. Ibid., p. 182; see also Eremin, 'Literaturnoe nasledie Feodosiya', *TODRL*, vol. 5, pp. 159–66.
36. *Kyyevo-Pechers'kyy pateryk*, No. 37, pp. 190–2; Eremin, *TODRL*, vol. 5, pp. 170–3.
37. *Kyyevo-Pechers'kyy pateryk*, p. 190; Eremin, *TODRL*, vol. 5, pp. 170–1.

literature filtered down to the people themselves? And, if it did, how intelligible to them was the significance of even the simplest differences in practice between the Latins and the Greeks? Could it have worried them that the Roman bishops wore rings on their fingers?

It was not the early Crusades that alerted the Russians to the growing differences between Rome and Constantinople. It was their good fortune that the West did little to involve them in the holy war against the Saracens and that the Crusaders' routes to the Middle East lay far to the south of Kievan Russia – through Greece and Asia Minor.

The Russians were aware of the Crusades themselves. But still there is no hint of disapproval of them in the sources. Daniil, abbot of one of the Chernigov monasteries and author of the earliest extant example of pilgrimage/travel literature in Russia,[38] spent sixteen months in Palestine (1106–07) after the first Crusade, met and was warmly welcomed and assisted by King Baldwin I ('Prince Baldwin of Jerusalem') and expressed almost no ill-feeling for the Latins – bar a fleeting mention of the azyme controversy[39] – or the crusading movement. In 1164 Andrey Bogolyubskiy, grand prince of Vladimir, compared his victorious campaign against the Volga Bulgars with the emperor Manuel's participation in the second Crusade against the Saracens (*na Sratsintsy*).[40] As for the third Crusade, the Ipat'evskiy Chronicle under the year 1190 contains a stirring passage relating to Frederick Barbarossa's Crusade against the infidels which ended in his accidental death near Seleucia in June 1190. 'In that year,' the chronicler interrupts his story of the waning fortunes of the first princely house of Galicia, 'the German emperor (*tsar' Nemetskiy*) went with all his people to fight for the Sepulchre of the Lord, for the Lord had bidden him by an angel to go. And when they came they fought fiercely with those £godless sons of Hagar [i.e. Moslems].' After breaking off to digress for a moment on the Saracens' occupation of the Holy Land as God's punishment for the erring Christians ('God brought all these things upon us because of our sins'), the chronicler continues: 'These Germans, *like Holy Martyrs*, spilt their blood for Christ together

38. *Zhitie i khozhdenie Daniila rus'skyya zemli igumena* in PLDR, *XII vek*, pp. 24–114.
39. In the description of Melchizidek's cave on Mount Tabor, he talks of Melchizidek 'bringing forth bread and wine' and adds: 'This was the beginning of Liturgies with bread and wine *and not azymes (a ne opresnokom)*'. Ibid., p. 99.
40. In *The Tale of the Victory over the Bulgars (Skazanie o pobede nad Bolgarami*), reprinted in Hurwitz, *Prince Andrej*, pp. 90–1. See also Rybakov, *Russkie letopistsy*, p. 110.

with their emperor's'[41] – hardly illustrative of disapproval of the crusading spirit of the Latin West!

If there was, in the pre-Mongol period, a turning point in the attitude of the Russians to Rome, then it was probably the capture and sack of Constantinople by the Latins in 1204. Not that the Russians were physically involved in the ghastly fourth Crusade. As far as we know they weren't – except probably for the eyewitness author of the description of the capture of Constantinople which first appeared in the older redaction of the Novgorod First Chronicle,[42] and which in places supplements the contemporary account of the Byzantine historian Nicetas Choniates. Many must have learnt of the last days of Constantinople and the atrocities of the Latins from this chronicle story, which, although it omits some of the more lurid details – French prostitutes rampaging in the sanctuary of the Cathedral of St Sophia, for example – nevertheless describes in great detail the pillaging of the churches in the city. Furthermore, the full horror of the events in Constantinople must have been relayed to the Russians by the last three Greek metropolitans of Kiev before 1240. After the fall of the city and the installation of a Latin patriarch in Constantinople, Nicaea became the main centre of Greek Orthodoxy – and of the empire of the Laskarids – and was to remain so until the recapture of Constantinople in 1261; and it was there – in the greatest anti-Latin centre in the East – that during the next five and a half decades metropolitans of Kiev were consecrated and indoctrinated. After the demise of Metropolitan Nikifor II, his successor Matfey became metropolitan of Kiev. The date is not known, but it was before 1210. It seems improbable that he was elected by Patriarch John X Camaterus, who fled from Constantinople to Thrace in 1204 and died there two years later.[43] More likely he was consecrated by Michael Autoreanus in Nicaea, who was elected patriarch in 1208. In either case he would have been well and truly briefed in the current official Orthodox attitude to Rome. The same applies to his two successors, Kirill I and Iosif, who were appointed to the Russian metropolitanate in 1223 or 1224 and 1235 or 1236 respectively. Unfortunately there is no record of the attitude to Rome, or the teaching, of any of the three. But there is no reason to believe that it was in any way different from that of the Greek hierarchs in Nicaea.

41. *PSRL*, vol. 2, col. 667.
42. *NPL*, pp. 46–9.
43. Runciman, *The Kingdom of Acre*, p. 127.

The time had not yet come, however, for the hostile reaction of Church – *and* State – in Russia to the Latin West to be openly manifested in propaganda and polemics. This was only to appear in the centuries following the Tatar-Mongol invasion when Russia found itself faced on its western boundaries with the aggressive might of Catholic Lithuania and Poland, to say nothing of the Teutonic Knights on its north-western Baltic frontier.

CHAPTER EIGHT

Christian Writing in Kievan Russia

The Primary Chronicle contains a panegyric to Yaroslav 'the Wise' under the year 1037 – the date is really immaterial as it is some seventeen years before his death. After listing his building achievements in Kiev – fortifications, churches, monasteries – and noting his devotion to 'Church statutes, priests and monks', the chronicler turns to Yaroslav's love of books and his creation of what looks like a scriptorium in Kiev:

> he applied himself to books and read them frequently by night and by day. And he gathered together many scribes and they translated from Greek to Slavonic. And they copied many books by means of which the faithful are instructed and enjoy divine teaching. For as one person ploughs the land, another sows it and others reap and eat the abundant food – so did he. For his father Vladimir ploughed and softened the land, that is to say he enlightened it with baptism. But this one [Yaroslav] sowed the written word in the hearts of the faithful, while we reap the harvest on receiving book-learning.

This is followed by a description of the benefits accruing from the knowledge acquired from books: 'Great is the advantage of book-learning, for by books we are instructed and taught the path of penitence and from written words we gain wisdom and restraint.' In the end the chronicler returns to Yaroslav: 'As we have said, [he] was a lover of books', and adds: 'Having copied [*napisav*, lit. 'written' – surely in error for *spisav*: 'copied'] many, he placed them in the church of St Sofia which he himself had created.' The passage ends with a description of Yaroslav's embellishments of St Sofia, his building of other churches elsewhere and his joy at the growth of Christianity.[1]

---

1. *PVL*, vol. 1, pp. 102–3.

From all this it would seem that the author of this particular encomium was intent on stressing amongst Yaroslav's other cultural achievements his initiative in fostering translated literature. But, as is so often the case in any study of the chronicles, it is virtually impossible to say for certain when exactly this particular passage was written – except that it must have been before 1117, the final entry in the Primary Chronicle. However, it seems likely that it *was* written during Yaroslav's lifetime, as it makes no mention of original literature, none of which – with the possible exception of early chronicle entries and perhaps the sermons of Metropolitan Ilarion and Bishop Luka of Novgorod – can be dated before the middle of the eleventh century.

Needless to say, literature in translation from Greek formed the bulk of all written works in the pre-Mongol period; and of this literature books essential for the maintenance and spread of Christianity especially at the parish level – liturgical and biblical works, service-books, prayer-books, hymn-books, the Gospels and the Psalms[2] – comprised the majority.

Of less immediate importance for the expansion of the faith was patristic literature – the works mainly of the Greek theologians from the third to the eleventh centuries. These were of use for the fostering of the faith at all levels of society, containing as they did codes of behaviour, anti-heretical teaching, highly practical instructions on how to lead a Christian life, monastic rules, and so forth. Many such works were put together in miscellanies (*sborniki* or *izborniki*). Sometimes these were merely anthologies of extracts from the works of one or more of the Church Fathers; sometimes semi-encyclopaedias containing a mixture of religious and lay wisdom. Of considerable importance for later 'original' Russian writing were such gnomological collections as *The Bee* (*Pchela*, Greek *Melissa*), which contained quotations and aphorisms from the Gospels, the Epistles and the Wisdom of Solomon, from the Church Fathers and from classical and Byzantine writers. As these gobbets of information were grouped under various rubrics such as 'wealth and poverty', 'truth and falsehood', they proved of considerable assistance to Russian authors in search of ideas and quotations in support of them.

It was the same with most of the other genres of translated literature which proliferated in Kievan Russia – apocryphal literature, hagio-

2. From the Old Testament, only extracts for reading in church (*paremii*, from the Greek *paroimia*, lit. 'proverb', 'maxim').

graphy, *paterica*, homilies, historiography (the chronicles of John Malalas and George Hamartolus), secular tales (the exploits of Alexander of Macedon, Josephus Flavius's *History of the Jewish War*), natural history miscellanies (the *Hexaèmera* – commentaries on the six days of Creation; the *Physiologus* – a treatise on animals, minerals and trees) – all of which gave the Russians a glimpse, albeit often a distorted, ill-proportioned and misleading glimpse, of Byzantine religious and secular thought.[3]

It was not that this translated literature provided the Russians with a true concept of Byzantine culture or that it acquainted them with the theology of the Fathers of the Church, still less with classical literature and philosophy. It did not. In many cases all the Russians received were ill-assorted fragments, some mistranslated into a poor language that was not capable of rendering all the subtleties of Byzantine Greek. Whether this meant, as one scholar has dismissively asserted, that 'Kievan Russia was not heir to the intellectual world of Byzantine culture but the obscurantism of Byzantine monasticism' and that 'any ideas of a high level of intellectual culture in Kievan Russia must be dismissed',[4] is open to question. But what *is* certain is that much translated literature was of inestimable value to medieval Russian writers. For so much early Russian religious writing is compilatory: it is not original but largely borrowed from what were taken to be acceptable – in some cases 'safe' – sources. It was of course a type of plagiarism. But then in medieval Russia plagiarism was never considered to be a literary failing. Instead, it was something that came to be expected of authors. Many a Russian cleric writing on ethical or dogmatic subjects was not giving his own views; he was expounding those of others, sometimes acknowledging his source, sometimes not. As writers in the sixteenth century were to learn to their cost, it was often dangerous to put forward an opinion without backing it up with a string of 'witnesses' (*svidetel'stva*), i.e. *evidence* from accepted sources (the Bible, the Fathers, etc.). This could be done with a certain amount of tact and grace, and it frequently was in the Kievan age. But later much of the dry anti-heretical, polemical and purely didactic literature was often poorly linked together and introduced by the magic words, 'I have put together a little from much' (*se az skladokh maloe ot mnogogo*). It was all too easy for writing to degenerate into selecting what recognized 'safe' source to quote.

The trouble is, of course, that much of this imitative creation

3. See Thomson, 'The Nature', pp. 107–15.
4. Thomson,'Quotations', pp. 65, 73.

tended to influence non-religious writing as well. The medieval Russian scribe so often resorted to commonplaces while describing battles, burials, physical and moral qualities, while composing speeches, especially military ones, and obituaries, that 'realism' rarely emerges. The stock phrases used to enumerate the moral or physical qualities of, say, a dead prince give us no idea whatsoever of his personality, his appearance, or even of his virtues. Not even Vladimir Monomakh, writing about himself, gives us a clear picture of what sort of man he was. Nor does this stereotyped phraseology enable us to differentiate between the qualities of one virtuous prince and another – it is often only the wicked and the evil-doers who are allocated something approaching graphic characteristics. Likewise, the clichés used to describe a battle often make it difficult to know what exactly happened – even who won.

If the reliance on translated literature was inevitable in a land which had no known autochthonous culture before the coming of Christianity and if, as a result of this reliance, plagiarism and clichés became the hallmarks of much of the original literature of the early period, it does not mean that all writing was stereotyped, lacked aesthetic or visual values, or was incapable of moving the reader or listener. If we take, for instance, two examples from eleventh-century hagiography, the anonymous *Narrative and Passion and the Encomium of the Holy Martyrs Boris and Gleb* and Nestor's *Life of Saint Feodosy of the Monastery of the Caves*, both of which lean to some extent on foreign patterns, we can see just how emotive and absorbing the first is and how vividly descriptive and entertaining is the second.

The first of these two works, the most vivid of the three extant accounts of the murder and martyrdom of two of Vladimir's youngest sons (see above, p. 11), is a remarkable mixture of brevity and crispness in the action passages and a rhetorical, dramatic and passionate style used to portray the emotions of the heroes when faced with death. Take, first, the description of Boris's death:

> . . . the body of Boris was pierced: spears were thrust in by Put´sha, Tal´ts´, Elovich´, Lyashko. Seeing this his servant hurled himself on the body of the blessed one . . . He was a Hungarian by birth, Georgy by name; and Boris had put a golden necklace on him. And they transfixed him . . . not being able to remove the necklace, they cut off his head, they threw it away and because of this no one could recognize the body. They wrapped Boris in a tent-cloth, put [him] on a waggon, drove it off.[5]

5. *AHE*, pp. 35, 37; *PLDR, XI – nachalo XII veka*, pp. 286, 288.

The bare precision and tension of the extract, the lack of decorative additives, the primitive syntax uncluttered with subordinate clauses and non-essential descriptive adjectives – all witness the objectivity and impartiality of the author, who stands aside from his text, makes no comments, passes no judgements.

But when it comes to describing the emotional experiences of the two victims, the tone and texture are entirely different. Gleb's appeal to his murderers, for all its implausibility, is aimed at moving the reader to pity and tears:

> 'Do not touch me, my dear sweet brothers, do not touch me who have done you no ill! Spare me, brothers and masters, spare me! . . . Have mercy on my youth, have mercy, my masters! . . . Do not cut me down, for my life is not yet ripe, do not cut off the ear of corn that is not yet full but bears the milk of innocence. Do not cut the branch of the vine that is not yet fully grown but still bears fruit . . . I, my brothers, am still an infant in wickedness and age – this is not murder but the cutting of unseasoned timber.'[6]

The description of the moments before the murderers burst into Boris's tent is pervaded with excitement:

> And when he heard the evil whispering around his tent, he trembled and began to shed tears from his eyes . . . And his priest and his servant . . . looked upon him, and when they saw their master morose and bathed in sorrow, they burst into tears and said: 'Our sweet dear master, how much goodness were you filled with that you did not wish to resist for the love of Christ, yet how many warriors did you hold in your hand!' And having said this they were filled with pity.[7]

Both these extracts, with their extravagant and unoriginal commonplaces, contrast strongly with the objective, matter-of-fact descriptions of action. The author's stance has altered radically. Instead of standing aloof from what he describes, he now moves closer to his characters, explaining their emotions and fears, giving their intimate thoughts, suffering with them in order to make the reader experience their sufferings. Needless to say, the contrast between the two styles of writing is not deliberate on the part of the 'author': indeed, there are probably at least two if not more different redactions of the *Life* sewn together in some stage or other in its textual history – and not always sewn together with care, as the seams at times betray contradictions, clumsiness.[8] But in general the overall effect is breathtaking. As one

6. *AHE*, p. 41; *PLDR, XI – nachalo XII veka*, p. 292.
7. *AHE*, pp. 34–5; *PLDR, XI–nachalo XII veka*, p. 286.
8. For a detailed 'socio–cultural' analysis of the three versions, see Lenhoff, *The Martyred Princes*. See also Fennell and Stokes, *Early Russian Literature*, pp. 11–32.

modern scholar puts it: 'the events retain their immediate freshness . . . the *Narrative* is saturated with deep piety and strong feeling. It is a literary work of art which enables even the modern reader to experience the piety of the age.'[9]

Nestor's *Life of Saint Feodosy*, on the other hand, is of importance from a literary point of view not for its emotive power or for its influence on future Russian hagiography but for its startlingly realistic portrayal of two human beings – Feodosy's mother and Feodosy himself – which was to have few if any parallels in pre-seventeenth-century Russian literature. Just as the anonymous *Narrative* owes much to foreign patterns, so too Nestor's *Life* is closely linked both with traditional hagiography and with Greek *paterica*. But the character-portrayal in the work owes little to the sources.

The first mention of Feodosy's mother shows her in the traditional hagiographical role of the parent blocking the future saint's entry to monasticism: she attempts to stop her 13-year-old son from 'working with the serfs' and urges him to dress decently like the other children of his own age and class.

> . . . he would go into the fields and toil with all humility. But his mother
> would stop him, forbidding him to work and begging him to dress
> cleanly and to go and play with his fellows. She said: 'Going about like
> that, you are a disgrace to yourself and to your family.'

Of course he refuses, with the result that his mother flies into a rage and beats him: 'Many a time she would flare up and beat him, for she was tough and strong of body, just like a man. Indeed, anyone not seeing her but hearing her speak would think that she *was* a man.'[10]

On another occasion, after he had secretly set off on a pilgrimage to the Holy Land, his mother pursued him, caught him up and 'in her wrath and fury seized him by the hair, hurled him to the ground and kicked him . . . and brought him back home like an evil-doer. So overwhelmed was she by her wrath that she beat him until he lost consciousness . . . She then tied him up, locked him up and went away.'[11] It was all, Nestor tells us, 'because she loved him exceedingly, more than all others, and could not bear to be without him'.[12]

Eventually Feodosy manages to escape, make his way to Kiev and persuade Antony of the Monastery of the Caves to tonsure him. His mother meanwhile becomes distraught with grief: 'she wept fiercely

9. Lilienfeld, *Der Himmel*, p. 67.
10. *Sbornik XII*, p. 44; *PLDR, XI–nachalo XII veka*, pp. 308, 310.
11. *Sbornik XII*, p. 45; *PLDR, XI–nachalo XII veka*, p. 310.
12. *Sbornik XII*, p. 45; *PLDR, XI–nachalo XII veka*, p. 312.

for him, beating her breast as though he were dead.' Four years later she traces him to the Caves Monastery. The story of the titanic struggle between the two ends with Feodosy's mother at last reconciling herself to his monasticism and agreeing to take the tonsure in a Kievan nunnery.

In Feodosy's mother Nestor created a truly memorable character, not just because she is violent, obdurate and headstrong, but because she evokes pity in the reader for her plight, especially in her last desperate attempt to extract her son from his cave. We *know* she cannot win and we suffer with her in her unequal struggle with Antony. And what better contrast could one wish for than that between her and her son? 'Where he is gentle, she is violent; where he is submissive, she is overbearing; and where he is ethereal, she is earthbound.'[13]

The second part of Nestor's *Life of Feodosy* need not concern us for long. It describes in considerable – and not always original – detail Feodosy's ascetic practices: his sleeping in a sitting posture, the exposure of his body to mosquitoes, his wearing of a hair-shirt, his refusal to wash, his constant struggle with temptation in the shape of vast hordes of teasing demons ('riding in carriages, beating drums, playing pipes, all shouting so loud that the cave shook from the din and the evil spirits'[14]). Much space is given to the practical side of his office as abbot: his nightly rounds of the cells, his strict discipline, his concern with the monastery's food supplies, his building of almshouses and above all his refusal to isolate himself from the political life of the State which is reflected in his close ties, both friendly and hostile, with the princes of Kiev. Although much of this has its origins in conventional saints' *Lives* and *paterica* and although much of it is patently and at times tediously didactic, it still has a remarkable freshness and liveliness. What is more, the monks themselves are portrayed as human beings in their fight to observe the harsh discipline of the Caves, not as superhuman automata. But, above all, its importance lies not so much in its literary influence on future Russian hagiography as in its image of Feodosy the competent administrator, the founder of coenobitism, monastic landownership and monastic social service in Russia, the active participator in the political life of the State. Indeed, in many ways Nestor's *Life* helped to shape the future of Russian monasticism.

13. Fennell and Stokes, *Early Russian Literature*, p. 38.
14. *Sbornik XII*, p. 58; *PLDR, XI–nachalo XII veka*, p. 336.

Of course, these two works of 'original' literature are not the only examples either of home-grown hagiography or of other genres of native literature written in pre-Mongol Russia. They have been discussed here merely because both are based on antecedents – that is to say, on translated literature – and yet both contain specifically autochthonous qualities which sharply distinguish them from their foreign precursors. The same goes for other genres of original Kievan literature: homiletics, chronicle-writing, travel literature, autobiography. The important point is that Kievan creative writing was bound to be influenced by the literature in translation which came into Russia with Christianity. Curiously enough, this 'original' Russian writing of the pre-Mongol age, dependent though it was on foreign patterns, was by and large fresher and more spontaneous than most of the literature produced in the following three-and-a-half centuries and indeed was less conditioned by exemplars. Certainly, few chronicles of the thirteenth to the sixteenth centuries can equal the spontaneity and vigour of the Primary Chronicle and few saints' *Lives* can match those we have just discussed, nor can any sermons hold a candle to Ilarion's oration on Law and Grace. This is not to say that the Kievan age witnessed a number of literary masterpieces. It did not. And many of the major works of the age in fact had little or no influence on the writings of succeeding periods. But it is important to remember that by and large it was a literature created by – and often for – the Church. The remarkable thing is that, during the complex and difficult process of spreading Christianity throughout the country, any original writing was produced at all. But it was. And it was produced by the Church.

CHAPTER NINE
The Church's Involvement in Politics

Before leaving our survey of the Russian Church in the Kievan period there is one more question to be answered: to what extent did the Church involve itself in the political life of the State? The princes, we have seen, occasionally meddled with the duties and privileges of the metropolitans and attempted to have prelates to their liking rather than those of the metropolitans' choice appointed in their principalities (see above, pp. 49 ff.); from time to time they also successfully managed to have their own candidates for the metropolitanate appointed (see above, pp. 47–8). But what of the Church itself? How far were the clergy prepared to enter into the sphere of politics, to cooperate with the lay authorities or to hamper them? Unfortunately, not a great deal is known on this score, mainly because the sources were produced largely by clerics themselves, who were usually only ready to mention those lay activities of abbots, bishops and metropolitans which redounded to their glory and were never prepared to suggest their motives.

The remarkable tenacity with which the Monastery of the Caves and its first abbot Feodosy openly criticized and harried the rulers of Kiev when they disapproved of their political activities has already been mentioned (see above, pp. 65–6). No less striking was the role played by Grigory, abbot of the Kiev Monastery of St Andrey, who in 1128 managed to avert war between Vladimir Monomakh's son Mstislav of Kiev and Svyatoslav of Chernigov's grandson Vsevolod Ol'govich. The latter had driven out his uncle Yaroslav Svyatoslavich from Chernigov and had called in 7,000 Polovtsians to help him resist Mstislav. It was neatly done. A congress of all the clergy in Kiev (*sbor iereyskiy*) was convoked by Grigory. By its authority Mstislav was released from his oath on the Cross to protect Yaroslav and was thus enabled to avoid what would certainly have proved to be the first major confrontation in the ensuing long fratricidal war between the descendants of Vladimir Monomakh and the princes of Chernigov. Normally such action would have been taken by the metropolitan had he been so inclined. But the see was vacant at the time.[1]

Of all the metropolitans of Kiev, Nikolay (1092–1104) emerges as the first to intervene in Kievan politics. Five years after his arrival in Russia the powerful West-Russian prince Vasil'ko Rostislavich, great-grandson of Vladimir I, was blinded at the instigation, so we are told in the Primary Chronicle, of his cousin David Igorevich and with the approval of the prince of Kiev, Svyatopolk Izyaslavich. The reasons for the blinding do not concern us here. But the outcome does. The reaction of Vladimir Monomakh, not yet ruler in Kiev, but the most powerful prince in the land, was what one would expect from a scribe always ready to pay tribute to his virtues: 'hearing that Vasil'ko had been captured and blinded, [he] was horror-struck. He burst into tears and said: "Such an evil thing has never happened in the Russian land at the time of either our grandfathers or our fathers." '[2] Svyatopolk's explanation failed to hold water, and Vladimir with two of his cousins was on the point of attacking him when Metropolitan Nikolay and Vladimir's stepmother approached him. They begged him 'not to destroy the Russian land by fighting the prince of Kiev'. 'If you fight amongst each other,' they said, 'the pagans [i.e. the Polovtsians] will rejoice and take your land . . . You will ruin the Russian land.'[3] After still more tears Vladimir agreed to call off the attack. Unfortunately, the chronicle gives no indication as to what the real reasons for the metropolitan's intervention were: both he and Vladimir's stepmother appear to have acted at the behest of 'the people of Kiev', for they merely repeated to Vladimir Monomakh what the Kievans had told them to say. But still it was effective and fighting was averted.[4]

The only other recorded interventions by metropolitans in pre-Mongol Russian political life are again all connected with attempts to

---

1. *PSRL*, vol. 1, cols. 296–7; vol. 2, cols. 290–2.
2. *PVL*, vol. 1, p. 174.
3. Ibid., pp. 174–5.
4. Vasil'ko may have been considered by the Greeks as a military threat to the Empire and hence Nikolay may have been acting on instructions from Constantinople. See *PVL*, vol. 2, p. 461. Note that four years later Metropolitan Nikolay again intervened in the affairs of State. Svyatopolk had attacked and arrested his nephew Yaroslav Yaropolchich for initiating some unexplained military activity in Brest and brought him shackled to Kiev. Nikolay intervened with Svyatopolk and had him liberated. No explanations are given in the chronicle (*PVL.*, vol. 1, p. 182).

prevent or stop internecine wars among the princes. From 1134 to 1140 Metropolitan Mikhail on at least four occasions acted as intermediary in the complex and vicious political struggle between the Monomashichi and the Ol'govichi;[5] Metropolitan Feodor in 1161 managed to reconcile his protector, Rostislav Mstislavich of Kiev (see above, p. 48), with Svyatoslav Ol'govich of Chernigov;[6] while in the period of respite between the Tatar-Mongol invasions of 1223 and 1237 Metropolitan Kirill I was at least twice instrumental in successfully mediating between the various princely branches: in 1226 Grand Prince Yury of Vladimir was about to aid his distant kinsman Mikhail of Chernigov against Oleg of Kursk, in what appears to have been a family feud between the Chernigov princes, when Kirill patched up the quarrel – so delighted was Yury that 'he gave him many gifts and kept him in his presence'.[7] Two years later we find him attempting to make peace between Daniil Romanovich of Volynia and Vladimir Ryurikovich of Kiev;[8] finally, in 1230, Kirill and Bishop Porfiry of Chernigov were instrumental in averting a war between Mikhail of Chernigov and Yury's brother Yaroslav.[9] On all three occasions Kirill appears to have been working as the grand prince of Kiev's agent, and it is impossible to say to what extent the initiative was his own.

On the whole, then, the scale of the Church's involvement in the political life of Kievan Russia was, as far as we can tell, relatively modest. This is not really surprising in view of the fact that nearly all the metropolitans and many of the bishops were Greek and in some cases had little opportunity of acquainting themselves with the complexities of inter-princely relations: after all, the administration of their huge dioceses required – or should have required – much time and effort. As for the heads of monasteries, the monks and the white clergy, too little is known for us to be able to form any conclusions about their involvement in worldly matters. Furthermore, as we have noted, virtually all ecclesiastical intervention in lay affairs was limited to mediation and peace-keeping. Again, there is nothing surprising in this: the good offices of the Church in inter-princely squabbles were often essential, for who else but the clergy, and the senior clergy at

5. 1134 (*NPL*, pp. 23, 208); 1136 (*PSRL*, vol. 2, col. 299); 1138 (ibid., vol. 1, cols. 306–7); 1140 (ibid., vol. 2, cols. 302–3). See above, p. 48.

6. Shchapov, *Gosudarstvo*, p. 198.

7. *PSRL*, vol. 1, col. 448; vol. 25, p. 122. See Fennell, *The Crisis*, p. 71.

8. *PSRL*, vol. 2, col. 753: 'the most blessed and holy metropolitan Kirill had come to make peace but was unable to do so.'

9. Ibid., vol. 1, cols. 455–6; vol. 25, p. 125; Fennell, *The Crisis*, p. 71.

that, could release a combatant from an oath taken on the Cross or actually administer the ceremony of kissing the Cross which normally marked the end of quarrels and hostilities? And it is more than likely that in many cases the initiative for such arbitration came not from the clergy but from the combatants themselves. The era of the Russian Church's active intervention in the political life of the State was yet to come.

PART TWO

CHAPTER TEN

Russia under the Mongols: A Political Survey

1

In 1242 Khan Baty suddenly ordered the withdrawal of the Tatar-Mongol armies from the westernmost limit of their advance in Europe. Returning through Serbia and Bulgaria and the south-Russian Kipchak steppes – the Desht-i-Kipchak – Baty established his headquarters in Saray near the mouth of the Volga. From there the khans of what was later to be called the Golden Horde controlled much of the political and economic activities of the Russian princes until the battle of the Field of Kulikovo in 1380. It was the beginning of the so-called 'Tatar Yoke'.

It is difficult to come to any valid conclusions about the immediate consequences for Russia of the Tatar-Mongol invasion. We do not know how many towns were sacked or destroyed, how many of the population were put to the sword or led away in captivity, how many buildings were destroyed. Did agriculture suffer? Was internal and external trade affected? To what extent was subsequent Russian culture influenced by the invasion? In the view of this author the overall *physical* destruction was considerably less than a reading of the contemporary sources would lead us to believe,[1] a view strongly rebutted by Soviet scholars.[2] But whether or not many of the cities, small towns and villages were depopulated; whether or not whole groups of the population – in particular the craftsmen – were expatriated; whether or not culture – in the shape of literature (chronicle-writing, hagiogra-

1. Fennell, *The Crisis*, pp. 86 ff.
2. e.g. A. L. Khoroshkevich and A. I. Pliguzov in Fennel (*sic*), *Krizis*, pp. 20 ff.

phy, travel–literature and homiletics), architecture, painting and applied arts – suffered catastrophically in the two or three decades
following the invasion, the Russian State and the Russian Church in
the first hundred and thirty years after the inception of the Horde in
Saray were very different from what they had been before Baty
invaded.

What, then, were the differences? One of the most important of
them resulted from the breach between north and south Russia. After
1240 the north – that is, Suzdal', Novgorod and Pskov – as well as the
central districts of Smolensk and Ryazan' seems to have lost touch
with the south, the early Kievan empire, i.e. Kiev, Chernigov and
Pereyaslavl'. As for the south-west, Volynia and Galicia were mostly
under the leadership of Daniil Romanovich and his family, deeply
absorbed in local and East-European affairs. Furthermore, for the time
being the Tatar-Mongols appear to have left Volynia and Galicia to
their own devices and in relative control of their own affairs: there is
no evidence of census-taking or of the permanent presence of Tatar
officials in the two principalities. But apart from one short-lived
alliance between Daniil and Aleksandr Nevskiy's brother Andrey in
the early 1250s, there was very little contact between the north-east
and the south-west. Altogether, in the second half of the thirteenth
century few north–south contacts are mentioned in the contemporary
sources, apart from the activities of the metropolitan, whose seat
remained officially in Kiev until 1299.

From a purely political point of view, the authority and effectiveness
of the rulers of the north were drastically enfeebled by the setting up
of Baty's Horde. Princes were obliged to present themselves at Saray,
and often at Karakorum in Mongolia as well, to receive their patents
for office (*yarlyki*) and to pay obeisance to the khan of Kipchak and to
the supreme khan. Their authority was further weakened by Tatar-
Mongol census-taking and the levying of tribute, and still more by the
establishment of *baskaki*, senior Mongol officials stationed in centres of
strategic importance to maintain order, crush rebellions and oversee
the collection of taxes. In the second half of the thirteenth century we
find Russian princes even requesting help from the *baskaki* and the
troops at their disposal, not only to take part in foreign ventures but
also to assist them militarily in their purely internal squabbles.[3]

Yet it was not only the Mongol control that weakened the Russian
rulers in the second half of the thirteenth century – it was the

3. Fennell, *The Crisis*, pp. 128 ff.

outmoded system of lateral inheritance, or rule by seniority (see above, pp. 12 ff.), which governed succession to the senior grand principality of Vladimir amongst the descendants of Yaroslav Vsevolodovich (grand prince from 1238 to 1246). The system led to the proliferation of minor principalities – the larger the families grew, the more family nests were needed for the offspring – the rulers of many of which were often totally cut off from whoever was grand prince at the time; and to him they owed no visible signs of fealty. And not one of the grand princes of Vladimir (the descendants of Yaroslav Vsevolodovich) was able to develop his own family patrimony – such as Northern Pereyaslavl', Suzdal', Kostroma or Yur'ev – so that it might emerge as the supreme principality of north-east Russia. It was only in the last decade of the thirteenth century that the rulers of two such patrimonies, Moscow and Tver', were showing signs of breaking the system. Horizontal succession had not long to survive.

Disorganized, fragmented, lacking in any sense of national unity, the Ryurikovichi of the thirteenth century had little chance of standing up to their overlords. Nor did they show much will to do so even when the Horde was temporarily weakened by dichotomy in the 1280s and 1290s. As for enemies from the West, it was the princes' good fortune that Lithuania in the thirteenth century was occupied with consolidating the territories it had gained in south-west Russia, while the Teutonic Knights were more concerned with subjugating the Balts than penetrating Russia's western frontiers. And any idea of a concerted plan, a crusade, masterminded by the pope, to invade and conquer Novgorodian territory in the north-west seems unlikely, to say the least of it.

There were, of course, exceptions amongst the weak princes who ruled from Vladimir from 1238 to the end of the century. Yaroslav, easily the most capable and politically the toughest of Vsevolod III's many sons, acceded to the grand-principality at the death of his elder brother Yury in 1238, having gained valuable experience in controlling Novgorod during the 1220s and 1230s, dealing with its difficult citizens and combating his volatile and adventurous enemy, Mikhail of Chernigov. But little is known of his rule as grand prince, except that he was twice summoned to the Kipchak Horde (1243 and 1245) and on the second sent to Mongolia, where he died, most probably poisoned.

However, it was his son Aleksandr (called 'Nevskiy' in a fifteenth-century chronicle in honour of his victory over the Swedes on the Neva river in 1240) who stole the limelight. Not only was he canonized, but he was also regarded throughout Russian history as the great Russian warrior, indeed by some as the saviour of Russia, who by his careful diplomacy in Saray and Karakorum and his valiant defence of the frontiers against the Latin West saved Russia from being overrun by the creatures of the pope; indeed, it is significant that in July 1942, at the height of the German offensive, Stalin resuscitated the Order of Aleksandr Nevskiy, founded by Catherine I in 1725, 'for Toil and Fatherland'. Aleksandr's defeat of the Swedes (1240) and of the Teutonic Knights (1242) on the ice of Lake Peypus are lauded in his *Life*, written some forty years later. But whether these were the great victories the author of his *Life* made them out to be is open to question:[4] probably his campaigns against invading Lithuanians (1242, 1245, 1248) were of greater import in the history of Russia's defence of the western borders in the period immediately following the Mongol invasion.

Aleksandr did not in fact become grand prince at the death of his father. There was still one of Yaroslav's brothers alive, Svyatoslav, who lasted as grand prince of Vladimir for only one year before being ousted by Aleksandr's younger brother Andrey. From the contemporary chronicle accounts of the years of Andrey's reign (1248–52) it would appear that he and his father-in-law, Daniil Romanovich of Volynia and Galicia (Andrey married Daniil's daughter in 1250/1), as well as another brother Yaroslav, had no wish to be vassals of the khans of the Kipchak Horde and indeed may well have been planning military resistance to the Mongols. Aleksandr clearly had no part in Andrey's schemes. In 1252 he went to Saray. Whether as a result of his influence over the khan or not, two expeditions were dispatched, one against Andrey and Yaroslav in Suzdalia and the other against Daniil. While the latter had little difficulty in resisting the Mongol army sent against him, Andrey and Yaroslav were decisively beaten at the battle of Pereyaslavl' and Andrey fled to Sweden 'rather than serve the khans', as the contemporary chronicler puts it. In the same year, presumably as soon as the news of Andrey's defeat had been received at the Horde, the Mongols 'sent him [Aleksandr] off with great honour, having given him seniority amongst all his brothers . . . Grand Prince Aleksandr came to the city of Vladimir and was met with Crosses at the Golden Gates by the metropolitan and all the abbots and the citizens, and was placed upon the throne of his father Yaroslav.'[5]

---

4. See ibid., pp. 103–6.
5. *PSRL*, vol. 1, col. 473; Fennell, *The Crisis*, pp. 106–9.

Aleksandr's brief reign of eleven years as grand prince (1252–63) was marked first and foremost by his friendly relations with the Mongols, by his uncompromising attitude towards any opposition to his own policy – especially in Novgorod – and by his unwillingness to support anti-Mongol feeling amongst the population: the spontaneous popular uprising of 1262 was neither inspired, and certainly not encouraged, by Aleksandr, who, it seems, was summoned by the khan to explain away his failure to restrain the citizens of the northern towns of Rostov, Vladimir, Suzdal', and Yaroslavl'; he could only beg Khan Berke to take no reprisals or order mass conscription in Suzdalia.

During his reign his many relatives caused him no serious trouble – even his old enemies, his brothers Andrey and Yaroslav, he somehow managed to appease; indeed, Andrey, after his return from Sweden, behaved, and was treated, as a compliant service prince, while Yaroslav offered no challenge whatsoever. The Church, as we shall see, treated him with the utmost respect and fostered in his *Life* the image of him as the champion of Orthodoxy. As for the West, his activities consisted for the most part in frontier-skirmishing, the Lithuanians again proving to be the only serious adversaries.

Novgorod provided Aleksandr with even more intractable problems than the rebellious northern cities and illustrated still more sharply his subservient attitude to the Mongols. Soon after his accession to the grand-princely throne he appointed his son Vasily – not more than 12 years old at the time – prince and ruler of Novgorod. But strong elements in the city which favoured links with the West drove Vasily out and in 1255 invited in, of all people, Yaroslav, who had been sheltering from his brother in nearby Ladoga after his and Andrey's defeat by the Mongols at the battle of Pereyaslavl'. It was an act of open defiance on the part of the Novgorodians. Aleksandr marched in, dismissed the mayor (*posadnik*), appointed his own creature in his place and, a year later, sent back Vasily to rule. But the majority of the population, though not, significantly, the archbishop, were in opposition to Aleksandr. A sort of fragile peace was patched up, but only by means of a compromise.

The real trouble began two years later when news reached the city of the impending visit of Mongol census officials intent on levying taxes. They were accompanied by Aleksandr himself. This time Vasily, who by now had come under the influence of the anti-Aleksandr element in Novgorod, fled to Pskov. In fact, the Novgorodians managed to bribe the census officials to leave. Only Aleksandr remained in the city to deal with his son's followers by cutting off their noses or gouging out their eyes. Vasily was captured and banished by his father to Suzdal'. In the following year, 1258, Aleksandr was sent for by the khan to explain why the Novgorodians had failed to accept the census. The outcome was predictable: Aleksandr returned in 1260 once again with the census officials, but this time with a detachment of Russian and Mongol soldiers. Opposition eventually collapsed when Aleksandr, who had been biding his time in the fortress of Gorodishche south of the town, 'rode in[to the city] and the accursed Tatars with him'. The Novgorod chronicler described the scene: 'the accursed ones began to ride through the streets, writing down the houses of the Christians; for our sins God has brought these wild beasts from the desert to eat the flesh of the strong and drink the blood of the boyars'.[6]

It is hard to believe that Aleksandr's brief reign was anything but a setback in the struggle of the Russian people to free themselves from Mongol overlordship. It could of course be argued, and it often is, that his policy of appeasement gave the Russians a breathing space – time to recover from the trauma of the invasion – and that it saved the population from the Mongol reprisals which would have resulted from the Novgorodians' refusal to submit to the census and from the northern cities' insurrection of 1262 had Aleksandr not been able to mollify the khans. Yet it cannot be denied that he showed no inclination whatsoever to support the coalition of his brothers and Daniil of Galicia in 1252, and it seems more than likely that the dispatch of the Mongol expeditions against them and the presence of Aleksandr at the Horde at the time were not coincidental. Still, the question remains: would the Russians have been capable of throwing off the 'Tatar Yoke' in the early 1250s even with Aleksandr's support and leadership and of resisting further reprisals? It is one of those questions that cannot be answered. All we can say is that Aleksandr's reign was followed by many decades of passive subservience to the Horde. The spirit of resistance had faded.

2

The forty-one years following Aleksandr's death were the low-water mark of Russia's existence under the Mongols. All four grand princes

6. *NPL*, pp. 82–3, 311.

of Vladimir – two of Aleksandr's brothers, Yaroslav and Vasily, and two of his sons, Dmitry and Andrey – ruled a loose and feeble federation of princes with a singular lack of cohesiveness. None of the four were able to exercise any control over their relatives; none had sufficiently strong family bases on which to build and from which to initiate military operations; and none were parochially minded enough to develop their patrimonies – Tver', Kostroma, Pereyaslavl' and Gorodets; instead, they concentrated their rule on the capital Vladimir and spent much of their energy trying to keep Novgorod under their sway and to stop their authority there being whittled away.

But by far and away the most disastrous aspect of the futile struggle of the four successors of Aleksandr Nevskiy somehow to control north-east Russia was their dependence on Mongol military assistance, not just against foreign enemies but, more deadly still, against their own brothers and cousins. Time and again they called in Mongol troops. At first it was to bring Novgorod to heel (1270, 1272, 1273); then to war on Lithuania (1275); finally, in the internecine wars which raged between Dmitry and Andrey from 1277 until 1294, the year of Dmitry's death, both princes attempted to benefit from the civil war which was taking place in the Horde at the time and called in the armies of opposing khans. The result of this senseless dependence on their masters to fight their own wars was a vast increase in the number of Mongol troops on Russian soil, who used every opportunity to ravage the country. And it did little to help either prince strengthen his authority. Any idea of opposition to the Horde became totally unrealizable. Subservience to the various khans was the order of the day.

As for the districts of the old Kievan empire, nothing was done, or could be done, by Aleksandr's successors to spread their influence to the south or the south-east of Suzdalia. During Yaroslav's reign Lithuania gradually expanded eastwards into Polotsk, northern Volynia and the western areas of the old principality of Turov. But most of south-west Russia and the heartlands of Kiev – the districts of Kiev, Chernigov and Pereyaslavl' – seems to have been under firm Mongol control. And so these territories remained until the middle of the fourteenth century.

3

The year 1304 marked the end of a critical period in the history of Russia. With the old Kievan empire in ruins, with Volynia and

Galicia looking to the West and having fewer and fewer links with Suzdalia, with European trade reduced to a trickle, with the senior prince of the Ryurikovich dynasty enjoying less authority than at any time previously and with the Mongols of the Kipchak Horde still very much in control of the subjects, Russia must have seemed to many at the time on the brink of disintegration.

During the last decade of the thirteenth century two relatively insignificant principalities, Moscow and Tver', were showing signs of economic and political superiority over the other patrimonies of north-east Russia. Under Daniil, Grand Prince Andrey's younger brother, who died in 1303, and his son Yury the territory of the principality of Moscow was enlarged roughly threefold by the annexation of neighbouring lands, so that by 1304 it was already a self-sufficient economic unit based on the Moskva river and a stretch of the Oka and the upper Klyaz'ma rivers, which provided a certain amount of protection from Mongol incursions as well as access to Ryazan' and the grand-princely capital of Vladimir. To the north-west of the district of Moscow lay the principality of Tver'. There were no natural defences of the area, but it was remote from the southern and eastern boundaries of Suzdalia and thus relatively safe from Mongol attack. The main advantage of its geographical position lay in the fact that the Volga flowed from the western to the eastern frontiers of the principality and that its many tributaries, especially the Tvertsa river which flowed into the Volga at the capital Tver', provided access to east–west trade and controlled the main water-routes from Novgorod to Suzdalia and beyond.

In 1304 there began a bitter struggle for supremacy between Moscow and Tver', which lasted twenty-four years. In this period Tver' managed to secure the grand-princely patent for three of its princes – Mikhail Yaroslavich (1304–08) and two of his sons, Dmitry (1322–25) and Aleksandr (1326–27) – while Moscow provided only one grand prince of Vladimir – Yury Danilovich (1318–22). By 1328, however, Tver' had shot its bolt, had lost all political and economic advantage and was no longer a serious rival to Moscow. In 1331 the great Kipchak khan Uzbeg (1312–41) bestowed the patent for the grand principality of Vladimir on Yury of Moscow's brother, Ivan I, the first of a long and only spasmodically interrupted succession of Muscovite princes who were to rule part or most of Russia from 1331 until the extinction of the line of Ivan's direct descendants with the death of Tsar Fedor Ivanovich in 1598.

Ivan's reign was distinguished by his servile dependence on Uzbeg: from the point of view of the khan, he was the ideal ruler of north-east Russia, malleable, obedient and prepared to do what he was told to do by his masters. In return he was allowed to get on with the business of dealing with the grand-principality of Vladimir and trying to cope with a touchy Novgorod and an intractable Pskov. Suzdalia under Ivan was no longer an object of concern for Uzbeg. Instead Uzbeg's attention was drawn to the nascent expansionist tendency of Lithuania. For under its intelligent and far-sighted grand prince Gedimin (Gediminas) (1316–41) Lithuania gradually encroached eastwards, infiltrating into, and annexing where possible, the old southern possessions of Kiev and at the same time putting out feelers towards Novgorod, Pskov and Tver'. Small wonder then that the Mongols were prepared to back, or at any rate not to harass, Moscow in the face of the growing menace of Lithuania. And yet, Ivan's achievements were few. True, he managed to gain the support of the Church (see below) and, true, he secured the patent for the grand-princely throne for his sons. But he never managed to gain more than a shaky control over Novgorod, where Lithuanian pressure and infiltration led to the emergence of a pro-Lithuanian faction within the city, and his reputation amongst many historians as the 'gatherer of the Russian lands' cannot hold water any more: during his reign no territories are known to have been annexed by Moscow.[7]

Ivan's two sons, Semen (Simeon) (1340–53) and Ivan II (1353–59), who succeeded him as rulers of Moscow and grand princes of Vladimir, for the most part carried out his policy of subservience to the Horde, which entailed resistance to the ever-growing power of Lithuania under the forceful son of Gedimin, Ol'gerd (Algirdas). The nineteen years of their reigns were an age of relative stability in north-east Russia. No new accessions to the territory of the principality of Moscow were made – indeed, Moscow's political authority in Suzdalia was deliberately kept at the same level as it had been under Ivan I by the shrewd policy of Uzbeg's son, Khan Jani-Beg (1342–57); Tver''s fragmentation was accelerated both by Moscow and by the Horde; and the Church continued to give strong support to Moscow. In the north-west of Russia Moscow's influence in Novgorod, especially during Semen's rule, increased to such an extent that any danger from a pro-Lithuanian party within the city faded. At the same time Pskov, which achieved a degree of semi-independence from its old mother-State Novgorod by the treaty of Bolotovo in 1348, fell for the first

---

7. Fennell, *The Emergence*, pp. 181–6; Crummey, *The Formation*, p. 49; Vodoff, 'A propos des "achats"'.

time under the sphere of Moscow's influence by the end of the 1340s.[8]

4

A new era in the history of Russia can be said to have started with the reign of Ivan II's son Dmitry, prince of Moscow from 1359, grand prince of Vladimir from 1362. Not only was Dmitry able to consolidate his position as undisputed leader of north-east Russia by annexing the majority of the hitherto uncommitted districts and thus doubling the area of the principality of Moscow, but he also succeeded in altering the whole attitude of the Russian people to the Mongols; for, indeed, Moscow had enjoyed relative stability as far as the Mongols were concerned for some thirty years before Dmitry's reign – little military interference, no reprisal raids. As a result the new generation of Russians lacked the vivid memories of their ancestors of the preceding century. Furthermore, the old creaking Russian military machine with its total lack of liaison between the armies of the disunited princes had disappeared. In its place was a single army consisting of the troops of the united principalities under the command of the grand prince of Moscow and Vladimir. There were few to oppose Dmitry amongst the Russian districts. Indeed, there was only one prince strong enough to offer any military resistance: Mikhail Aleksandrovich of Tver', who had somehow managed to restore a semblance of unity to a highly fragmented Tver' thanks largely to an alliance with Ol'gerd of Lithuania. But it was an uneven struggle that took place between 1368 and 1375, for Mikhail was no match in wealth or popularity for Dmitry, and, as he found to his cost, the Lithuanians turned out to be totally unreliable as allies. In 1375 a vast allied army under Dmitry defeated Tver', and Mikhail was obliged to recognize Dmitry as his elder brother and sovereign and never again to oppose Moscow in any conflict against the Mongols or against the Lithuanians.

But the real *élan* in Russian spirits resulted not from the victory over the Tverites but from the first military confrontations with the Mongols not to end in defeat. In the twenty-three years from 1357 to 1380 the Horde was in disarray, khan succeeding khan in quick

8. Fennell, *The Emergence*, pp. 268 ff.

succession. But still they represented a formidable power, and in 1377 a Russian army was soundly beaten on the River P'yana in the district of Nizhniy Novgorod. In the following year, however, the Russians won their first decisive victory over the Mongols on the Vozha river near Ryazan'. The powerful emir Mamay, who had dispatched the Mongol army north, decided that the time had come to punish the Russians. Having secured an alliance with Yagaylo (Lithuanian: Jogaila; Polish: Jagiełło), the new grand prince of Lithuania, and with Oleg of Ryazan', he led a large army to the southern borders of Russia and on 8 September 1380, at Kulikovo Field near the river Don, confronted Dmitry's forces. Mamay's allies from Lithuania and Ryazan' failed to turn up at the battlefield, and the Mongol army was put to flight. It was hailed by contemporary and near-contemporary writers as a great victory, and Dmitry was given the sobriquet *Donskoy* (Dmitry of the Don). But the fruits of victory were not enjoyed for long. In 1382 a descendant of Chinghis Khan, Tokhtamysh, who had captured Saray in 1378, had reunited the old Horde and had defeated Mamay's stricken army in 1381, took revenge on the Russians, sacking and burning Moscow and reimposing tribute. Nevertheless, in spite of Tokhtamysh's invasion and in spite of further Mongol inroads (Tamerlane in 1395, Edigey in 1408), the attitude of Muscovite Russia to the 'Tatar Yoke' was never the same as it had been before 1380. And although tribute was still demanded, if not always paid, until exactly one hundred years after the battle of Kulikovo, the aura of Mongol invincibility was shattered.

Towards the end of his life Dmitry Donskoy achieved a diplomatic and legal triumph to match his military successes. In his final will drawn up shortly before his death on 19 May 1389, after listing the distribution of various districts within the principality of Moscow to his five sons, he included a clause bequeathing his 'patrimony the grand principality' to his eldest son Vasily.[9] It meant that the grand principality of Vladimir was now the inalienable possession of the house of Moscow, universally recognized, both in north-east Russia and in the Horde – indeed, it had been stipulated in treaties with Ol'gerd (1371) and with Mikhail of Tver' (1375) ('you shall defend and not offend our patrimony of Moscow and all the grand principality'[10]). Nevertheless, this was the first time that the principle of the

9. 'Lo, I bless my son Prince Vasily with my patrimony, the grand principality.' *DDG*, p. 34.
10. Ibid., p. 26.

right of one branch of the Ryurikovichi to the title of grand prince of Vladimir and to all the land that went with it was sanctioned by law in a document ratified by the Horde. From now on until the extinction of the House of Moscow in 1598 not only the titles of grand prince of Vladimir and grand prince of Moscow but also the lands of Vladimir and Moscow were legally recognized as the possessions of Dmitry's direct descendants.

Vasily I's long reign (1389–1425) was one of fluctuating fortunes.[11] Apart from Tamerlane's abortive incursion of 1395 (his army inexplicably withdrew after reaching the southern borders of Ryazan´) and Edigey's destructive raid of 1408, Russo-Mongol relations were on the whole uneventful. In Lithuania Ol´gerd's brilliant and ambitious nephew Vitovt (Vitautas) took control of the grand principality in 1392, his cousin, Ol´gerd's eldest son Yagaylo, grand prince of Lithuania, having become king of Poland in 1386 (negotiations of Krewo). Apart from border skirmishes with Vasily I over Pskov from 1406 to 1408, the two princes, their alliance sealed by the marriage of Vasily to Vitovt's daughter, managed to coexist amicably. And even when Vitovt occupied the still uncommitted principality of Smolensk in 1395, Vasily took no action to hamper him. At home the only gain of territory was the annexation of the geographically important district of Nizhniy Novgorod based on the middle reaches of the Volga and the lower reaches of the Oka, Klyaz´ma and Unzha rivers. Tver´ and Ryazan´ both maintained their independence.

When Vasily I died in 1425 his 9-year-old son Vasily II (1425–62) acceded to the throne, only to be challenged by his formidable uncle, Yury of Northern Galich. Unfortunately for Russia, Dmitry Donskoy had left no explicit instructions in his will as to what was to happen at Vasily's death. Only a clause stipulated that 'should God remove my son Vasily', his next eldest brother (i.e. Yury) was to receive 'Prince Vasily's appanage'.[12] But at the time the will was drawn up Vasily was only 17, and Dmitry had no intention of abrogating primogeniture: he clearly had in mind the death of his eldest son unmarried, heirless and intestate. Yury, however, thought otherwise. But he had few supporters except in the districts left him by his father, Galich in the north-east and Zvenigorod west of Moscow, while Vasily II enjoyed the support of his three remaining uncles and the metropolitan Foty.

---

11. For a balanced view of his reign, see Crummey, *The Formation*, pp. 56–68.
12. 'Should . . . God remove my son Vasily, then whichever of my sons be below him [i.e. next in lateral succession], this son of mine shall receive Prince Vasily's appanage.' *DDG*, p. 35.

Yury was obliged to submit. But immediately after Foty's death in 1431 the conflict flared up again with renewed intensity and Yury went to the Horde 'with chronicles, old documents and the will of his father'[13] to dispute Vasily's right to the patent. Although the khan sanctioned Vasily's claim to the throne, it was the start of a singularly vicious and bloody civil war which was to last another sixteen years during the course of which Vasily II was thrice ousted by Yury and his sons, once captured by the Mongols, blinded, having himself had Yury's eldest son blinded, and eventually restored to the throne of Moscow as grand prince on 17 February 1447.

In the following year Iona, bishop of Ryazan', who had loyally supported Vasily II in the final stages of the conflict, was elected to the vacant metropolitan see without the blessing of Constantinople. An era in the history of the Russian Church had come to an end.

13. *PSRL*, vol. 25, p. 249.

CHAPTER ELEVEN

The Metropolitans of Russia: From Kirill II to Aleksiy

1

Of all the metropolitans who headed the Russian Church from 1240[1] to 1448 the great majority played a far more active role in the political life of the State than did their predecessors of the Kievan period. Of course this may appear so simply because the contemporary sources paid more attention to them than they did to the metropolitans of the previous age; or it may be that the senior hierarchs of the two centuries after the Mongol invasion were endowed with greater intelligence and tougher moral fibre. By and large they were certainly more aware of their own powers and ability to help or hinder the lay rulers – indeed, to such an extent that it is sometimes hard to decide whether it was the grand prince who used his metropolitan to shape the history of the emergent State, or the other way round. They lasted longer too: the seven major metropolitans ruled their dioceses for an average of twenty-three years, while their twenty-two pre-Mongol brothers managed an average of only nine years.

The first of the great metropolitans, Kirill II (c.1250–81), almost certainly a Russian and the first Russian metropolitan since Klim in the twelfth century, was the candidate of Daniil Romanovich of

1. The last metropolitan of the previous period was Iosif, a Greek, who arrived from Nicaea in 1237 (*NPL*, pp. 74, 285) and about whose activities nothing is known: he either returned to Nicaea during the Mongol invasion or died in Kiev. It is not known if there were any metropolitans in Russia between 1240 and 1250: there is, however, mention of a shadowy 'Archbishop Petr of Russia' present at the Council of Lyons in 1245 ('Quidam archiepiscopus de Russcia, Petrus nomine', Matthew of Paris, in Matuzova, *Angliyskie srednevekovye istochniki*, p. 124); Stökl, 'Kanzler', pp. 165–6.

Galicia, having probably been previously his chancellor (*pechatnik*).[2] How his nomination and election were carried out – when? by what council of bishops? with or without patriarchal approval? – is simply not known. Presumably he left Russia some time after 1244, for there had been no patriarch in Nicaea for the previous four years, and was consecrated some time in the second half of the 1240s.

He never returned to what was probably his native south-west Russia, nor do the sources mention any links between him and Volynia or Galicia, although it is clear that 'Little Russia' (ἡ μικρὰ 'Ρωσία), as the area was known in Byzantium, was under his jurisdiction as metropolitan of Kiev.[3] Instead he spent the rest of his life in Kiev and north Russia. He never went to the Horde, or if he did the sources are silent about it. Kiev of course was his base – he was, after all, 'metropolitan of Kiev and all Russia' – but owing to the thinness of the thirteenth-century chronicles it is hard to judge just how long he spent there. Certainly for most of the first half of his metropolitanate he was in north Russia, where, apart from the consecration of bishops and the celebration of Andrey's marriage to Daniil's daughter in 1250/1 (see above, p. 122), his only recorded actions are all connected with Aleksandr Nevskiy: he visited him in Novgorod in 1251; he cured a 'grievous sickness' of his in the same year 'by means of his prayers';[4] he met and enthroned him as grand prince of Vladimir in 1252; he accompanied him on the first leg of a military campaign against the Swedes in 1256; he buried him in 1263; and in all probability he set in motion the initial local veneration in Vladimir and wrote his *Life*.[5] But he never transferred his official residence to Vladimir and for the last fourteen years of his life he is reported mainly as resident in Kiev. All the bishops he appointd in this last period were consecrated by him in Kiev (Feognost of Saray in 1269; Serapion of Vladimir in 1273; Kliment of Novgorod and Fedor of Vladimir in 1275/6) and a major synod of bishops was convoked by him and held there in 1273.[6] His only known visits to northern Russia were in 1270, when he intervened in Novgorod on behalf of Grand Prince Yaroslav (see below, pp. 218-19); 1274, when he enthroned Serapion as bishop of Vladimir; 1280–81, when he settled a conflict with the

<hr/>

2. See Stökl, 'Kanzler'.
3. See Podskalsky, *Christentum*, pp. 299–301.
4. *PSRL*, vol. 1, cols. 472–3.
5. See Fennell and Stokes, *Early Russian Literature*, pp. 120–1.
6. For the date and place, see Shchapov, *Vizantiyskoe i yuzhnoslavyanskoe pravovoe nasledie*, pp. 183–4.

bishop of Rostov and died in Northern Pereyaslavl' (27 November 1281). His remains were transferred ten days later to the cathedral of St Sofia in Kiev where they were interred.[7]

Like him, his successor Maksim (1283–1305), a Greek, spent much of his twelve years as metropolitan in Kiev, but, unlike him, he visited the Horde[8] – most probably on his way to Kiev from Constantinople – and in 1299 transferred his see from Kiev to Vladimir-on-the-Klyaz'ma, 'being unable to tolerate Tatar violence'.[9] Apart from convening a synod of bishops in Kiev in 1284 and in all probability formally canonizing Vladimir and Ol'ga at it (see above, pp. 60-1), and apart from consecrating a number of bishops and visiting many of his dioceses in the north of Russia ('teaching, instructing and administering'[10]), little is known of his ecclesiastical activities, and one can only speculate about his political leanings or his relationship with Byzantium.

As mentioned above, during Kirill II's primacy most of the old Kievan State, including 'Little Russia' (Volynia and Galicia) as well as northern Russia (Suzdalia, Novgorod and Pskov), came under his jurisdiction. In 1303, however, the ruler of Galicia, Yury I L'vovich, grandson of Daniil Romanovich, managed to persuade the emperor (Andronicus II) and the patriarch (Athanasius I) to raise the bishopric of Galich to a metropolitanate – the metropolis of Little Russia – consisting of four of the bishoprics of Volynia and Galicia (Vladimir-in-Volynia, Peremyshl', Lutsk and Kholm) and Turov, which was probably under Yury's control at the time. The new metropolitan see came under the old bishop of Galich, Nifont.

Nothing is known of the short-lived existence of this, the first breakaway metropolitanate in the Russian lands, or of Metropolitan Nifont: he either died or resigned his see in 1305, for after Maksim's death in that year Yury of Galicia dispatched one Petr, a local abbot, to Constantinople as his candidate for the metropolitanate either of 'Kiev and all Russia' or, more likely, of 'Little Russia'. At the same time the grand prince of Vladimir, Mikhail Yaroslavich, sent *his* candidate, Abbot Geronty, to replace Maksim. Alas, we do not know what exactly transpired in Constantinople. All we do know is that the emperor and the patriarch decided to liquidate the metropolitan see

---

7. Podskalsky, *Christentum*, p. 300.
8. Only mentioned in the Nikon Chronicle (*PSRL*, vol. 10, p. 161).
9. *TL*, p. 349. On Maksim's move to Vladimir, see Ostrowski, 'Why Did the Metropolitan Move'.
10. *PSRL*, vol. 10, p. 166.

they had so recently created, to ignore the grand prince of Vladimir's candidate and to appoint Petr sole metropolitan of Kiev and all Russia. The first metropolitanate of Little Russia had lasted barely two years.[11] There were others to come.

But not during the metropolitanate of Petr. No mention is made in any of the sources of attempts to resuscitate the short-lived 'metropolis of Little Russia' during Petr's tenure of the see of Kiev; nor is Petr, himself a Little Russian, reported as having shown much interest in the south-west even though the sees of Volynia and Galicia came under his jurisdiction as metropolitan of Kiev and all Russia. Yury L'vovich, not unexpectedly, was dismayed by the abrupt liquidation of his 'metropolis', so much so that he even approached Pope Clement V with the aim of discussing the possibility of a union with the Latin Church.[12]

Petr arrived in Vladimir from Constantinople in 1309 at the height of the conflict between Tver' and Moscow for supremacy in north-west Russia. From the first, circumstances placed him in the Moscow camp. This was hardly surprising in view of the fact that Mikhail of Tver' was unlikely to welcome as metropolitan the opponent of his own candidate for the supreme see in Russia. Indeed, Petr was accused of simony by Mikhail's bishop of Tver', Andrey, but was vindicated at a council (1310 or 1311) at which were present a representative of the patriarch, two Russian bishops, two sons of Mikhail of Tver' and in all probability Yury of Moscow.

Petr's actions illustrate his political leanings: in 1309 he interfered in the affairs of Bryansk in support of a prince protected by Moscow (see below, p. 196); he successfully baulked a Tverite expedition to Nizhniy Novgorod in 1311 (see below, pp. 220–1); he appointed bishops who were his adherents, if not his own nominees (David of Novgorod in 1309 and Prokhor of Rostov in 1311), with the result that Tver' suffered constant trouble in both these districts;[13] and in 1315 he replaced Andrey, who retired discreetly to a monastery, with his own nominee, Varsanofy, as bishop of Tver'.

In many ways the most significant year of his life from a purely ideological point of view was his last, 1326. In the beginning of the year he was already resident in Moscow, where Ivan I had taken over following the murder of his brother Yury at the Horde by Dmitry of

---

11. On Nifont and the first metropolitanate of Little Russia, see Fennell, *The Emergence*, pp. 68–9, 125; Meyendorff, *Byzantium*, pp. 91–3.

12. Paszkiewicz, *Jagiellonowie*, p. 317 n. 5.

13. For details, see Fennell, *The Emergence*, p. 73 n. 2.

Tver´. In February, together with his appointee bishops (Moisey of Novgorod, Prokhor of Rostov and Varsanofy of Tver´), he buried Yury of Moscow; in August, 'with his own hands', so we are told in his *Life*, he began building a burial-vault for himself in the early stages of the construction of the cathedral of the Dormition in Moscow. On 20 December 1326 he died and was buried by one of the bishops of Little Russia in the presence of Ivan I. By his residence in Moscow and his choice of burial place Petr had virtually designated Moscow as the future centre of the Russian Church. The official residence of the metropolitan, however, was not transferred from Vladimir to Moscow either by Petr or by his successor, but by the next Russian metropolitan, Aleksiy.

Metropolitan Petr's great contribution to the cause of Moscow and its princes was recognized by Ivan, who not only is believed to have granted him a small estate near Moscow,[14] but also was the inspiration and initiator of Petr's canonization at the Council of Vladimir in 1327. The list of miracles occurring at Petr's grave which were read out at the Council – miracles being the indispensable condition of canonization – was clearly prepared by Ivan, while the Council itself was presided over by the faithful Bishop Prokhor. Shortly afterwards the first version of Petr's *Life*, full of pro-Moscow and anti-Tver´ flavouring, was composed by an unknown Muscovite, later to be reworked at the end of the fourteenth century by Metropolitan Kiprian.[15]

2

If Ivan I had cause to be grateful to Metropolitan Petr for his political support and collaboration, both he and his son Semen were even more indebted to Petr's successor, the Greek Feognost (Theognostos) (1328–53). Tough, cultured, probably the friend of the Byzantine historian Nicephorus Gregoras, shrewd and intelligent, he acted throughout his primacy as the true friend of Moscow. Like his predecessor, he interfered in the affairs of Bryansk (see below, pp. 196–7) and adopted a political stance in his appointment of, and attitude to, the bishops of his see (Fedor of Tver´ and Vasily of Novgorod: see below, pp. 225–7); he foiled Lithuanian plans for an independent bishopric of Pskov

---

14. Veselovsky, *Feodal´noe zemlevladenie*, p. 332.
15. On the *Life* of Petr, see Kuchkin, ' "Skazanie" '.

(see below, p. 224); but, above all, again like Petr, he fought, and fought successfully, to maintain the indivisibility of the see of Kiev and all Russia and to protect it from the splinter metropolitanates of Little Russia and Lithuania.

It was in this opposition to the establishment of rival metropolitan sees that Feognost's main contribution to Moscow's struggle against Lithuania lay. Little Russia – Volynia and Galicia – was the main area of dispute. His first recorded act on arrival in Russia was to appoint Fedor (Theodore) as bishop of the town of Galich in the presence of the bishops of Peremyshl', Kholm, Vladimir, Lutsk and Turov.[16] Of course this may simply have been the statutory filling of an empty see. But the presence of all the bishops of Little Russia at the ceremony looks as though Feognost was anxious publicly to declare the dependence of the bishoprics of Volynia–Galicia on his metropolitan see of Kiev–Vladimir–Moscow – an act of defiance, as it were, in the face of Yury L'vovich's Polish successor as ruler of Little Russia, Bolesław-Yury II,[17] son of the prince of Mazovia.

Fedor, however, was not to prove an ally of Feognost for long. In April 1331 an unnamed 'metropolitan of Galicia' was listed as present at a synod in Constantinople, and it may well be that this was the first of Fedor's appointments to the see of Little Russia.[18] If it was in fact Fedor who was made metropolitan, his prelacy was short-lived, for in August 1331 he is known to have been present at the consecration of Archbishop Vasily of Novgorod in (Volynian) Vladimir, and named merely as the *bishop* of the town of Galich.[19] In the following year Feognost was in Constantinople, probably to confirm this the second closure of the metropolitanate of south-west Russia.

Whether or not it was Fedor who was the metropolitan, it was clearly a triumph for Feognost, and for some thirteen years no more attempts were made to resuscitate the metropolitanate of Galicia (i.e. of Little Russia). In the middle of the 1340s, however, during the civil war in Byzantium between Ann of Savoy and John VI Cantacuzenus, Little Russia, now under Gedimin's son Lyubart-Dmitry,[20] became

16. Fennell, *The Emergence*, p. 126.
17. Bolesław, Gedimin's son-in-law, became Orthodox and took the name of Yury (II) when he became ruler of Volynia and Galicia in 1325.
18. Fennell, *The Emergence*, p. 128. Meyendorff, however, calls the presence-list of the synod 'somewhat dubious' and doubts whether Fedor was in fact consecrated. See *Byzantium*, pp. 154–5.
19. *NPL*, p. 343.
20. Lyubart (Lithuanian: Liubartas) – his pagan name; Dmitry – his Christian name after his Orthodox baptism.

once again a metropolitanate outside the jurisdiction of Feognost.[21] It was the work of Patriarch John Calecas, the enemy of Emperor John Cantacuzenus, and when at the end of the civil war the latter returned to power in 1347, the metropolitanate of Little Russia was for the third time liquidated. Again, it was Feognost who contrived the liquidation: Grand Prince Semen, at the prodding of his metropolitan, wrote to Cantacuzenus asking him to return the bishoprics of Volynia and Galicia to the metropolitanate of Kiev. As the letter was accompanied by a sweetener in the shape of considerable funds for the repair of the church of St Sophia, it produced the required result. The emperor replied, in August 1347, with a chrysobull decreeing that

> the most holy dioceses in the said Little Russia – Galich, Vladimir, Kholm, Peremyshl′, Lutsk and Turov – be submitted again to the . . . most holy metropolitanate of Kiev . . . and that the God-loving bishops of those most holy dioceses should pay proper obeisance to the same most sacred Metropolitan of Kiev . . . the Lord Theognostos (and to those metropolitans who would succeed him) as to their First Bishop . . .[22]

Far less is known about the other splinter-see which Lithuania was anxious to establish as a rival to, or a supplanter of, the metropolitanate of Kiev, namely that of Lithuania. It was first created *c.*1300[23] and there is evidence of its primate (or primates?) in Constantinople in 1317, 1327 and 1329[24] and that his name, given on the last occasion only, was Feofil (Theophilus).[25] The residence of the metropolitan was in Novgorodok (Lithuanian: Naugardukas; Polish: Nowogródek), some 80 kilometres west of Minsk, and his diocese consisted of 'Black Russia' – the western district of modern Belorussia watered by the upper Nieman river which Lithuania had annexed in the middle of the thirteenth century – probably the old principality of Polotsk, perhaps part of Turov and possibly even Chernigov, Kiev and Smolensk.

If Metropolitan Petr was aware of this see's existence, he took no steps to have it closed by the patriarch; at any rate the sources are silent on the matter. As for Feognost, all we know is that in 1329 or 1330 Feofil died and that Feognost was evidently responsible for the subsequent closure of the see. There were no more 'metropolitans of

21. For the dating (1345–6), see Meyendorff, *Byzantium*, pp. 159–60; cf. Golubinsky (*IRTs*, vol. 2, I, pp. 157–8), who hazards 1337–8.

22. *RIB*, vol. 6, app., cols. 17, 19. See Meyendorff, *Byzantium*, pp. 280–2 for a translation of Cantacuzenus's letter.

23. See Giedroyc′, 'The Arrival', pp. 15–17.

24. *APC*, vol. 1, pp. 72, 143, 147.

25. Ibid., p. 147: Τοῦ Λιτβῶν καὶ ὑπερτίμου Θεοφίλου.

Lithuania' until the last year of Feognost's life. And doubtless whatever bishoprics had been under Feofil's aegis were transferred back to the metropolitanate of Kiev.

Clearly, however, Ol'gerd was not pleased with the situation. It was not at all in his interest that the Orthodox districts now controlled or occupied by Lithuanian governors should owe spiritual allegiance to a metropolitan close to the grand prince of Moscow. In 1352 he sent one Feodorit (Theodoret) to Constantinople for consecration as 'metropolitan of Russia'. Not surprisingly, Ol'gerd's request was turned down – after all, Feognost was still alive and, although he had fallen ill in 1350, was still active in the following two years.[26] In 1352, however, Feodorit managed to get himself consecrated – quite illegally –metropolitan of Russia by the Bulgarian patriarch of Trnovo. He then took up residence in Kiev where he remained for at least two years. Meyendorff considers that 'sponsored and supported by Ol'gerd, he was in the process of building up an all-Russian Church independent of Constantinople and based in the historic see of Kiev'.[27] Eventually he was deposed. No details are known of his ultimate fate.[28]

If proof were needed of the benefits accruing to the grand prince of Moscow from the policy of keeping the western sees under Suzdalian control, one has only to consider the immediate political results of the third closure of the metropolitanate of Little Russia. In 1349, two years after the return of the Volynian and Galician bishoprics to the Muscovite fold, Lyubart Gediminovich, the Lithuanian ruler of Volynia and Galicia, sent envoys to Semen asking for peace and for the hand of his niece in marriage.[29] It is true that Lyubart's brother Ol'gerd, also in 1349, asked Semen for permission to marry his wife's sister (Iuliania, the daughter of Aleksandr Mikhaylovich of Tver'),[30] and Lyubart's act was probably dictated by a wish to keep in line with his brother, all the more so in the year when not only were the Lithuanians crushed by the Teutonic Knights at the battle of the

26. *TL*, p. 371 (nomination by Feognost of Daniil as bishop of Suzdal'). In 1352 Archbishop Moisey of Novgorod complained to the emperor and patriarch of 'unbefitting things' and 'violence' allegedly committed or caused by Feognost (*NPL*, p. 363).

27. Meyendorff, *Byzantium*, p. 166.

28. The only information on Feodorit's activities comes from a patriarchal letter (July 1354) addressed to the archbishop of Novgorod, warning him that if Feodorit has not cast off his episcopal rank (τὰ ἀρχιερατικὰ), then he is to be considered excommunicated. *APC*, vol. 1, pp. 350–1; *RIB*, vol. 6, app., col. 61.

29. *TL*, p. 370.

30. It is interesting to note that Semen first approached Feognost (*dolozha Feognosta mitropolita*) before giving his sister-in-law in marriage to Ol'gerd. Ibid.

Strawa (February 1349), but also King Casimir III of Poland, no longer the ally of Lithuania, extended his rule over the whole of Galicia and occupied virtually all Volynia in the great Hundred Days war against Little Russia (September–December 1349).[31] Nevertheless, the temporary alignment of Little Russia with Moscow was a considerable triumph for Semen and his prelate. Feognost's ecclesiastical policy had undoubtedly reaped its political rewards.

Feognost died on 11 March 1353. Three months earlier he had taken the precaution of appointing as bishop of Vladimir-on-the-Klyaz′ma Aleksiy Byakont.[32] Son of a boyar in Chernigov, Aleksiy, baptized with the lay name of Semen and with Ivan I as godfather, had been brought up at the court of Moscow. Tonsured as Aleksiy in the Moscow Bogoyavlenskiy (Epiphany) Monastery, he had eventually found favour not only with Feognost but also with Semen, to the writing of whose will he had been a witness (March/April 1353).[33] Immediately after his investiture as bishop of Vladimir an embassy was sent off to Constantinople by Feognost and the grand prince requesting his appointment as metropolitan-elect.[34] The envoys returned not long after Feognost's death 'with letters from the emperor [John VI Cantacuzenus] and the patriarch [Philotheus]' and the command that 'Bishop Aleksiy proceed to Constantinople to be consecrated [as metropolitan] . . . by the holy patriarch'.[35] Aleksiy was kept waiting a year in Constantinople and only returned to Moscow in 1354.

The agreement of the patriarch and the emperor to appoint Aleksiy was undoubtedly a victory for Moscow and a setback for Lithuania. In December 1354, however, John VI Cantacuzenus abdicated and was supplanted by his son-in-law John V Palaeologus, and Philotheus was replaced by his predecessor Patriarch Callistus (1354–63). This could only mean one thing: a change of attitude towards Ol′gerd, whose

31. See the probably exaggerated account found in the Novgorod Fourth Chronicle *s.a.* 1349 (*PSRL*, vol. 4, I, p. 279): 'The king of Cracow [i.e. Casimir the Great] came and took the land of Volynia by cunning and did much evil to the Christians and converted the Christian churches to the Latin faith abhorrent to God.' Later chronicles repeat this, e.g. *PSRL*, vol. 25, p. 177. The invasion of Little Russia is described in Knoll, *The Rise*, pp. 140–2.
32. *PSRL*, vol. 15, I, col. 62; *TL*, p. 373. Aleksiy had previously been his 'vicar' (*namestnik*) in Vladimir, where there had been no bishop since Maksim had transferred his see there from Kiev in 1299.
33. *DDG*, p. 14.
34. *PSRL*, vol. 15, I, col 62; *TL*, p. 373.
35. *PSRL*, vol. 15, I, col. 63; *TL*, pp. 373–4.

own candidate, Roman, the son of a Tverite boyar[36] and a relative of Ol'gerd's wife Iuliania, was consecrated in Constantinople as 'metropolitan of the Lithuanians'.[37]

Not surprisingly, most of the Russian contemporary chronicles, duly censored of course by Moscow, say little or nothing about Roman's activities; the Moscow Trinity Chronicle does not even mention his name. Still, we know that in 1355 both he and Aleksiy went to Constantinople to establish the areas under their respective jurisdictions. The Tver' (Rogozhskiy) Chronicle merely says that 'between them there was a great quarrel' and that 'the Greeks [received] great gifts from them' – a clear indication that both metropolitans resorted to large-scale bribery to gain their ends. It adds, somewhat unhelpfully, that in the following year 'Metropolitan Aleksiy came from Constantinople to the Russian land and Roman to the Lithuanian and Volynian land'.[38] Roman's see, however, was defined by Callistus in 1355–56 as that of the previous metropolitan of Lithuania (i.e. Black Russia, Polotsk and Turov[39]), as well as 'the sees of Little Russia' – in other words, virtually all the territories outside Lithuania proper controlled by Ol'gerd.

Although Aleksiy retained the title of 'metropolitan of Kiev and all Russia', there was little he could do to stop Roman from maintaining or increasing his hold over Ol'gerd's lands. After their return from Constantinople the two metropolitans went their own ways. Roman, now 'fearlessly' styling himself 'metropolitan of Kiev and all Russia', took up his residence in Kiev, causing 'much confusion and trouble for the eparchy'.[40] How long he remained there is not known. The only information from the Russian sources on his activities in Russia before his death in 1362 is that in 1360 he 'came to Tver'' in fury and shamelessness without having been in friendly contact with the Most Reverend Metropolitan Aleksiy; and nothing happened according to his will . . . and Fedor, the bishop of Tver', did not see him, nor did he

---

36. *PSRL*, vol. 15, I, col. 61.

37. See Meyendorff, *Byzantium*, pp. 168–9. Note that according to the Tver' (Rogozhskiy) Chronicle *s.a.* 1354, it appears that Aleksiy and Roman were both appointed at the same time: 'In Constantinople two metropolitans of all the Russian land, Aleksiy and Roman, were appointed and there was great hostility between them . . .' *PSRL*, vol. 15, I, col. 62.

38. Ibid., cols. 64–5.

39. In fact the decree merely states: 'Polotsk and Turov together with Novgorodek (μετὰ καὶ τοῦ Νοβογραδοπουλίου), the seat of the metropolitan' (*APC*, vol. 1, p. 426; *RIB*, vol. 6, app., col. 75), but presumably 'Novgorodek' includes the whole of Black Russia. See Meyendorff, *Byzantium*, p. 170.

40. *APC*, vol. 1, p. 428; *RIB*, vol. 6, app., col. 77.

render him honour. And after a short time he went back to Lithuania.'[41]

A little more is known about Aleksiy in the five years after his return from his second visit to Constantinople in 1356. In 1357 he was in Vladimir-on-the-Klyaz'ma, where much of his time was taken up dealing with the problems of Tver': two of the contending princes, Vsevolod Aleksandrovich of Kholm and Vasily Mikhaylovich of Kashin – the latter supported by the pro-Moscow bishop of Tver', Fedor 'the Good', as he was styled – brought their cases before him (see below, pp. 229-30). In the same year he went to Saray to heal Uzbeg's widow Taydula from an unspecified illness.[42] In 1358 he was in Kiev. On the first leg of his journey there he was accompanied by Bishop Fedor of Tver', greatly harassed by the inter-princely struggle in his diocese. Fedor begged to be allowed to retire from his post, but Aleksiy 'instructed him with great love', urged him to persevere and sent him back to Tver' from Kolomna.[43] Aleksiy stayed in Kiev until 1360[44] without even returning to Moscow to bury Ivan II, who died in 1359. He was back in Moscow in 1360 and, after a visit to Tver' in 1361 to appoint a new bishop to replace the long-suffering Fedor, who had finally succeeded in retiring to a monastery,[45] returned once more to Moscow. Here his presence as regent was needed: Dmitry, who had succeeded his father Ivan II in 1359, was only 11 years old at the time.

There can be no doubt that Patriarch Callistus underwent a change of heart towards Roman, reports of whose impingement on Aleksiy's rightful title and territory must have reached Constantinople. At any rate, after Roman's death (1362) the damage was undone. All the districts which had come, legally or illegally, under Roman's sway – in other words, the two metropolitanates of Lithuania and Little Russia and any other lands which Roman had claimed were under his jurisdiction – were now officially returned by Callistus to Metropoli-

---

41. Only in the sixteenth-century Nikon Chronicle. *PSRL*, vol. 10, p. 231. But see Meyendorff (*Byzantium*, p. 186), who says that in 1360, after Aleksiy's departure, he 'invaded the see of Kiev' and 'extended his power over Bryansk' (see *APC*, vol. 1, p. 428; *RIB*, vol. 6, app., col. 79 – 'he acquired the larger Russian diocese of Bryansk').

42. *PSRL*, vol. 15, I, col. 66; *TL*, p. 375.

43. *PSRL*, vol. 15, I, col. 67; vol. 10, p. 230.

44. *TL*, pp. 376, 377. Presumably, then, Roman left Kiev before 1358. According to a patriarchal act of 1380, Aleksiy on arrival in Kiev was arrested by Ol'gerd, but managed to escape (*RIB*, vol. 6, app., col. 167). None of the Russian chronicles (Trinity, Nikon, *et al.*), however, mention this. Cf. the version of N. S. Borisov, who has Aleksiy spending 'about two years in prison' (*Russkaya tserkov'*, p. 80). Cf. Skrynnikov, *Gosudarstvo i Tserkov'*, p. 14.

45. *PSRL*, vol. 15, I, cols. 70, 72.

tan Aleksiy.[46] For at least three years Aleksiy's by now vast metropolitanate was secure, doubly so after his great patron in Constantinople,
Philotheus, replaced Callistus as patriarch in 1364.

The unity of the Orthodox Church under Aleksiy was not to last
for long. The fluid political situation in south-west Russia was about
to enter into a new phase. After King Casimir the Great's occupation
of Galicia and most of Volynia in 1349 (see above, p. 140, n. 31) Little
Russia underwent three years of inconclusive warring, Lithuanians
and Poles both attempting to control as much of Roman Mstislavich's
old principality as they could. Eventually in 1352 a compromise was
reached: Catholic Casimir emerged as ruler of much of what had been
Galicia (L'vov, Galich, Peremyshl' and Sanok), while the still pagan
descendants of Gedimin of Lithuania were recognized as masters of
Volynia (Vladimir, Lutsk, Bel'z and Kholm).[47] For fourteen years the
position remained more or less static. But in Poland preparations were
going on for the conquest of the whole of Little Russia – *regnum
Galiciae et Lodomeriae*. In 1366 Casimir invaded. Within two months
most of Volynia was in his hands as well as all of his previous
possessions in Galicia.

The annexation of south-west Russia by the Poles could only mean
one thing as far as the ecclesiastical administration of the area was
concerned: Metropolitan Aleksiy's hold on the Orthodox population
was certain to be disputed by the king. And yet nothing happened for
nearly four years. The Russian sources are ominously silent: not a
word is said of Casimir's invasion; the metropolitan seemingly took
no steps to investigate the situation in the western wedge of his
diocese, let alone in Kiev, which the Lithuanians had captured in 1362.
All he is reported as doing between 1366 and 1370 is assisting Dmitry
Donskoy to lure Mikhail Aleksandrovich of Tver' to Moscow in 1368
(see below, pp. 231–2); taking refuge in the Kremlin at the time of the
first Lithuanian-Tver' invasion of Moscow in the same year; and in
1370 baptizing the son of Boris Konstantinovich of Suzdal' in Nizhniy
Novgorod.[48] Nor did Casimir or Ol'gerd, the latter by now in
aggressive opposition to Moscow, do anything to lessen Aleksiy's
spiritual hold over his flock in Little Russia. Nothing, that is, until

---

46. Meyendorff, *Byzantium*, p. 171; *APC*, vol. 1, pp. 525–7; *RIB*, vol. 6, app., cols.
91–7.

47. Knoll, *The Rise*, pp. 153–5.

48. *TL*, pp. 386, 388, 391 (and other near-contemporary chronicles); *PSRL*, vol. 4,
I, p. 295.

1370,[49] when Casimir wrote to Patriarch Philotheus requesting that his candidate, one Bishop Antony, presumably one of the west-Russian bishops, be consecrated metropolitan of Little Russia, 'so that the law of the Russians may not be reduced to chaos, so that it may not disappear.'[50] The letter ends with the threat that should Antony not be consecrated, then 'we will be forced to baptize the Russians into the faith of the Latins'.[51]

The threat indeed must have appeared only too real to Constanti-nople, for although the majority of the population in Volynia and Galicia was Orthodox, there were by now considerable numbers of Latins in residence there – in L'vov alone there were two Catholic monasteries and four churches[52] – and the number was undoubtedly growing. Philotheus, after his return to the patriarchal throne in 1364, had for six years shown remarkable – remarkable even for him – readiness to back Dmitry Donskoy against Ol'gerd of Lithuania and to assert the authority of Aleksiy: he approved and sanctioned the metropolitan's canonization of three Lithuanian Christians martyred in 1347 by Ol'gerd;[53] and in June 1370 he wrote a number of letters – to Dmitry Donskoy, Aleksiy, 'the princes of Russia', Archbishop Aleksiy of Novgorod – as well as two acts of excommunication against Ol'gerd's Russian allies;[54] all of which incontrovertibly placed him firmly on the side of the lay and spiritual rulers of Moscow. But on receipt of Casimir's letter he appears to have caved in. In May 1372 a patriarchal synod issued a decree confirming the appointment of 'dearest to God ($\theta\epsilon o\phi\iota\lambda\acute{\epsilon}\sigma\tau\alpha\tau os$) Bishop Antony', 'who had come from Little Russia', to the 'most holy Galician metropolitanate'. The decree is curiously imprecise concerning the actual limits of Antony's metropolitanate: it was to include 'the most holy dioceses of Kholm,

49. Or perhaps 1369. It appears that Casimir's candidate, Antony, whose consecration by the patriarch was confirmed in Philotheus's letter to Casimir dated May 1371, had spent 'a long time' ($\chi\rho\acute{o}\nu o\nu$ $\pi o\lambda\grave{\nu}\nu$) in Constantinople. See *APC*, vol. 1, p. 578; *RIB*, vol. 6, app., col. 129.

50. *APC*, vol. 1, pp. 577–8; *RIB*, vol. 6, app., cols. 125–8; Meyendorff, *Byzantium*, p. 287.

51. Ibid.

52. Knoll, *The Rise*, p. 173.

53. For their martyrdom, see *PSRL*, vol. 25, p. 177; for their canonization and translation of part of their relics to Constantinople, see Meyendorff, *Byzantium*, pp. 187–8. See also below, p. 233.

54. The six documents are printed in *APC*, vol. 1, pp. 516–25; *RIB*, vol. 6, app., cols. 97–123. Translations into English of the letter 'to the princes of Russia' and the first act of excommunication are found in Meyendorff, *Byzantium*, apps. 2 and 3, pp. 283–6.

Turov, Peremyshl' and Vladimir', no mention being made of Lutsk. Furthermore, the control over these four sees – or perhaps the entire metropolitanate was meant? – was only to last 'until the quarrels which are now going on there are resolved and until there is peace and an end to the offences (διάλυσις τῶν σκανδάλων)'.[55]

In order to justify his volte-face, Philotheus three months later wrote again to Aleksiy. After an effusive expression of his love and respect for the metropolitan, he goes on to complain about his 'forsaking all the Christians there [i.e. in Little Russia]' and leaving them 'without teaching and spiritual care'. His accusations became more specific: 'because you have abandoned Little Russia for so many years . . . the king of Poland, Casimir, who [now] rules Little Russia, as well as other princes have sent a bishop from there [i.e. Antony] and letters with him saying that "all the land is without the law because the law is in chaos since there is no high priest (ἀρχιερεύς); therefore we have chosen [for this post] this good man . . . Bishop Antony"'. He repeats Casimir's threat to 'baptize the Russians into the faith of the Latins (εἰς τὴν τῶν Λατίνων πίστιν βαπτίζειν τοὺς 'Ρώσους)' and justifies the appointment and dispatch of Antony to his Galician metropolitanate (with the sees of Vladimir, Peremyshl' and Kholm) by asking what would have happened had he not sent him. In any case, Philotheus adds, 'you should not be distressed, for it is all your fault that this has occurred'. After repeating the contents of a bitter letter of complaint against Aleksiy's political behaviour sent by Ol'gerd, the patriarch concludes by requesting Aleksiy to come to Constantinople or send an envoy to discuss all the problems of the metropolitanate of Little Russia.[56]

What happened to Metropolitan Antony when and after he arrived in Galich is not known. The Russian sources are silent and the patriarchal records say no more about him. Even Casimir appears to have lost all interest in his protégé. In spite of the fact that Philotheus had in fact done what the king had asked him to do and consecrated Antony, the threat of baptizing the Russians 'into the faith of the Latins' soon began to materialize: in 1372 Pope Gregory XI ordered the archbishop of Cracow to appoint a Latin bishop to what was Antony's metropolitanate (Galich, Peremyshl', Vladimir and Kholm) and to remove the 'schismatic [i.e. Orthodox] bishops'. The order was carried out in 1375 and Antony was forced to leave his residence. His

---

55. The synodal decree is printed in *APC*, vol. 1, pp. 578–80; *RIB*, vol. 6, app., cols. 129–33. See Meyendorff, *Byzantium*, pp. 191–2.

56. *APC*, vol. 1, pp. 582–3; *RIB*, vol. 6, cols. 141–3.

eventual fate is not known.[57] Presumably, once again Aleksiy was able to resume spiritual control over all his Russian dioceses.

The resumption, however, if in fact it was a resumption, was only temporary, for at the end of 1373 or the beginning of 1374 a new figure had arrived in Kiev who was radically to reinterpret the authority of the metropolitan of Kiev and all Russia and to contribute eventually to the establishment of new and peaceful relations between Moscow, Lithuania and Poland. This was the Bulgarian Kiprian.

He had been sent by Patriarch Philotheus as his special envoy to investigate and calm the troubled waters of eastern Europe, especially in so far as Metropolitan Aleksiy was concerned. Judging from the sparse references in the Russian chronicles, he appears to have achieved some success, certainly in winning Ol'gerd's confidence and perhaps even that of Grand Prince Dmitry and Aleksiy.[58] His mission accomplished, he returned to Constantinople, perhaps with yet another request from Ol'gerd for a separate metropolitan for Lithuania and Little Russia, or perhaps simply with a full report on the sorry state of affairs within the Russian metropolitanate.[59] On 2 December 1375 Patriarch Philotheus consecrated Kiprian metropolitan. According to the synodal decree of 1380,[60] he was given the title of 'metropolitan of Kiev and the Lithuanians' as well as that of 'metropolitan of Little Russia and the Lithuanians'; according to the pro-Kiprian decree of 1389,[61] 'metropolitan of Kiev, Russia and the Lithuanians' on the understanding that at Aleksiy's death he was to be 'metropolitan of all Russia'. Whatever his true title – and it certainly could not have been

57. Meyendorff, *Byzantium*, p. 193 n. 60. Obolensky is of the opinion that Antony died in 1391, having 'probably shortly before his death . . . consecrated two bishops . . . for the Moldavian Church'. See Obolensky, 'A Late Fourteenth-Century Byzantine Diplomat', pp. 301–2, 311. If it is the same Antony, then he may have been operating in Moldavia after 1375. Prokhorov thinks he was still metropolitan of Galicia in 1382, but has nothing to support this view (*Povest'*, p. 170). Kartashev and Golubinsky both think he remained in Galicia until his death in 1391–2 (*Ocherki*, p. 337; *IRTs*, vol. 2, I, p. 342).

58. A temporary peace was made between Tver' and Moscow in early 1374, and on 9 March Kiprian was in Tver' together with Aleksiy (*PSRL*, vol. 15, I, col. 105).

59. According to a synodal decree of 1389 (distinctly favourable to Kiprian), Ol'gerd and his allies sent their envoys to Constantinople asking that 'another high priest [i.e. metropolitan] be given them', threatening to apply to the Latins if this fell through. According to a decree of 1380 (hostile to Kiprian), Kiprian conveyed a letter 'from Ol'gerd' to the patriarch (which he himself allegedly had composed!) asking that he be appointed metropolitan. Parts of both decrees are printed in *APC*, vol. 2, pp. 14, 18; *RIB*, vol. 6, app., cols. 171, 181; Meyendorff, *Byzantium*, pp. 304, 306.

60. *APC*, vol. 2, p. 120; *RIB*, vol. 6, app., col. 203; Meyendorff, *Byzantium*, p. 307.

61. Ibid.

'of Kiev and all Russia', for Aleksiy was still stubbornly alive – he went straight to Kiev. He arrived there on 9 June 1376.[62]

Little is known of his activities for the next two years. According to his own testimony, his attitude towards Dmitry at this period was exemplary: 'no single word against Grand Prince Dmitry came from my mouth; I have not spoken against his princess . . . I am not guilty against him either in action, or in word, or in thought . . . I loved him with my whole heart and I wish well to him and to all his domain . . .'[63] No less exemplary were his actions in Lithuania:

> I liberated many Christians from bitter bonds . . . I erected holy churches,
> I confirmed Christianity, I restored ecclesiastical domains, waited for many
> years in order to appropriate them for the metropolitanate of all Rus'.
> Novgorodok, in Lithuania, was lost for a long time, but I restored it and
> obtained the tithe and villages for the metropolitanate. For how long in
> the land of Volynia did the diocese of Vladimir remain empty without a
> bishop? But I consecrated a bishop and restored the area . . .[64]

Needless to say, the Russian chronicles say nothing to confirm this. The only information in them about Kiprian is found in the Novgorod First Chronicle under the year 1376:

> that winter Metropolitan Kiprian sent his envoys from Lithuania bringing
> with them patriarchal decrees (*patriarshi gramoty*) to the archbishop in
> Novgorod saying: 'Patriarch Filofey [Philotheus] has blessed me as
> metropolitan for all the Russian land.' And Novgorod, having heard the
> decree, answered them: 'Send to the grand prince; if the grand prince
> receives you as metropolitan of all the Russian land, then for us you are
> metropolitan . . .' And hearing Novgorod's answer, Metropolitan Kiprian
> did not send to Moscow to the grand prince.[65]

However fraternal and amicable were Kiprian's professed feelings towards the grand prince at this time, they were clearly not reciprocated.

---

62. For the date, see his second letter to Sergy of Radonezh: Prokhorov, *Povest'*, p. 199; Meyendorff, *Byzantium*, p. 296.

63. Ibid.

64. Prokhorov, *Povest'*, p. 200; Meyendorff, *Byzantium*, p. 297.

65. *NPL*, p. 374, repeated in the Moscow *svod* of 1479 (*PSRL*, vol. 25, pp. 192–3). Cf. the Nikon Chronicle *s.a.* 1376 (*PSRL*, vol. 11, p. 25) which omits the Novgorod episode, but says that Dmitry Donskoy 'did not receive [Kiprian], but said: "we have Metropolitan Aleksiy; why are you appointed while the metropolitan is alive?" Kiprian went from Moscow to Kiev and abode there' – i.e. infers that Kiprian himself went to Moscow. See Prokhorov, *Povest'*, p. 53.

CHAPTER TWELVE

Metropolitan Kiprian

On 12 February 1378 Metropolitan Aleksiy, now in his eighties, at last died, later to be canonized – the first act of Iona as metropolitan in 1449.[1] His death saw the beginning of twelve years of chaos and upheaval in the political and ecclesiastical affairs of Russia, Lithuania and Byzantium, twelve years of bewildering changes of direction, disorder and violence in which Grand Prince Dmitry of Moscow and his allies forced the army of Mamay to retreat in disorder (1380) and Moscow was sacked by Khan Tokhtamysh (1382) (see above, p. 129); in which the grand prince often appeared incapable of maintaining a consistent policy towards his prelates; in which patriarchs replaced patriarchs of different hues, and metropolitans – 'of great Russia', 'of all Russia', 'of Kiev and Great Russia', 'of Kiev and Lithuania', 'of Little Russia': titles often so vague and confusing as to make it difficult to understand what exactly they meant – interchanged and journeyed with such alarming speed between Moscow, Kiev, Lithuania, the Kipchak Horde and Constantinople as to make it frequently impossible to know what they were after, why they fled, who chased them; twelve years in which allegiances and loyalties were switched seemingly without rhyme or reason, canons were flagrantly ignored or simply misunderstood by confused clerics. Even Kiprian, whose integrity of character and purpose has been staunchly defended by most modern historians of the age, by no means always emerges unblemished from the contemporary sources.

As soon as the news of Aleksiy's death reached him, Kiprian set off from Kiev to Moscow. Grand Prince Dmitry, deeply suspicious

---

1. Golubinsky, *Istoriya kanonizatsii*, pp. 74–5.

perhaps of his Lithuanian sympathies and connections, had him arrested, subjected to 'blasphemies, insults, derision, thefts, hunger', locked 'in the dark, naked and hungry' and eventually expelled.[2] Having attempted in vain to persuade Abbot Sergy of the Trinity Monastery to succeed Aleksiy as metropolitan, Dmitry had turned to his father-confessor, Mikhail, known in contemporary sources as Mityay (probably a diminutive of Dmitry, which may have been his secular name), as candidate for the see. He was supported in this by Patriarch Macarius, Philotheos's successor, who wrote immediately he heard of Aleksiy's death to warn Dmitry not to accept Kiprian as 'metropolitan of Russia', but to send Mityay to Constantinople for consecration.[3]

Kiprian's reaction to his treatment in Moscow was to set off for Constantinople. On his way south he wrote to Abbots Sergy (of Radonezh) and Fedor, justifying his past actions in Russia, complaining of his treatment at the hands of the grand prince, excommunicating 'all those who plotted these acts', expressing his disgust at Mityay's behaviour ('a monk occupies the metropolitan seat, wearing a hierarchical robe and cowl . . .'), asserting his right to the primacy of Russia ('since my brother [Aleksiy] is dead, I am high priest after him: the metropolitanate [i.e. of all Russia] is mine') and announcing that he is 'travelling to Constantinople, seeking protection from God, the holy patriarch and the great synod'.[4]

Kiprian was the first to leave for Constantinople in the winter of 1378/1379. On arrival in the spring of 1379 he found himself in the

2. Kiprian describes his treatment in a bitter letter written to Sergy of Radonezh, abbot of the Trinity Monastery, and Sergy's nephew Fedor, abbot of the Simonov Monastery. *En route* to Moscow from Kiev, he also wrote to them: 'I am on my way to see my son, the grand prince in Moscow. I am coming bringing peace and blessing.' Both letters are printed in Prokhorov, *Povest'*, pp. 195–201, and in English translation in Meyendorff, *Byzantium*, pp. 292, 293–9.

3. See the patriarchal act of 1389 (in *APC*, vol. 2, pp. 116–29; *RIB*, vol. 6, app., cols. 193–207; translation in Meyendorff, *Byzantium*, pp. 307–10). For Mityay's background and his curious behaviour in Moscow (on Aleksiy's death, 'with the permission of the grand prince (*po velikago knyazya slovu*), he took up residence in the metropolitan's palace and wore his regalia'), see *PSRL*, vol. 15, I, cols. 125–7. On Macarios and his political connections, see Meyendorff, *Byzantium*, pp. 208–9; Prokhorov, *Povest'*, p. 64 ('acting in the opposite direction to Patriarch Philotheos's Russian policy'). See also the patriarchal act of 1389: '[Macarios] is the real culprit of all these events' (in Meyendorff, *Byzantium*, p. 308).

4. Prokhorov, *Povest'*, pp. 198–201; Meyendorff, *Byzantium*, pp. 296, 298–9. Sergy and Fedor evidently approved of the contents of Kiprian's second letter to them: on 18 October 1378 he wrote to them from Kiev expressing his satisfaction at their reaction. For the text of his third letter to them, see Prokhorov, *Povest'*, p. 202.

midst of 'all kinds of imperial and patriarchal disorder (*vsyako nestroenie v tsarekh i v patriarshestve*)'. In the place of his great patron Philotheus, who had been imprisoned in August 1376 by Emperor Andronicus IV and who had died a year later, was Macarius, uncanonically elected by Andronicus and not by a synod. In his highly autobiographical *Life of Metropolitan Petr of Moscow* Kiprian describes Macarius as 'evilly appointed . . . mad, who without synodal election . . . dared to jump upon the lofty patriarchal throne, solely by the emperor's wish'.[5] It was hardly a warm welcome that awaited Kiprian in Constantinople, for, as has been mentioned above, Macarius had already written to Grand Prince Dmitry warning him not to accept Kiprian as 'metropolitan of Russia', i.e. as Aleksiy's successor, but to send Mikhail-Mityay for consecration. However, he had not long to wait for a change of fortune. On 1 July 1379 Andronicus IV's father, the old emperor John V Palaeologus whom Andronicus had overthrown two years previously, managed to escape and to recapture Constantinople in August. As a result of the change of government Macarius was deposed. Kiprian had the pleasure of being present at the synod: 'Macarius, who had been appointed by the emperor [Andronicus], is deposed by divine judgement at the synod and, as of evil repute, is condemned to expulsion and imprisonment, I and other bishops were present at that synod and I signed that very act of expulsion.'[6]

Meanwhile in Moscow Mityay, now resident in the metropolitan's palace, decided that before consecration as metropolitan he should at least be appointed bishop. He told the grand prince that according to canon law 'five or six bishops . . . may consecrate a bishop'.[7] As a result Dmitry ordered the bishops to assemble. None of them, with the exception of Dionisy of Suzdal' and Nizhniy Novgorod, 'dared to say anything against Mityay'. But Dionisy, a close associate of Abbot Sergy of Radonezh and probably of Kiprian as well, 'rebuked the grand prince, saying: "It is not right that this should be."' The

---

5. The text of Kiprian's version of the *Life of Metropolitan Petr* is printed in Prokhorov, *Povest'*, pp. 205–15 (see p. 214).

6. *Life of Metropolitan Petr* by Kiprian, ibid., p. 215. He signed his name, somewhat prematurely, as 'metropolitan of all Russia'. See Meyendorff, *Byzantium*, p. 213.

7. Meyendorff, however, points out that 'canon law did not allow the consecration of bishops without confirmation by the metropolitan of the province' (canon 4 of the First Oecumenical Council), but that a synod of bishops could ordain a metropolitan 'without seeking the approval of one patriarch' (ibid., pp. 215–16). There is nothing in the account of the Tver' (Rogozhskiy) Chronicle to show that Mityay *was* attempting to pre-empt patriarchal consecration as metropolitan. He clearly only wanted appointment as bishop.

squabble ended with Mityay upbraiding Dionisy: 'It was not befitting for you, a bishop . . . not to have asked for blessing from me . . . You did not consider me worthy of attention. Do you not know who I am? I have power in all the metropolitanate.' Dionisy countered: 'You have no power over me. You should have come to me and asked for my blessing and you should have bowed down before me, for I am a bishop, whereas you are a [mere] priest.' The last word was Mityay's: 'I shall not avenge myself now. But [just] wait until I return from Constantinople!'[8]

In July Mityay set off for Constantinople, having first obtained from Dmitry several blank sheets of parchment with the grand-princely seal on them. His suite was vast. It included the senior member of the grand-princely duma as Dmitry's envoy, six boyars of the metropolitan court, two interpreters, three archimandrites and a large number of lay and clerical members.[9] After a momentous journey – in the Polovtsian Horde Mityay was apprehended and briefly held by Mamay – the party approached Constantinople in September 1379. Suddenly Mityay 'fell ill and died at sea'. His corpse was transferred for burial to Galata, the Genoese-held right bank of the Golden Horn where the recently overthrown Andronicus IV was sheltering. So ended Mityay's quest for Aleksiy's see.

Mityay's death left his suite in disarray. There can be little doubt that foul play was suspected by many. The sixteenth-century Nikon Chronicle, maybe repeating rumours current in Moscow, reports that Dmitry was later told by some 'that Mityay had been strangled; but others said that he had been drowned, for all the bishops, archimandrites, abbots, priests, monks, boyars and people did not wish to see Mityay as metropolitan and that only the grand prince wanted [his appointment]'.[10] Whether or not the members of Mityay's retinue suspected – or knew – that he had been murdered, instead of returning to Moscow or waiting for further instructions from Dmitry and the bishops, as they should have done, they arbitrarily decided that one of the three archimandrites in the party should be presented as the grand prince's candidate for the metropolitanate. Not surprisingly, they were unable to agree on which of the three should be chosen. Some voted for Archimandrite Ioann ('Ivan Petrovsky'), described as the 'head of the senior coenobitic monastery in Moscow',[11] one of the co-

8. *PSRL*, vol. 15, I, cols. 126–7.
9. For details, see ibid., cols. 128–9.
10. *PSRL*, vol. 10, p. 40.
11. *Moskovskago kinoviarkha, nachalnika obshchemu zhitiyu*, ibid., vol. 15, I, col. 130.

founders of the hesychastic movement in Russia, together with Dionisy of Suzdal' and Sergy of Radonezh (see below, pp. 207–9).[12] But 'the boyars [of the metropolitan's court] opted for Pimen'[13] ['archimandrite of Pereyaslavl''[14]] and arrested Ioann. Eventually Pimen, using one of the blank sheets of parchment with the grand-princely seal attached with which Dmitry had so thoughtlessly provided the party, forged a missive 'from the grand prince of Russia to the emperor and patriarch. I have sent Pimen to you. Appoint him metropolitan for me. For he is the only candidate I have chosen in Russia and I have found no other than him.'[15]

Macarius's successor, Neilus, was only elected in June 1380. In the same month he and the members of a patriarchal synod accepted the forged document in spite of the fact that most if not all of those present must have been aware that Macarius had in fact asked Dmitry to send Mityay and that Pimen was an impostor. And so Pimen was duly elected 'metropolitan of Kiev and Great Russia'.[16] According to the decree issued by the patriarch, the ambassadors from Russia – Mityay's retinue – also claimed that Philotheus's consecration of Kiprian was uncanonical in so far as Aleksiy was still alive at the time. Kiprian, however, who attended the synod, requested that his title be 'metropolitan of Kiev and Great Russia'. Although he had been defended by Theophanes, the pro-hesychast metropolitan of Nicaea who claimed that his appointment by Philotheus was justified, he was nevertheless relegated to the metropolitanate of 'Little Russia and the Lithuanians' with a rider to the effect that if he predeceased Pimen, then his see was to revert to Pimen.[17]

Early in the proceedings of the synod of 1380, indeed before a decision was taken about Pimen's consecration, Kiprian 'secretly fled, without talking to anyone'.[18] It was the eve of the great military confrontation between Dmitry and Mamay. By now the political outlook of the Moscow government had radically altered. Heartened by the memory of the defeat of the Mongols on the Vozha river (1378; see above, p. 129) and encouraged by the recent defections of two of Ol'gerd's sons, Andrey of Polotsk (1377) and Dmitry of

12. Prokhorov, *Povest'*, p. 89.
13. *PSRL*, vol. 15, I, col. 130.
14. Ibid., col. 129.
15. Ibid., col. 130.
16. See the patriarchal act of 1380 (in *APC*, vol. 2, pp. 12–18; *RIB*, vol. 6, app., cols. 165–83; Meyendorff, *Byzantium*, pp. 303–6).
17. Ibid.
18. *APC*, vol. 2, p. 17; *RIB*, vol. 6, app., col. 179; Meyendorff, *Byzantium*, p. 305.

Trubchevsk (1379), Dmitry and his numerous Russian allies were ready to meet Mamay's army on its approach to Moscow at the beginning of September 1380. Had Mamay's allies, Ol'gerd's son Yagaylo, grand prince of Lithuania, and Oleg of Ryazan', provided their promised military support, the outcome might have been very different. But neither turned up at the Field of Kulikovo. Could it have been, asks Meyendorff, that Kiprian went straight to Lithuania from Constantinople in the summer of 1380 and advised Yagaylo not to join Mamay's forces? As he points out, there is no evidence to show that such advice was sought or given.[19] Nevertheless, as we shall see, after Kulikovo Dmitry's attitude towards Kiprian changed abruptly from one of bitter hostility to warm friendship.

It was when he heard of Mityay's death and Pimen's appointment that Dmitry, enraged by the news, decided to send for Kiprian from Kiev. He told Fedor, his father-confessor and Sergy of Radonezh's nephew and close collaborator – both firm supporters of Kiprian – to fetch him. On 23 May 1381 Kiprian arrived in Moscow 'to his metropolitanate . . . All the bells were rung and many people gathered to meet him. Grand Prince Dmitry Ivanovich received him with great honour and love.'[20] The fact that he returned to his metropolitanate (*v svoyu mitropoliyu*) presumably implies that Dmitry had nominated him – without patriarchal approval and thus quite uncanonically – 'metropolitan of Kiev, Great Russia, Lithuania and Little Russia'. At last, it seemed, Kiprian had achieved his aim: the consolidation of all the Orthodox of Suzdalian Russia and of all those areas of southern and south-west Russia under Lithuanian or Polish control. And all under one metropolitan.

In the new atmosphere that prevailed in Moscow – manifest in the growing ascendancy of Sergy of Radonezh and his nephew, the triumphant spirit of hostility to the Horde, the resumption of a united metropolitanate and the benevolence of the grand prince – all went well for Kiprian, at least for the time being. He and Abbot Sergy baptized Dmitry's nephew Ivan Vladimirovich. He wrote his own version of the *Life of Metropolitan Petr of Moscow* (see above, p. 150), and Pimen, when he finally turned up as 'metropolitan of Kiev and Great Russia' in Kolomna in the autumn of 1381, was immediately arrested, humiliated, banished and imprisoned, the grand prince being 'unwilling to receive him'.[21]

19. Ibid., pp. 223–4.
20. *PSRL*, vol. 15, I, cols. 131, 142.
21. Ibid., cols. 131–2, 142–3.

Kiprian's good fortune was short-lived. Khan Tokhtamysh, now master of Saray and conqueror of Mamay's fugitive army, crossed the Volga in the late summer of 1382 and marched on Moscow. Dmitry lost no time: 'without raising a hand against the khan', he set off for remote Kostroma, not far from Chukhloma where Pimen was incarcerated. Before Tokhtamysh reached the capital, 'the people [of Moscow] met in assembly (*stasha vechem*), plundered the metropolitan and the grand princess, and barely let them leave the city'.[22] After Moscow had been burned and sacked, the Mongols withdrew and Dmitry returned to the remnants of his capital. On 7 October Kiprian arrived back in Moscow from Tver' where he had been waiting for the Mongols to withdraw.

The Dmitry he found in Moscow was very different from the the one who had so warmly welcomed him the previous year. The Rogozhskiy Chronicle merely states that 'in the autumn Kiprian departed (*s"ekha*) from Moscow to Kiev together with Abbot Afanasy',[23] yet another of Sergy of Radonezh's disciples. Other, later, chronicles hint at Dmitry's anger with Kiprian 'for not having remained in Moscow during the siege'[24] – hard to believe in view of Dmitry's own precipitous flight at the approach of Tokhtamysh – while one source even declares that 'Grand Prince Dmitry expelled (*vygna*) Kiprian' and that 'from then on there was upheaval (*myatezh'*) in the metropolitanate'.[25]

In whatever circumstances Kiprian left Moscow, one thing is certain: Dmitry Donskoy's attitude to the Horde, to Kiprian and to Pimen had reversed since the heady days of anti-Mongol belligerence preceding Kulikovo and of support for a metropolitanate of *all* Russia. Following Tokhtamysh's withdrawal, many of the princes of northeast Russia duly presented themselves at the Kipchak Horde to have their patents renewed or confirmed, while Dmitry, according to the Soviet historian I.B. Grekov, was granted a *yarlyk* for the grand-principality of Vladimir-on-the-Klyaz'ma.[26]

22. Ibid., cols. 143–4; II, col. 441. In an attempt to minimize Dmitry's seemingly craven behaviour, the Nikon Chronicle talks about 'conflicts and squabbles between the prince and his boyars and impoverishment of the military . . . as a result of the battle with Mamay', as one of the causes of Dmitry's flight. Ibid., vol. 11, p. 72.

23. Ibid., vol. 15, I, col. 147.

24. The Sofiyskiy First Chronicle (ibid., vol. 5, p. 238); copied in the Moscow *svod* of 1479 (ibid., vol. 25, p. 210) and repeated in the Ermolinskiy Chronicle (ibid., vol. 23, p. 129) and the L'vov Chronicle (ibid., vol. 20, p. 204).

25. The Moskovsko–Akademicheskiy MS of the Suzdal' Chronicle (*MAK*): ibid., vol. 1, col. 537. For the sources and origins of *MAK*, see Fennell, 'K voprosu ob istochnikakh'. Cf. Dmitriev, 'Rol' i znachenie', p. 219.

26. Grekov, *Vostochnaya Evropa*, p. 166. He makes no mention of sources confirming this.

The most unexpected of all Dmitry Donskoy's about-turns was his sudden espousal of Pimen's cause. In the autumn of 1382 Dmitry sent for him 'from his banishment to Moscow and received him in the metropolitanate in honour and love'.[27] Once again the metropolitanate was split: 'Kiev and all Russia' or 'Kiev and Great Russia' was under Pimen, while Kiprian, with his seat nevertheless in Kiev (if that is where he remained after his flight from Moscow), reverted to the old title of 'metropolitan of Little Russia and the Lithuanians'.[28]

Very little is known of Pimen's activities in Russia for the first two-and-a-half years of his metropolitanate. There is nothing to show that he travelled outside Suzdalia or that he ever set foot in Kiev, which is not surprising, assuming that that was Kiprian's residence at the time. It may be that he convoked a small synod in Pereyaslavl'-Zalesskiy, where he had previously been archimandrite, in the autumn of 1382, for it was there that, together with the bishops of Rostov and Zvenigorod, he consecrated one Savva bishop of Saray.[29] A year later, in the winter of 1383/1384, he appointed two more bishops, Mikhail of Smolensk and Stefan of Perm', the latter a close associate of Sergy of Radonezh. All appeared calm on the surface. It would, however, have been surprising had there been no opposition to Pimen. And opposition there was. This time it came from two of Sergy of Radonezh's circle of monastic followers: his nephew Fedor, still the grand prince's father-confessor, and Bishop Dionisy of Suzdal' and Nizhniy Novgorod.

Dionisy, it will be remembered, had been the only bishop in 1379 temerarious enough to oppose Mityay after his selection as metropolitan-elect and to upbraid Dmitry for his choice. He had planned to go to Constantinople to block Mityay's consecration.

---

27. *PSRL*, vol. 15, I, col. 147. Cf. ibid., vol. 15 (1st edn.), col. 442, where Dmitry 'brought Pimen with honour from Tver' to Moscow, and he was metropolitan of all Russia'. According to the *Tale of Mityay*, Pimen, after one year (or one summer?) was 'brought from Chukhloma to Tver'' (ibid., vol. 15, I, col. 132), but why or at whose order he was transferred to Tver' of all places is not stated.

28. Prokhorov is of the opinion that 'Galicia' (i.e. Little Russia) was still under Metropolitan Antony (*Povest'*), in spite of the fact that the patriarchal act of 1380 states that Kiprian was to be 'metropolitan of Little Russia and the Lithuanians'. See above, p. 152.

29. *PSRL*, vol. 15, I, col. 147; *TL*, p. 425. Meyendorff thinks that the fact that he was *persona grata* with Tokhtamysh enabled him to appoint Savva. However, it is hard to see what evidence there is to make him *persona grata* with the khan, *Byzantium*, pp. 229–30.

Dmitry had tried to restrain him by force, but Dionisy, having promised him not to go without his permission and having named the most respected of all the abbots, Sergy of Radonezh, as his sacred guarantor (*poruchnik*), had set off immediately.[30] In Constantinople he gained the ear of Patriarch Neilus, who in 1381 made his see an archbishopric (of 'Suzdal', Nizhniy Novgorod and Gorodets') and loaded him with honours (a polystavrion with four crosses) and relics.[31] At the very end of 1382 he returned to Moscow.

He spent only six months in north-east Russia, both in his see of Suzdal' and Nizhniy Novgorod and in Pskov, where the patriarch had instructed him to investigate the heresy of the *Strigol'niki* (see below, p. 215) and to 'confirm coenobiticism in the local monasteries'.[32] At the end of June 1383, Dmitry Donskoy, evidently having forgotten Dionisy's broken promise of 1379, sent him off to Constantinople together with Sergy's nephew, Abbot Fedor, 'concerning the management of the Russian metropolitanate'.[33] Doubtless Dionisy had wasted no time in insinuating himself into the grand prince's confidence and at the same time blackening Pimen's character.

Once in Constantinople, Dionisy set to work in earnest on Patriarch Neilos, informing him of various misdeeds of Pimen and of the grand prince's desire to be rid of him. According to the patriarchal act of 1389, Dionisy's report on the sorry state of the Russian metropolitanate produced the desired effect: it was decided to dispatch a delegation to Moscow headed by two Greek metropolitans to 'make an enquiry concerning Pimen and to depose him if they find out that indeed he had been consecrated on the basis of deceit and forged documents'. The two metropolitans were also given authority in the likely case of finding him guilty to excommunicate him and to install Dionisy instead.[34]

Leaving Abbot Fedor behind, Dionisy left for Russia in early 1384. He arrived in Kiev on his way to Moscow and was promptly arrested by Prince Vladimir of Kiev,[35] one of Ol'gerd's many sons, and kept in

30. *PSRL*, vol. 15, I, cols. 127–8, 137.
31. Ibid., cols. 147–8.
32. Prokhorov, *Povest'*, pp. 172–3.
33. *PSRL*, vol. 15, I, col. 148.
34. Meyendorff, *Byzantium*, p. 308. There was no question of Dionisy previously having been consecrated metropolitan in Constantinople; after all, both Pimen and Kiprian were canonically elected metropolitans. The Rogozhskiy Chronicle, however, states that Dmitry '*was appointed* metropolitan for Russia in Constantinople' (*PSRL*, vol. 15, I, col. 149). Prokhorov considers that Neilos in fact consecrated Dionisy metropolitan (*Povest'*, pp. 175–6).
35. *PSRL*, vol. 15, I, col. 149.

gaol until his death on 15 October 1385. Even though Kiprian was probably in Kiev at the time, there is no firm evidence to show that he was in any way connected with the imprisonment and death of Dionisy.[36]

In the winter of 1384/1385 Abbot Fedor and the Greek delegation with its two metropolitans in tow arrived in Moscow. They examined the Pimen affair, concluded that all the accusations against him were correct, excommunicated him and told him to go to Constantinople.[37] On 9 May Pimen made his way back to Constantinople, followed soon after by the Greek delegation together with Kiprian and, in 1386 or 1387, by Abbot Fedor, sent by Dmitry to disentangle the affairs of the metropolitanate.[38] Three years of utter confusion and chaos followed, during most of which time there was no metropolitan in Russia. Fedor, far from doing what Dmitry Donskoy had asked him to do – his brief was not only to report on 'many accusations against Pimen' but probably also to secure confirmation of his deposition at a patriarchal synod – suddenly turned about and threw in his lot with the unseated metropolitan. The two of them went to the Turkish-occupied east bank of the Bosporus, where Pimen rewarded his erstwhile opponent with the archbishopric of Rostov. In their absence both were deposed and excommunicated – Pimen for the second time – by Patriarchal decree.[39] They returned to Russia in July 1388. Pimen, still 'metropolitan of Great Russia', acted as though nothing untoward had occurred, his authority seemingly accepted by the grand prince and by his bishops. Nor was Fedor's archiepiscopacy publicly questioned by anyone.

However, Pimen's stay in Russia was short. In 1389 the new patriarch, Antonius – Neilus had died in the previous year – confirmed the previous depositions of Pimen and decreed that Kiprian was now 'the one and only metropolitan of Russia'.[40] Pimen left Russia for Constantinople shortly after the decision had been taken. On 11

36. See the views of Meyendorff (*Byzantium*, p. 233) and Obolensky 'A *Philorhomaios anthropos*'). Golubinsky (*IRTs*, vol. 1, II, p. 223) and Kartashev (*Ocherki*, p. 332) both consider he was involved in Dionisy's death. Dmitriev ('Rol' i znachenie', p. 219) calls Vladimir 'Kiprian's protector', while Prokhorov (*Povest'*) vaguely hints at Kiprian's involvement.

37. Patriarchal act of 1389 (*RIB*, vol. 6, app., pp. 213–14; *PSRL*, vol. 15, I, col. 150).

38. 'o upravlenie mitropolia' (*PSRL*, vol. 15, I, col. 152).

39. *RIB*, vol. 6, app., cols. 215–18. For a possible explanation of Pimen's extraordinary behaviour, see Prokhorov, *Povest'*, pp. 180–1; Meyendorff, *Byzantium*, pp. 234–5.

40. Patriarchal act of 1389, in *APC*, vol. 2, pp. 127–8; *RIB*, vol. 6, app., col. 223, and Meyendorff, *Byzantium*, pp. 309, 310.

September 1389, having been once again deposed in his absence, he died in Chalcedon.[41]

Meanwhile Kiprian, who had been sent on a brief visit to Little Russia by Emperor John V,[42] returned to Constantinople. Reinstated as 'metropolitan of Kiev and all Russia' and in the knowledge that Dmitry and Pimen were now both dead,[43] he left Constantinople on 1 October 1389, accompanied by the two Greek metropolitans and a number of Russian bishops (including Fedor of Rostov) who had escorted Pimen on his last journey. On 6 March 1390 the party arrived in Moscow and were met 'with great honour' by the new grand prince Vasily I.[44] 'And the confusion (*myatezh'*) in the metropolitanate ceased, and there was one metropolitanate [of] Kiev and Galich and all Russia'.[45]

Much of the energy expended by Kiprian during the last sixteen years of his life went on enlarging and strengthening relations with Poland and Lithuania. His first recorded act after arriving in Moscow was to officiate at the wedding of Vasily I and Sofia (9 January 1391)[46] – a wedding which may well have resulted from Kiprian's brief visit to Little Russia in 1387,[47] for Sofia was the daughter of Ol'gerd's nephew Vitovt, who in 1392 was to be recognized by King Władysław II Jagiełło of Poland as grand prince of Lithuania. Soon afterwards he went to Tver' at the invitation of its ruler, Mikhail Aleksandrovich, to depose Bishop Evfimy, responsible for some sort of unexplained ecclesiastical 'upheaval' (*myatezh'*) in the diocese; the striking warmth and affection shown by Mikhail Aleksandrovich – the former enemy

41. For Pimen's last journey to Constantinople and his death, see Meyendorff, *Byzantium*, pp. 235–8; Prokhorov, *Povest'*, pp. 181–7.
42. For the possible purpose of his visit – to investigate the situation in Eastern Europe resulting from the negotiations of Krewo between Lithuania and Poland – see Prokhorov, *Povest'*, p. 179. At the Union Yagaylo (Polish: Jagiełło) of Lithuania, Ol'gerd's son, married Jadwiga, Louis of Hungary's daughter, and was crowned king of Poland and Lithuania (1386).
43. Dmitry Donskoy: 19 May 1389; Pimen: 11 September 1389.
44. *PSRL*, vol. 15, I, cols. 157–8.
45. Ibid., vol. 1, col. 537.
46. Ibid., vol. 11, p. 124: *venchyan byst . . . Vasiley s Sofeyu . . . Kiprianom . . .* The Tver' and Trinity Chronicles make no mention of Kiprian's presence at the wedding. Note that in 1394 Vasily I gave his sister Maria in marriage to Ol'gerd's son, Lugveny (Lithuanian: Lengvenis)- Semen (ibid., vol. 15, I, col. 164).
47. Meyendorff considers that Kiprian 'prepared an alliance between [Vitovt] and the grand principality of Moscow' resulting in the marriage between Vasily and Sofia. *Byzantium*, p. 244.

of Moscow, close ally of Lithuania and brother-in-law of Ol'gerd – to Kiprian is stressed in no uncertain terms in the local (Rogozhskiy) Chronicle.[48]

Twice he paid prolonged visits to Poland and Lithuania (1396–97 and 1404–06). In the first of these Kiprian not only went to Smolensk, which had just been captured by Vitovt, and appointed a bishop there,[49] but, during his one-and-a-half years spent in Polish and Lithuanian territory, was closely connected with Jagiełło and Vitovt and with them discussed a scheme for union between the Orthodox and Latin Churches. A letter was written to the patriarch suggesting that a council be held in 'Russian' – which probably meant 'Lithuanian' – territory. The plan, however, came to nothing: the patriarch answered both Kiprian and Jagiełło, saying that both the time and the venue were misplaced – Constantinople was under heavy siege by the Turks and routes for the Greek participants at such a council were closed. Instead he begged Kiprian to urge the king of Poland together with his brother-in-law King Sigismund of Hungary to aid the Greeks against the Turks.[50] During his second visit to Poland and Lithuania (1404–06) he was received – probably in Vil'na, the capital of Lithuania – by Vitovt 'with great honour' and later by Jagiełło and Vitovt 'in the town of Milyubra' (var. Milolyuba = Lublin?), where again he was paid 'great honour' and was loaded with gifts.[51] What the purpose of these two meetings was is not, alas, disclosed, and all we hear of Kiprian's ecclesiastical business is that he appointed a bishop in Vladimir (in Volynia) and deposed one, at Vitovt's request, in Turov.[52]

In spite of Kiprian's excellent relationship with Jagiełło and Vitovt in the last sixteen years of his life and in spite of the chronicle's jubilant entry of 1390 to the effect that at last there was 'one metropolitanate [of] Kiev, Galich and all Russia', the question of who exactly *was* responsible for the overall ecclesiastical administration of the Orthodox populations of the lands governed by Jagiełło and Vitovt was as vague, to say the least of it, as it ever had been. The 'metropolitanate of the Lithuanians' was, presumably, under Kiprian.

48. *PSRL*, vol. 15, I, cols. 159–60.
49. Ibid., vol. 11, pp. 162, 164.
50. Golubinsky, *IRTs*, vol. 2, I, pp. 338–9; Meyendorff, *Byzantium*, pp. 252–4; Halecki, *From Florence*, pp. 23–5. The original letters of Kiprian and Jagiełło to the patriarch have not survived. For Patriarch Antonius's answers, see *APC*, vol. 2, pp. 280–2, 282–5.
51. *PSRL*, vol. 11, pp. 191, 192.
52. Ibid.; *TL*, p. 459.

At least, there are no reports to the contrary, and, as mentioned above, we do know that he consecrated a bishop in Lithuanian-held Smolensk. But Little Russia, or Galicia, was a different proposition altogether.

It will be remembered that after King Casimir's invasion of Galicia and most of Volynia (in 1366), Antony had been appointed by the patriarch as metropolitan of Little Russia in 1371 and that in 1375 he had been obliged to quit his see. It is hard to say who had been in charge of the metropolitanate for the next five years, but it does appear that Kiprian, from 1380 to 1391, was, in name at least, metropolitan of Galicia as well as of the other sees under his control.[53]

However friendly Kiprian's relationship with Poland and Lithuania may have been at the beginning of the 1390s, in 1391 Jagiełło suddenly – and, it seems, unilaterally – nominated Bishop Ioann of Lutsk (nicknamed Baba: Βάβα ἐπίσκοπος Λουτικὸς[54]) as metropolitan of Galicia. As might be expected, Kiprian protested to Patriarch Antonius. But although in 1393 Ioann was deposed both by the patriarch and by Kiprian,[55] he continued to exercise some sort of control over the bishoprics of Little Russia. Perhaps as a result of Kiprian's contacts with Jagiełło in 1396–97, a temporary solution appears to have been found in 1397 when the patriarch not only requested Jagiełło to remove Ioann from his metropolitanate but also appointed the archbishop of Bethlehem as his agent for Little Russia and Moldavia in his place.[56] His job was 'to see to and inspect . . . the

53. According to Meyendorff (Byzantium, p. 202 n. 11), Patriarch Neilus appointed a new metropolitan to Galicia in 1381 (name unknown). However, there is nothing in any of the Russian or Greek sources to indicate that Kiprian was not the metropolitan of Galicia from 1380 until at least 1391.

54. APC, vol. 2, pp. 284; RIB, vol. 6, app., col. 307. 'Baba' could be a nickname for either 'woman', 'midwife' or 'pelican'.

55. Antonius wrote to Kiprian (October 1393) saying that Ioann had come to Constantinople, but had refused to attend the synod at which the question of his metropolitanate was to be discussed. Antonius told Kiprian to depose him, to strip him of his episcopal rank and to appoint another bishop of Lutsk (APC, vol. 2, pp. 282–5; RIB, vol. 6, app., cols. 303–10). See also Antonius's letter to King Władysław II Jagiełło (January 1397) telling him that Ioann must leave Galicia, go to Kiprian, bow down to him and ask forgiveness (APC, vol. 2, pp. 280–2; RIB, vol. 6, app., cols. 297–302).

56. See Patriarch Antonius's instructions to Archbishop Mikhail (APC, vol. 2, pp. 278–80; RIB , vol. 6, app., cols. 291–8; Meyendorff, Byzantium, p. 250). It may be that in 1397 Kiprian succeeded in appointing a new bishop of Lutsk to replace Ioann Baba. One 'Fedor [bishop] of Lutsk' is mentioned s.a. 1397 in the Trinity Chronicle (TL, p. 448). By 1401 he too had been replaced by Bishop Sava (PSRL, vol. 11, p. 185). On Archbishop Mikhail's three missions to Russia (1393, 1397 and 1400), see Obolensky, 'A Late Fourteenth-Century Byzantine Diplomat', pp. 300–3, 310–15. On the Moldavian Church at the end of the fourteenth century, see ibid., pp. 310–12.

holy metropolitanates of Moldavia and Galicia, as our exarch'.[57]

What did the archbishop of Bethlehem manage to achieve in Little Russia and Moldavia during his mission of 1398? When and how was Bishop Ioann Baba finally removed from his quite illegally held see of Galicia? Did Kiprian, before his death on 16 September 1406, succeed in reclaiming Little Russia as part of his metropolitanate and thus finally bring about the restitution of an undivided metropolitanate of Kiev and all Russia? Alas, these are questions that cannot be answered with any degree of certainty, for the sources – even the Greek sources, usually so helpful in elucidating Russo-Byzantine ecclesiastical diplomacy – seem somehow to have lost interest in Kiprian's quest for control over all the Orthodox in the lands owing allegiance to the rulers of Moscow, Lithuania and Poland.

57. 'ἵνα ἴδῃ καὶ ἐπισκέψηται . . . τὰς . . . ἁγιωτάτας μητροπόλεις τὴν Μαυροβλαχίαν καὶ τὴν Γάλιζαν, ὡς ἔξαρχος . . . ἡμέτερος' (*RIB*, vol. 6, app., col. 309).

CHAPTER THIRTEEN

Metropolitan Foty

Kiprian's Greek successor, Metropolitan Foty (Photius), was a man of strong moral fibre and great determination. He worked tirelessly for the unification of his province brooked no impediments from Vitovt of Lithuania and lived in amity with Vasily I, only once rebuking him for appropriating dues assignable to his own office. He staunchly supported Vasily's son and heir against his mutinous uncle Yury and in general showed himself a firm upholder of the grand principality of Moscow.

The two great aims of this single-minded and businesslike metropolitan were first to refurbish and safeguard the possessions of the 'metropolitan's house' (*mitropolichiy dom*) – in other words, the landed property donated by the State (i.e. the grand princes) and by individual laymen to him and his predecessors (see below, pp. 212–15); and secondly to ensure that all the Orthodox in Russia and in the lands annexed by Poland and Lithuania came directly under his jurisdiction.

Already at the death of Kiprian, at the same time as Vasily I sent his envoys to Constantinople to request that 'a holy bishop of Kiev and all Russia be appointed according to the old custom (*po staroy poshline*)',[1] Vitovt attempted to have his own candidate consecrated either as metropolitan of Kiev and all Russia or, more likely, as metropolitan of Lithuania and perhaps Galicia as well:[2] Feodosy, bishop of the old principality of Polotsk, annexed by Lithuania at the beginning of the fourteenth century, was dispatched to Constantinople. His fate, so

---

1. See Foty's circular letter of 1415–16 to the Lithuanian bishops. *RIB*, vol. 6, col. 330.
2. Ibid., col. 329. Vitovt is not mentioned in Foty's letter, but it seems unlikely that anyone else would have sent him.

Foty tells us in tones of withering contempt, was a humiliating rebuff. Not even attempts at bribery saved him:

'Tell me, O deluded non-bishop of Polotsk, at the demise of Metropolitan Kiprian who died in holiness, did you not go [to be appointed to] the metropolitanate? You yourself know, O accursed one, how much silver and gold you promised for that appointment! Had it been possible to effect [your appointment] by bribery, you would not have been sent away empty-handed. But with great disparagement and shame they dismissed you, saying, "May your gold and silver be your downfall!" '[3]

Foty was consecrated metropolitan on 1 September 1408. Exactly a year later he arrived in Kiev, where he stayed for just over six months. What precisely his relations with Vitovt were at the time it is hard to say. Vitovt later (1415) alleged that he had no wish to accept Foty but that 'as he agreed to stay with us and to care for the Church [in Kiev], we accepted him for the metropolitanate of Kiev'.[4] It seems that Foty at least made an effort to abide by his promises, if such they were, for he is known to have spent a whole year in Kiev and south-west Russia (autumn 1411 to autumn 1412).[5] But this was not enough for Vitovt. A clash with the metropolitan was imminent.

According to the Nikon Chronicle, where Foty's doings are reported at considerable length and with obvious sympathy, the trouble started in the autumn of 1414, when a number of 'impious men rose up against Foty and slandered him to the grand prince'. At the same time they complained to Vitovt of Foty's neglect of Kiev:

From the beginning the metropolitans of all Russia have had Kiev as their see and sat there on the throne of the metropolitan of all Russia. But now Kiev has been reduced to nought and everything has been removed from it to Moscow. And Metropolitan Foty transfers all the adornments of the church [St Sofia] to Moscow and he has ruined all Kiev and all the land [of Kiev] by heavy taxes and great and intolerable tribute.

Vitovt retaliated by summoning all the Orthodox bishops not only of Lithuania but also of Galicia,[6] and telling them to appoint a separate metropolitan in Kiev. The bishops, however, were unwilling to comply and Vitovt had to force them to write a complaint against

---

3. Ibid.
4. *AZR*, No. 25, p. 36.
5. According to the Lithuanian Suprasl'skiy Chronicle, he appointed Sevastian bishop of Smolensk in Kiev, Evfimy bishop of Turov in Lutsk, and he 'left Galich for Moscow on 1 August [1412]'. *PSRL*, vol. 35, p. 55.
6. Chernigov, Polotsk, Lutsk, Vladimir (in Volynia), Galich, Smolensk, Kholm, Cherven' and Turov. Ibid., vol. 11, p. 223.

Foty. This they did in spite of their unwillingness to act against 'their father and master Foty, the metropolitan'. The document, dictated perhaps by Vitovt to the reluctant bishops, accused Foty of neglecting Kiev, not caring for his flock and transferring valuables from St Sofia to Moscow. It delighted Vitovt, who set about making an inventory not only of everything in St Sofia but of 'all the towns and districts and villages belonging to the metropolitan'. He could now try once again to have a candidate of his own appointed as metropolitan.

When Foty learned of Vitovt's intentions he decided to go to Constantinople in order to prevent at any cost the establishment of yet another breakaway metropolitanate of Lithuania and Galicia. But first he went to Kiev to investigate the situation and, if possible, to make his peace with Vitovt. But Vitovt had him arrested, robbed and returned to Moscow. He then distributed the landed possessions of the Kievan metropolis to his *pany* (lords), plundered Foty's vicars (*namest-niki*) and sent them back to Moscow.[7] The Nikon Chronicle, which is particularly rich in information concerning the landholdings of the metropolitanate at the time,[8] even adds a moralizing coda about one Savva Avramiev, one of the 'slanderers' of Foty who allegedly set the campaign against him in motion. During one of the periodic conflagrations in Moscow (1414), 'fire came down like a cloud from the top storey of Foty's residence and consumed him alive'.[9]

Vitovt's next move was to summon his bishops yet again (1415) and to tell them to select any one of their choice as metropolitan and send him to Constantinople for consecration. Some objected ('it were better to make peace with Foty', they said), but Vitovt forbade them to interfere. The choice fell on Grigory Tsamblak as future metropolitan of Kiev (i.e. as metropolitan of Kiev and the Lithuanians), a Bulgarian and a disciple of Metropolitan Kiprian. He had been in Lithuania in some capacity or other for the last eight years, but nothing is known of his activities or what position, if any, he held. It appears that he was not yet a bishop.

Grigory Tsamblak was sent to Constantinople together with the bishops' letter of complaint. Vitovt, himself since 1386 a rebaptized Catholic, can hardly have been so sanguine as to expect success. After all, Foty was the direct appointee of the patriarch. So, not surprisingly,

---

7. Nikon Chronicle (ibid., pp. 223–4).
8. See Kloss, *Nikonovskiy svod*, pp. 51–4.
9. *PSRL*, vol. 11, p. 224. This is immediately followed by the tale of yet another of Foty's slanderers, a merchant whose limbs became paralysed after the fire of Moscow but who, after confessing to Foty, was miraculously healed.

Grigory was rejected by 'emperor and patriarch'.[10] There was now only one thing left for Vitovt: to appoint Grigory Tsamblak by a synod of local bishops without reference to Constantinople. It was not all that easy. The same nine bishops were summoned again and were told to 'elect as metropolitan of Kiev Grigory Tsamblak the Bulgarian'.[11] Again they demurred on the grounds that even though the land of Kiev might now be in Vitovt's hands, there was already one metropolitan and that 'it is not right for two metropolitans to be in one province'. Vitovt resorted to threats: 'If you do not appoint my metropolitan [i.e. Grigory] in my land in Kiev, you will die a dire death (*to zlo umrete*).' There was no way out for the bishops. On 15 November 1415, meeting in Novgorodok, the old seat of the metropolitanate of Lithuania, 'against their will they appointed Grigory Tsamblak the Bulgarian as metropolitan of Kiev.' Once again the bishops were obliged by Vitovt to write a joint epistle, this time justifying their action. This curious document again enumerates the complaints against Foty – his neglect of the Church and the land of Kiev, 'laid waste and spurned', the shepherdless flock – and states bluntly, but presumably metaphorically, that 'we have exiled and expelled Foty from the throne of the metropolitanate of Kiev' and that, at a synod attended by 'all the Lithuanian and Russian princes subject to [Vitovt], all the boyars, grandees and all the archimandrites and abbots and pious monks and priests', Grigory was appointed 'metropolitan of our holy Kievan Church and of all Russia'. In order to justify their action, the bishops quoted canon law: 'it is right for us bishops to appoint a metropolitan at a synod, as it is written in the sacred canons: two or three bishops [may] ordain by imposition of hands, that is to say appoint, a metropolitan'; and to back their claim they referred to the practices of the Bulgarians and the Serbians and, still closer to hand, to the case of the appointment of Metropolitan Klim in the twelfth century 'during the rule of Grand Prince Izyaslav of Kiev' (see above, pp. 46–7).[12]

The bishops' letter soon produced a reaction – and a strong one – in Moscow. Foty thundered back with a remarkably angry, bitter and

10. Ibid., p. 225.
11. Ibid., p. 227 (*s.a.* 1416). In the justificatory 'synodal epistle of the Lithuanian bishops concerning the election of Grigory Tsamblak to the metropolitanate of Kiev', 15 November 1415 (*RIB*, vol. 6, cols. 309–14), only eight bishops signed: the bishops of Cherven′ and Galich are not mentioned, but the bishop of Peremyshl′ is added to the list. Cf. above, p. 163 n. 6.
12. See the synodal epistle of the Lithuanian bishops (*RIB*, vol. 6, cols. 309–14); and the close version of it in the Nikon Chronicle (*PSRL*, vol. 11, pp. 226–30).

lengthy screed, chock-full of quotations from the Bible and the canons and impregnated with insult and irritation.[13] It was addressed to clergy and laymen alike. After a long prelude on the evils of false pastors, he lays into the two main objects of his wrath: Grigory Tsamblak and the wretched bishops who appointed him. Grigory, he claimed, excommunicated and anathematized by the patriarch, brought nothing but ruin, confusion and corruption on the Church he had been so falsely appointed to. Next the Lithuanian bishops themselves are execrated for having appointed Grigory in the first place and thus for breaking their oath 'not to receive another metropolitan except for the one sent from Constantinople, from the catholic [i.e. Universal] and apostolic Church'.[14] He begs his flock to console him, 'plunged in deep despondency and sorrow'.[15] After a long string of quotations from the canons on all aspects of the excommunication of errant clergy – especially the prelacy – and on the 'need for obedience of bishops to metropolitans and archbishops', he ends with an exhortation to all to pray 'for the unity of God's Church' – in other words, for the undivided metropolitanate of Kiev and all Russia.

It is worthy of note that no blame whatsoever is attached by Foty to the real initiator of all the 'troubles and misfortunes', namely the grand prince of Lithuania himself. And yet Foty cannot have been unaware that the majority of the bishops acted grudgingly and only complied with Vitovt's demands when faced with sombre threats. Of course the reason for Foty's omission of Vitovt's prime role in the sorry story of Tsamblak's appointment can only be that he had no wish to antagonize the ruler of most of the vast Orthodox flock which would eventually return to him as sole shepherd of Kiev and all Russia.

The new patriarch, Joseph II, Euthemius's successor, answered Foty's epistle as soon as he received it, probably in 1416. The wording of the letter to Foty is somewhat vague in places, but nevertheless the main objects of his diatribe, apart from the obvious one of Grigory himself, are the bishops who appointed him. Yet they are not named and are only mentioned indirectly. Grigory, he points out, has again been excommunicated and anathematized at an *ad hoc* synod summoned especially to deal with the situation in Russia. But the bishops are also clearly involved in the turmoil, for he states that should Tsamblak be

13. Printed in *RIB*, vol. 6, cols. 315–56.
14. Ibid., col. 328.
15. Ibid., col. 330.

chased out, then 'you [Foty] should come to us with all speed, for it is essential that we should consider in council how those Christians there [i.e. the Lithuanian bishops] can be absolved from excommunication'. And at the end of the letter he adds that 'it would be good that all those bishops should be corrected in your presence (*pred toboyu ispravyatsya*)'. As for Vitovt, no blame is imputed to him. Indeed, quite the opposite. Joseph writes that 'the holy emperor, and we too, have written to Grand Prince Vitovt about rectifying this matter, and we hope, for he is an intelligent sovereign (*umnyy ospodar*), that he will rectify what has happened and expel him who has been dismissed [from his post]'.[16]

But for all Foty's protests and the patriarch's denunciations, nothing dislodged Grigory until his death. For four years after his appointment he remained firm and immovable as the pastor of Vitovt's Orthodox subjects. What is more, if we assume that the lists of those who appointed him which are found in the Russian sources are correct, then it is evident that most if not all of the bishops of Polish-ruled Little Russia (Volynia and Galicia) also came under his aegis. The huge Russian land now under Vitovt and the south-eastern annexe of King Władysław II Jagiełło's Poland were once more split off from the 'all-Russian' metropolitanate of Kiev and Moscow.[17]

Nothing is known of the last years of Grigory's life except that he was sent to Rome and to the Council of Constance.[18] The Nikon Chronicle describes, with a certain amount of imagination, his last encounter with Vitovt in September 1417 (misdated 1418). He is reported as asking Vitovt:

'For what reason, O Prince, are you in the Polish [i.e. Latin] faith and not in the Greek?' Vitovt answered: 'If you wish to see not only me but also all the people of my land of Lithuania in the Greek faith, then go to Rome and argue with the pope and all his wise men; and if you win the argument, then we will all be in the Greek faith and in the Greek custom; but if you do not win the argument, then we shall convert all the people of our land who are of the Greek faith to our western faith (*nemetskiy zakon*).' And he sent him together with his *pany* to Rome and to the pope.[19]

16. Ibid., cols. 357–60.

17. In two signatures Grigory Tsamblak styles himself 'Humble Grigory Tsamblak, metropolitan of Kiev, Galicia and all Russia'; and 'metropolitan of Kiev and all the land of Lithuania'. Golubinsky, *IRTs*, vol. 2, I, p. 384 n. 1.

18. On the Council of Constance, see *The Council*; Halecki, 'From Florence', pp. 28 ff.

19. *PSRL*, vol. 11, p. 233.

Nothing was gained from Grigory's perfectly amicable discussions with Pope Martin V at the Council of Constance, which was also attended by representatives of Emperor Manuel II, now urgently in need of military aid against the Turks. Grigory returned from Constance – perhaps via Rome – to Lithuania in 1418 without having outwitted or out-argued the pope. Vitovt seems either to have forgotten his threat to convert all his Orthodox subjects to Catholicism, or merely to have indulged in idle talk when Grigory allegedly attempted to persuade him to change his faith for the third time.[20] In any case Tsamblak died in the winter of 1419, and again the metropolitanate of the Lithuanians and Galicia reverted to Foty. Once more the metropolitanate was undivided and united.

If Vitovt had seen fit earlier to criticize Foty for ignoring and even ruining those parts of his diocese which were outside Suzdalia, he could not complain of his activities in the south-west as metropolitan of all Russia during the last twelve years of his life (1419–31). For in that time Foty showed astonishing zeal and vigour in travelling around, and presumably administering, the outposts of his metropolitanate. In 1421 and 1422 he was absent from Moscow for a good two years, moving from town to town in the 'lands of Lithuania' as well as in Polish-held Galicia. The list of towns visited by him speaks of his astonishing journeying and the vast distances covered by him and his entourage. From Moscow he travelled to Novgorodok, the seat of the Lithuanian sector of his province; from there his itinerary took him to Kiev, Slutsk, Mozyr', Galich, L'vov, Vladimir in Volynia, Borisov, Drutsk, Mstislavl' and Smolensk – many of the major towns in Vitovt's huge eastern empire and Jagiełło's Little Russia.[21] Seldom can a metropolitan of Russia before or after him have covered so many thousands of kilometres on episcopal circuit! We know little of what he did in the places he visited, except that in the first and last of the towns mentioned in his itinerary, Novgorodok and Smolensk, he met Grand Prince Vitovt and presumably discussed the problems of his diocese with him.

In 1423 he again visited Smolensk for talks with Vitovt.[22] By now Vitovt was clearly reconciled with Foty as the spiritual leader of all his Orthodox subjects and the right hand of his ally and son-in-law,

20. Originally pagan, Vitovt had first been baptized Orthodox. In 1386, together with Yagaylo/Jagiełło, he was rebaptized Catholic.
21. See map, p. 251. For the source of his itinerary, see the Suprasl'skiy and Slutskiy Chronicles. *PSRL*, vol. 35, pp. 56, 78.
22. Ibid., vol. 11, pp. 238–9.

Vasily I of Moscow. At the end of both their lives, their common cause was illustrated yet again by the events of 1430 when Vitovt invited Foty to his capital Vil'na for his coronation as king of Lithuania – a coronation which in fact never took place: the Poles saw to it, so the Suprasl'skiy Chronicle tells us, that the crown was never delivered in Vil'na.[23] After the departure of the large number of distinguished guests, including King Władysław II Jagiełło, Vasily II of Moscow and a cardinal from Rome, Vitovt retained Foty for a further eleven days in his company. On his return to Moscow, the metropolitan stopped in Novgorodok, where he learned that Vitovt had just died – on 24 October 1430.[24] Eight months later, on 2 July 1431, Foty himself died in Moscow. He was buried near the tomb of Kiprian in the cathedral of the Dormition in the Kremlin.[25]

23. Ibid., vol. 35, p. 57. 'Poles' is hazarded here for the curious *polyane*.
24. Ibid., vol. 12, p. 9. Zimin, *Vityaz'*, pp. 42–3.
25. *PSRL*, vol. 12, p. 10.

CHAPTER FOURTEEN

Metropolitans Iona and Isidor; the Council of Florence

Foty's throne remained vacant for nearly six years after his death. This is not really surprising, for most of the six years were occupied by the first phase of the bloody civil war between Vasily II and his turbulent enemies, Yury of Galich and his three sons – a war in which, in this the first stage, Vasily twice lost and twice regained his grand-princely throne of Moscow. No wonder he had little time or opportunity to press the emperor and patriarch to provide Moscow with a metropolitan. Their minds were engaged rather with the possibility of some sort of a union with Rome, a union which, it was hoped, would lead eventually to Western military aid.

However, in Russia preparations did begin, probably in the second half of 1432, for the election of a candidate. The choice fell on Iona, bishop of Ryazan' and Murom, who, by March 1433, was already styling himself metropolitan designate.[1] Evidently he had been elected by a synod of bishops.[2] But nothing could be done before Vasily II

1. *RIB*, vol. 6, col. 521; *Blagoslovenie Iony episkopa, narechennogo v svyateyshuyu mitropoliyu russkuyu*. Ya. S. Lur'e has 'serious doubts' as to the reliability of most of the epistles of Vasily II and Iona (all published in *RIB*, vol. 6) describing the ecclesiastical events in Russia from the death of Foty to the appointment of Iona as metropolitan in 1448 and the reactions of both to the Council of Florence and the 'apostasy' of Metropolitan Isidor. See Lur'e in: *Slovar' knizhnikov*, vol. 2, I, pp. 109–12, 420–6, 449–50; *Dve istorii*, § 8.9. There seems, however, to be little reason to query the authenticity of this document (No. 61) – a business-like missive from Iona to the Nizhniy Novgorod Pecherskiy Monastery dated 11 March 1433.

2. See Vasily II's letter to Emperor Constantine XI (1451 or 1452), *RIB*, vol. 6, No. 71. 'We took council with our mother [Sofia of Lithuania, Vitovt's daughter] . . . with the Russian grand princes and local princes and with the sovereign of the Lithuanian land, the grand prince, and with the bishops of our land and with all [the clergy], the boyars and with all the Russian land, [and] having chosen [him] we sent with our envoy . . . to Emperor John [VIII] and Patriarch Joseph [II] our father Iona' (cols. 578–9). 'An embryonic Assembly of the Land' (*zemskiy sobor*) according to Sinitsyna, 'Avtokefaliya', p. 133.

170

regained his throne for the second time in 1434. And even then there were more delays. Eventually, at the end of 1435 or the beginning of 1436, Iona was at last dispatched to Constantinople for consecration. He was too late. By the time he arrived, the brilliant and astonishingly mobile and adventurous Isidor, Greek abbot of the Monastery of St Dmitry in Constantinople, had already been elected and consecrated metropolitan of Kiev and all Russia by the patriarch. Nevertheless, according to Iona, writing to the Orthodox Lithuanian prince of Kiev, Aleksandr Vladimirovich (before 31 January 1451), it was decreed by Patriarch Joseph 'and the divine and holy council' that 'when Isidor either by God's will dies, or should anything else happen to him', then Iona was to be 'metropolitan in Russia'.[3] Vasily II in his letter to Emperor Constantine XI (1451/1452), quotes the words of John VIII and Joseph to Iona: 'What shall we then do? You did not come to us in time and we appointed another to that most holy metropolitan see and we cannot now do otherwise. Isidor is already metropolitan in Russia, and you, Iona, go back to your see, the bishopric of Ryzan'. And should God's will preordain that Isidor dies, or should anything else happen to him, then you, Iona, shall be metropolitan in Russia after him.'[4] Accompanied by Iona, Isidor arrived in Moscow in April 1437.

While the Russians had been obliged by the chaos of the civil war to delay the process of getting Iona recognized and consecrated in Constantinople, the Lithuanians showed no reluctance at all in attempting yet again to acquire a spiritual leader for their Orthodox subjects – perhaps even a replacement for Foty in Moscow. King Władysław II Jagiełło's brother Svidrigaylo (Lithuanian: Švitrigaila), who had been appointed grand prince of Lithuania at the death of Vitovt, sent Bishop Gerasim of Smolensk to Constantinople for consecration.[5] Just why the bishop of Smolensk was selected, who selected him and what his province was to consist of (Kiev and all Russia? Lithuania? Lithuania and Galicia?) are questions to which there are no firm answers. All we know is that he returned to Smolensk in 1434 as

---

3. *RIB*, vol. 6, col. 561.
4. Ibid., col. 579. See also Iona's encyclical to the 'Lithuanian princes and *pany*' of 1448 (ibid., cols. 539–40). Lur'e considers the announcement of John VIII and Joseph to be most unlikely and points out that there is no mention of it in Vasily II's earlier letter to Metrophanes (ibid., cols. 525–36). See *Slovar' knizhnikov*, vol. 2, I, p. 111).
5. *PL*, vol. 1, p. 40; vol. 2, p. 43.
6. Ibid., vol. 1, pp. 41–2; vol. 2, pp. 44, 128.

metropolitan,[6] presumably having been consecrated by Patriarch Joseph, that he appointed Evfimy II archbishop of Novgorod in May 1434 'because', as the Nikon Chronicle explains, 'after the death of Foty, metropolitan of Kiev and all Russia, there was no metropolitan in Moscow',[7] and that in the following year he was arrested in Smolensk by his patron Svidrigaylo, held in irons for four months in Vitebsk (in the old principality of Polotsk) and eventually burned to death at Svidrigaylo's orders for 'treasonous relations' with Vitovt's brother and Svidrigaylo's rival, Sigismund.[8] But what was the province of this unfortunate creature of Svidrigaylo? The most likely answer must be: the 'metropolitanate of the Lithuanians'. For it seems highly improbable that the patriarch would have consecrated an appointee of Svidrigaylo and thus risked incurring the wrath of Vasily II, whose cash and international support for the hapless Greeks could hardly be sacrificed.[9]

Whatever may have been the province Gerasim was assigned to, Isidor arrived in Moscow, duly consecrated by Patriarch Joseph as metropolitan of *all Russia*. From a Byzantine point of view he was the ideal candidate for Moscow. His erudition, his command of languages and his conciliar and diplomatic skills were known to and praised by many.[10] Furthermore, he had experience of the interchange of interdoctrinal argument, having been sent by the emperor in 1433 to attend discussions touching on the union of the Churches at the Council of Basel. The Greeks were in awe of his intellect, and even his enemy, Simeon of Suzdal', who accompanied him to Italy in 1437 and wrote his account of the Council of Florence, had to admit that 'the Greeks

---

7. *PSRL*, vol. 12, p. 20. See also *NPL*, p. 417 ('Archbishop Evfimy came to Novgorod, [having been] appointed and blessed by Metropolitan Gerasim').

8. *PL*, vol. 2, p. 45; cf. a more muddled version, ibid., p. 131.

9. There is, however, some textual evidence to support the view that he was appointed to fill Foty's place: (*a*) in the *Life of Evfimy* he is called 'Metropolitan of Kiev and all Russia'; (*b*) the Pskov First Chronicle's account of his arrival in Smolensk concludes with the words: 'but he did not want to go to [his see in?] Moscow, for the Russian princes were warring and fighting for the grand principality of the Russian land' (*PL*, vol. 1, p. 42); (*c*) in the Novgorod First Chronicle's list of Russian metropolitans (*A se rustei mitropolity*), none of whom were metropolitans solely of Lithuania or Galicia, the last named, after Foty, is Gerasim (*NPL*, p. 163). Other lists of Russian metropolitans fail to mention him, e.g. the list in the Simeonovskiy Chronicle (*PSRL*, vol. 18, p. 22): '... Kiprian, Foty, Isidor ...'. Lur'e in his work on the Common-Russian chronicles of the fourteenth and fifteenth centuries seems to imply that Gerasim was appointed metropolitan of all Russia. See *Obshcherusskie letopisi*, p. 114; *Dve istorii*, p. 104 § 8.3. See also Alef, 'Muscovy and the Council of Florence', p. 393 n. 32; Zimin, *Vityaz'*, p. 84.

10. Golubinsky, *IRTs*, vol. 2, I, p. 423 n. 1.

thought him to be more than all the others a great metropolitan and philosopher'.[11]

In view of his previous experience at the Council of Basel and in view of what appeared to be his surprising volte-face at the Council of Ferrara-Florence and his eventual commitment to the Latin Church, it might seem reasonable to assume that on arrival in Russia he was already a staunch, though secret, supporter of union with Rome. But at the time no one in Russia suspected the rigidity of his faith. His successor as metropolitan, Iona, later wrote to Bishop Misail of Smolensk, in 1461, asserting that nobody knew of his plans to subject Orthodoxy to Rome.[12] Vasily II, it is true, was at first unwilling to accept Isidor as metropolitan. 'Had we not,' he said in a letter of 1441 to Patriarch Metrophanes, 'maintained our original Orthodox Christianity and had we not had the fear of God in our hearts, we would in no way have been willing to receive him.' But this was not because Isidor was suspected of pro-Roman tendencies. It was simply because Iona had been overlooked in Constantinople. It was only

> as a result of the entreaties of the emperor's envoy and the blessing of the most holy patriarch that we agreed – but only just agreed – to receive him (*edva edva priyakhom ego*). But when his extreme grief and self-abasement won us over, then we accepted him with great honour and zeal as a father and a teacher . . . just like our former most holy metropolitans, thinking that he was one of them and not knowing what deed would eventually be done by him.[13]

Whether or not Isidor was already determined to work for the union of the Churches when he arrived in Moscow, he certainly showed anxiety to leave as soon as possible for Italy to attend the Council for which the emperor and patriarch were already planning their departure from Constantinople. According to the Russian chronicles, Vasily II did all he could to prevent him from going to 'the eighth Latin Council and not to be led astray by their [i.e. the Latins'] heresy';[14] Iona, too, claimed that 'however much my lord and son, Grand Prince Vasily, urged him not to go, he was unable to stop him'.[15] But both the chroniclers and Iona were writing *after* the disclosure of Isidor's 'betrayal of Orthodoxy' and were only too

---

11. Simeon of Suzdal''s *Tale of the Eighth Council of Florence*, printed in Popov, *Istoriko-literaturnyy obzor*, pp. 344–59. Here, p. 346.

12. *RIB*, vol. 6, cols. 659–60.

13. Ibid., cols. 530–1.

14. *PSRL*, vol. 25, p. 253; vol. 6, p. 152; vol. 12, pp. 23–4.

15. *RIB*, vol. 6, col. 660.

anxious to stress what they considered to be the monstrosity of his perfidy. It may well be, of course, that Vasily merely urged him to postpone his departure so that he could deal with the mountain of ecclesiastical business that had piled up since Foty's death in 1430.

On 8 September 1437, having promised Vasily II that he would 'strengthen the faith and unite the Church in Orthodoxy',[16] Isidor set off from Moscow. His suite of one hundred included one bishop, Avraamy of Suzdal', and a number of clerics. Bishop Avraamy's own retinue had in it not only the monk Simeon, who wrote his polemical *Tale of the Council of Florence*,[17] but also other scribes, one of whom was probably the anonymous author of *Journey to the Council of Florence (Khozhdenie na Florentiyskiy Sobor)*,[18] the earliest known Russian description of Western Europe.

The journey to Ferrara took just under a year,[19] three staging posts in Russia (Tver', Novgorod and Pskov) and eight weeks in Riga[20] accounting for some eight months of the total. For all his haste in leaving Moscow, Isidor was evidently in no hurry to reach his destination. On arrival in Ferrara (18 August 1438) he found that the emperor and patriarch and their party had been waiting since early March – waiting, so Simeon of Suzdal' tells us, for the arrival of the Russian delegation; but they were also waiting for the Western princes, who, the Greeks had vainly hoped, would provide military help against the Turks once an agreement was reached. They never came.[21]

In spite of the absence of the Western rulers and the delay of the Russian delegation, it was decided officially to open the Council on 9 April 1438. In the early months the question of Purgatory was

---

16. Popov, *Istoriko-literaturnyy obzor*, p. 345.

17. See above, p. 173 n. 11.

18. Kazakova, '"Khozhdenie"'; *PLDR, XIV–seredina XV veka*, pp. 468–93.

19. Details of the route are given in the anonymous *Journey to the Council of Florence* (see above, n. 18).

20. In an encyclical sent to 'the Lithuanian princes and *pany*' in 1459 Iona describes how in Riga Isidor was met by 'Latin priests with crucifixes (*kaplanove . . . s . . . kryzhi*)', went into their church 'with his protodeacon Grigory, who has now become metropolitan, and served in the Roman manner'. He imprisoned and tortured 'our elders . . . and laymen who were there and who saw this and began to talk to him about it'. Furthermore, he called himself 'legate and cardinal'. *RIB*, vol. 6, No. 85, cols. 636–7. This description of Isidor's activities in Riga, which is after all based purely on heresay (*slyshim*), must be discounted. Isidor could only style himself legate and cardinal *after* Florence. The whole aim of the encyclical was to warn Iona's addressees of the evils of Isidor and his pupil Grigory, who had been sent by the unionist patriarch Gregory Mammas from Rome as 'metropolitan of Kiev' in 1458.

21. On the Western princes, see Gill, *The Council*, pp. 131 ff.

discussed, a question which little concerned the Greeks and was barely understood by the majority of them. Not surprisingly, no agreement was reached, and neither side seemed particularly put out by the deadlock. After the arrival of the Russian party the serious discussions began – that is, the discussions on the question of the *filioque*, which was to be by far the most important of all the topics. From 8 October 1438 to 10 January 1439 sessions were held mainly concerning the addition of the word *filioque* to the Creed. The chief contestants were Cardinal Cesarini on the Latin side and Metropolitans Mark of Ephesus and Bessarion of Nicaea on the Greek side – was *filioque* an addition or a clarification? Clearly the arguments were leading nowhere. By the end of the year it was resolved that a switch must be made to the very heart of the matter – the dogmatic question of the Procession of the Holy Spirit. In the beginning of 1439 it was also proposed by Pope Eugene IV that in view of the plague which had struck earlier and which threatened to erupt again in the spring the Council move to Florence.

In Florence sessions on the burning question of the Procession of the Holy Spirit – from the Father; from the Father *through* the Son; from the Father *and* from the Son – went on from 2 March to 2 June 1439. On the Greek side the leading figures – Bessarion, Isidor and the lay philosopher George Scholarius – gradually moved into a unionist position, recognizing that the only hope for the success of the Council was for the Orthodox to accept the Latins' views. The anti-unionist stand was resolutely defended by Mark of Ephesus and Metropolitans Dositheus of Monembasia and Antony of Heraclea. The emperor, John VIII, desperate for the West to rescue Byzantium from the Turks, did what he could to urge his prelates to reach an agreement with the Latins.

By mid-summer 1439 the Greeks after months of difficult, often meandering and always highly technical theological disputes, short of money and provisions and anxious to return home at long last, were ready to sign the act of union with Rome. On Sunday, 5 July 1439 all the Greeks headed by the emperor, signed the Decree of Union – all, that is, except for Mark of Ephesus, who remained inflexible to the very end. The old and fragile patriarch, Joseph II, who would probably have signed, was saved from capitulating to the Latins by dying just under a month earlier. The only Russian prelate present at the Council, Bishop Avraamy of Suzdal', signed, but, if we can believe Avraamy's fellow-Suzdalian, Simeon, only under duress: in his *Tale of the Council of Florence* Simeon writes that Avraamy 'did not wish [to sign], but Metropolitan Isidor arrested him and gaoled him for a whole week. Then he signed under constraint.'[22] There is no other evidence to support this.

The rewards to those most responsible for persuading the Greeks to sign the union were impressive. Pope Eugene appointed Metropolitan Bessarion cardinal and granted him an annual pension of 300 florins if he remained in Constantinople or 600 should he stay at the papal court. Isidor was likewise made cardinal and Apostolic Delegate 'in the Province of Lithuania, Livonia and Russia and in the states, dioceses, territories and places of Lechia [Poland] which are regarded as subject to you in your right as metropolitan'.[23] Bessarion had certainly been one of the leading lights amongst the pro-union Greek delegates, especially in the dogmatic discussions on the *filioque* in Florence. Isidor, however, had taken little part in the theological debates on the Procession of the Holy Spirit, but towards the end was instrumental in urging those Greeks who were still hesitant to sign the decree. According to Simeon of Suzdal', he was the pope's favourite: 'not one metropolitan did the pope love as much as Isidor.'[24]

When the Greeks returned to Constantinople they found the city in disarray. Much of the population was opposed to the union and there was no one resolute enough to enforce it. True, a unionist, Metrophanes II (1440–43), was appointed patriarch in the place of Joseph II. But there was little he or his successor Gregory III Mammas (1445–51) could do other than commemorate the pope in their Liturgies, proclaim the decree of the Council and consecrate unionist bishops. There was no change, or so Metrophanes announced in an encyclical written just after his accession to the patriarchate, 'in all our ecclesiastical customs, in the holy celebration of the sacred Body of Christ and in the other services and the recitation of the Holy Creed'.[25] Meanwhile, several of the signatories of the union began to recant, notably Metropolitan Antonius of Heraclea, Metropolitan Dorotheus of Trebizond and Mark of Ephesus's pupil George Scholarius, who in 1450 took the tonsure under the monastic name of Gennadius. But by far the most damage to the unionist cause was done by the intransigent Mark of Ephesus, who tirelessly attacked the supporters of the union. As Joseph Gill writes:

the impression of enthusiastic zeal and sincerity that pervades his writings, of devotion to the traditional faith of his Church and of hatred and scorn

22. Popov, *Istoriko-literaturnyy obzor*, p. 354.
23. Gill, *The Council*, pp. 299–300, 358.
24. Popov, *Istoriko-literaturnyy obzor*, p. 351.
25. Gill, *The Council*, p. 351.

towards those who, as he thought, were bent on contaminating it with
falsehoods and heresies of the West, must have greatly encouraged those
who had already rejected the union and have won over to his side many
who still hesitated, for he was harping on a theme already familiar to the
Greeks who hardly needed the fiery words of such an advocate to believe
the worst of the Latin Church. Both East and West recognised in him the
greatest obstacle to union. He was the only one of the Greek prelates who
had openly refused to sign the decree in Florence, the only one, therefore,
whose conduct throughout was consistent, who was not open to reproach.
And with all that he was venerated for the sanctity of his life. No wonder,
therefore, that his influence with his fellow-countrymen was so great.[26]

However much men's minds tussled with the problems set by the
Union, the real anxieties which beset the population of Constantinople
were linked with the impending disaster at the hands of the Ottoman
Turks. Hopes of military aid had been raised by the promises of the
pope. But the crusade preached by Eugene IV had ended in the
disastrous defeat of the allied army at Varna by Sultan Murad in 1444.
There was no more hope of help after that. And although when John
VIII died in 1448 and the new emperor, his brother Constantine XI
Palaeologus, threw in his lot with the unionists, still no fleet, no troops
could be expected from the West. Whether or not the Grand Admiral
of the Fleet, Luke Notaras, an opponent of the Union, uttered the
words put in his mouth by the contemporary Greek historian Ducas:
'Better the Sultan's turban than the Pope's mitre',[27] there can be no
doubt that the majority of his fellow-citizens shared his view. Constantinople fell to the Turks on 29 May 1453. The monk Gennadius –
George Scholarius – who had been bought by a rich Turk and taken
to Adrianople in Thrace, was brought back to the capital in January
1454 and invested by the sultan as the first non-unionist patriarch since
the death of Joseph II.[28]

Metropolitan-Cardinal Isidor, *Legatus a latere*, left Florence on 6
September 1439. If his journey to Ferrara had taken an unconscionably
long time, his return to Moscow took nearly twice as long. The
reasons for his apparent dilatoriness are not hard to find. In the first
place, Isidor cannot have been unaware of the fact that the authorities
in Moscow knew all about what would have seemed to them his
unacceptable role at the Council long before he arrived back in 1441:

26. Ibid., p. 356.
27. For his actual words quoted by Ducas, see ibid., p. 375 n. 6.
28. Runciman, *The Fall*, pp. 154–5.

both Simeon of Suzdal' and Foma, the envoy of the grand prince of Tver', having fallen foul of Isidor, had fled from Venice in December 1439,[29] and although Simeon in fact took refuge in Novgorod and was eventually brought back a prisoner of Isidor to Moscow,[30] Foma presumably reached Tver' in early 1440, whence the news of the Council would have been relayed to Moscow. Furthermore, the probably Suzdalian author of the *Journey to the Council of Florence* left Isidor's retinue in Vil'na in August 1440 and arrived in Russia a month later. Isidor may well have been apprehensive of his reception in Moscow. In the second place, he had a considerable amount of ecclesiastical – and, no doubt, political – business to conduct in Hungary, Poland, Lithuania and Polish-controlled Galicia before tackling the Russian dioceses of his metropolitanate.

Three months were spent by Isidor in Venice (15 September to 27 December 1439). He then went via Zagreb to Buda, from where he issued an encyclical 'to the Polish, Lithuanian and German [i.e. Teutonic Knights'] lands and to all Orthodox Christian Russia' (March 1440). The encyclical contained a somewhat innocuous statement affirming that the Churches were now joined together and that there should be no more separation of the Orthodox from the Latins. He urged the Greeks when in Latin territory to attend Latin churches and the Latins in Greek territory to attend Greek churches, for, after all, the baptism of the Roman Church and that of the Greek Church were equally valid. In order to avoid the old disagreements about the use of leavened and unleavened bread in the Eucharist, churches were advised to have both. The encyclical wisely avoided all mention of the Creed or of the supremacy of the pope.[31]

After a brief stay in Poland Isidor moved into Galicia-Volynia. With L'vov as his headquarters, he spent the first half of the summer of 1440 visiting Bel'z, Kholm, Galich and Kamenets. By mid-August he was in the Lithuanian capital of Vil'na. During the next six months he was active in the Lithuanian sector of his metropolitanate. However, he clearly spent some time in Kiev[32] and from there moved to Smolensk. Here he caught up with the unfortunate Simeon. The local Lithuanian prince of Smolensk, Yury Semenovich-Lugvenevich,

29. Popov, *Istoriko-literaturnyy obzor*, p. 353.
30. Ibid.
31. See *PSRL*, vol. 25, p. 258; vol. 12, pp. 36–8.
32. The local prince of Kiev, Aleksandr Vladimirovich, wrote to him in February 1441, addressing him as though he was still in Kiev. See *AI*, p. 488; Golubinsky, *IRTs*, vol. 2, I, p. 448 n. 1; *PSRL*, vol. 25, p. 258; vol. 12, p. 39.

·Ol′gerd's grandson, dissatisfied with Simeon's negative description of what had happened at the Council, and at the behest of Isidor, sent for him from Novgorod. He came, 'relying on the prince as a Christian', was assured that no harm would come to him and was promptly imprisoned on arrival: 'they put two iron shackles on me,' he wrote, 'and I spent the whole winter bare-legged and wearing a small jacket, suffering cold, hunger and thirst.'[33]

Accompanied by the shackled Simeon,[34] Isidor arrived back in Moscow on Sunday, 19 March 1441. If we can believe the reports of Simeon and the Russian chroniclers, his entry was tactless and provocative in the extreme. 'With great pride, falsehood and Latin arrogance he [had] carried before him a Latin crucifix and a silver crozier . . . Should anyone not bow down before the crucifix he ordered them to be beaten with the crozier, as is done in the presence of the pope.'[35] Thirty-one years later yet another papal legate, Cardinal Antonio Bonumbre, accompanying Ivan III's future bride, Zoe-Sofia Palaeologa, also entered Moscow demonstratively preceded by a crucifix; some of the grand prince's advisers told Ivan: 'It has never happened before in our land that the Latin faith is so honoured – only Isidor attempted to do this, and he perished.'[36]

More arrogance was to come, or so we are told. 'The metropolitan entered the holy cathedral church of [the Dormition of] the Mother of God and served the holy Liturgy, commemorating in the first place Pope Eugene without mentioning the Orthodox patriarchs.'[37] At the end of the Liturgy his protodeacon – the same protodeacon Grigory who was later created unionist 'metropolitan of Kiev' in 1458[38] – was told 'to read out in a loud voice the decree of the Eighth Council'. The grand prince was then given a letter from the pope announcing that 'the Eastern Church is now one with us' and that much of the credit for this was due to 'our most holy brother Isidor, your metropolitan . . . of all Russia and legate from the Apostolic Throne . . . We ask

---

33. Popov, *Istoriko-literaturnyy obzor*, p. 355.
34. Simeon was released after Vasily II 'dismissed' Isidor and was sent to the Trinity Monastery, where presumably he wrote, or rounded off, his work on the Council of Florence.
35. Popov, *Istoriko-literaturnyy obzor*, pp. 355–6; cf. *PSRL*, vol. 25, p. 258; vol. 12, p. 40.
36. *PSRL*, vol. 25, p. 299.
37. Popov, *Istoriko-literaturnyy obzor*, pp. 355–6. According to the Tver′ Chronicle, he also 'commemorated the emperor before Grand Prince Vasily of Moscow' (*PSRL*, vol. 15, col. 491).
38. See above, p. 174 n. 20.

you in piety to receive this Metropolitan Isidor for his justice and for the good of the Church . . .'[39]

How much of all this actually took place is hard to say. Still more imponderable are the subsequent events as reported by Simeon and the Moscow chroniclers. According to the former, Vasily II, 'realizing the delusion of the metropolitan', ordered Isidor to be 'cast out from his spiritual rank' – something a layman had no authority to do – and, 'for such soul-destroying heresy, to be expelled from the town of Moscow and from all his land'.[40] The chronicles go still further: three days after arriving in Moscow and officiating at the Liturgy in the Kremlin, Isidor was arrested and placed under guard in the Chudov Monastery.[41] As Golubinsky points out, Isidor's support of the union can hardly have come as a surprise to Vasily and his close associates. Nor can Vasily have been upset by Isidor's commemoration of the pope or by Eugene's missive; after all, there was no question of the Russians being obliged to change their Creed and to insert the *filioque*, to accept unleavened bread for the Sacrifice, to acknowledge the supremacy of the pope, the Latins' teaching on Purgatory or the celibacy of the white clergy.

Clearly Simeon and the chroniclers distorted facts in their depiction of Isidor's reception in Moscow, colouring their accounts according to their prejudices. If evidence is needed to confirm this, we have only to look at the one contemporary record of Isidor's position *vis-à-vis* the grand prince after his return from Florence, the authenticity of which is not open to any doubt – namely the text of the treaty between Boris Aleksandrovich of Tver' and Vasily II. The contents of the agreement need not concern us here, only the opening words: these state that the treaty was concluded 'with the blessing of our father Isidor, metropolitan of Kiev and all Russia'.[42] Unfortunately, the document contains no dates, but a reference to Ulug-Mehmet's advance on Moscow, which in fact took place in July 1439,[43] and to Vasily II's cousin Dmitry Yur'evich the Fair, who died on 22 September 1441,[44] would indicate first that the treaty must have been concluded *after* Isidor's return to Moscow in March 1441, and secondly

39. *PSRL*, vol. 25, p. 259; vol. 12, pp. 40–1.
40. Popov, *Istoriko-literaturnyy obzor*, p. 357.
41. *PSRL*, vol. 12, p. 41.
42. *DDG*, No. 37, p. 105.
43. *PSRL*, vol. 25, p. 260. See Cherepnin, *RFA*, p. 124. According to Zimin, the treaty was signed *before* Isidor left Moscow for Ferrara. *Vityaz'*, pp. 86, 88.
44. *PSRL*, vol. 26, p. 194; vol. 25, p. 261.

that Isidor, between 19 March and 15 September 1441, when he left Moscow for good, was at some time recognized by Vasily II as the lawful metropolitan of all Russia, and not as the heretical apostate, as he was later to be called.

The grand-princely chroniclers, only too inclined to magnify the sterling Orthodoxy of Vasily, in their account of the events subsequent to the 'fateful' liturgy officiated at by Isidor on the day of his arrival in Moscow, go out of their way to laud the grand prince as the great protector of the faith. It was he who immediately recognized 'wolf-like predatory Isidor's heresy (*Sidora volkokhishchnogo eres'*),'[45] while 'the princes, the boyars and many others – and especially the Russian bishops – remained silent, slumbered and fell asleep'. Only when 'the divinely wise, Christ-loving sovereign, Grand Prince Vasily Vasil'evich . . . shamed Isidor and called him not his pastor and teacher, but a wicked and baneful wolf', did 'all the bishops of Russia who were then in Moscow wake up, and the princes and boyars and grandees and the multitude of Christians come to their senses . . . and begin to call Isidor a heretic'.[46]

Now Isidor, so the Nikon Chronicle tells us, was arrested three days after his arrival in Moscow.[47] The grand-princely Moscow codex of 1479[48] is not quite so precise. It merely states that Vasily II, having listened to Pope Eugene's letter which was read out to him and recognizing Isidor's heresy, 'refused to receive his blessing, called him a heretical Latin deceiver and quickly ordered that he be expelled from his throne . . . and that he stay in the [Chudov] Monastery until he be investigated according to the divine sacred canons of the holy Apostles and the seven Councils of the holy fathers'.[49] Both chronicles agree that eventually – after 'the whole summer' (*leto vse*)[50] – 'on 15 September 1441',[51] Isidor escaped[52] with two of his disciples, Grigory (the future Uniate metropolitan of Kiev) and Afanasy, and fled first to Tver', where, according to the Pskov chronicles, he was placed under

45. Ibid., p. 259.
46. Ibid., vol. 12, p. 41.
47. Ibid. *v sredu krestopoklonnuyu Velikogo posta* – i.e. Wednesday, 22 March (the correct date for 1441).
48. The Moscow *svod* of 1479 was compiled not at the metropolitan's but at the grand prince's court. See Lur'e, *Obshcherusskie letopisi*, pp. 122 ff.
49. *PSRL*, vol. 25, p. 259.
50. Ibid., vol. 12, p. 41.
51. Ibid., vol. 25, p. 261.
52. According to the Tver' Chronicle 'in Moslem [i.e. Tatar] dress'. Ibid., vol. 15, col. 491.

house arrest by Grand Prince Boris Aleksandrovich,[53] and then via Lithuania (Novgorodok) to Rome.[54] It would appear that Isidor 'fled' with the connivance of Vasily II. The Moscow *svod* of 1479 describes his 'secret escape by night like a thief' (*noshchiyu bez"dveriyem' . . . tat'stvom*) and adds that 'Grand Prince Vasily Vasil'evich sent no one to bring him back, nor did he have any desire to hold him back'.[55] It is true that Vasily II did write to Patriarch Metrophanes II in 1441, little suspecting that he too was a 'heretic-unionist', asking for permission to appoint a Russian candidate (i.e. Iona) by a synod of local bishops. The letter is mild in tone, mild that is by comparison with later anti-Latin Russian polemical writings: there is no mention of 'heresy' and 'apostasy', 'Arianism'(!) and 'Nestorianism'(!), words which were soon to be used by Iona when metropolitan to blacken Isidor and his disciple Grigory.[56] But, more important, he makes no mention whatsoever of Isidor's imprisonment and 'flight'. All he does is to describe Isidor's return from Florence calling himself *Legatus a latere* and carrying before him 'a Latin sculptured crucifix with [Christ's] two feet nailed with one nail'.[57] He 'commemorated the pope' and 'subjected us to the Roman Church and the Roman pope' and brought with him the pope's letter. The only action reported by Vasily was the summoning of a synod of six bishops,[58] who concluded that 'all Isidor's business . . . is alien and different from the divine and holy canons'. The result was a decision to send envoys to Constantinople to request the appointment of a Russian metropolitan by 'the God-loving bishops of our fatherland'.[59] In fact the letter was never sent — no doubt it transpired in Moscow that the patriarch was also a signatory of the Union? — but was rewritten two years later and addressed to Metrophanes's successor, Gregory III Mammas, yet another adherent of the Union.[60] It too was never sent to Constantinople.[61]

---

53. Ibid., and *PL*, vol. 1, p. 46; vol. 2, pp. 47, 135.

54. *NPL*, p. 422; *PSRL*, vol. 12, pp. 42–3; vol. 25, p. 261.

55. Ibid., p. 259; vol. 6, p. 162.

56. e.g. *RIB*, vol. 6, cols. 621, 638, 642 (comparison with Pope Formosus), 646, 654.

57. On Russian Orthodox Crosses the two feet are nailed separately.

58. Efrem of Rostov, Avraamy of Suzdal', Iona of Ryazan', Varlaam of Kolomna, Iov of Saray and Gerasim of Perm'.

59. *RIB*, vol. 6, cols. 525–36.

60. See ibid., cols. 529–30.

61. In his letter to Prince Aleksandr Vladimirovich of Kiev (before 31 January 1451) Iona, probably referring to Vasily II's letter to Metrophanes, wrote: 'There was no one to send [the letter] to; the emperor was not such a person, nor was the patriarch — wrong-thinking and drawing close to the Latins' (ibid., col. 559). See Belyakova, 'K istorii', p. 154.

What can we conclude from all that we know of the events connected with Isidor's last days in Russia? What did happen? Was he really deposed three days after his arrival by Vasily II, who, in that case, would appear to have acted uncanonically, without the advice or the consent of his bishops? If he *was* deposed, then when did he officiate at the signing of the treaty between Vasily II and Boris of Tver'? And why did Vasily II refrain from mentioning his deposition – or his arrest – in his letter to Patriarch Metrophanes? Indeed, was Isidor *ever* arrested, or placed under house arrest, by Vasily or even by Boris Aleksandrovich after his flight to Tver'?[62] Whatever the case, he was clearly an embarrassment to Vasily II, who seems to have been only too keen to be rid of him.

But why? In view of the contradictory nature of so much of the evidence, the only surmise that seems to be acceptable is that Vasily II, at this stage in his career – in the comparative lull in the civil war between his resumption of the throne of Moscow in 1434 and his capture by Ulug-Mehmet in 1445 – was not much concerned with the niceties of the theological debates that had taken place in Ferrara and Florence or with such matters as the commemoration of the pope before the patriarch. What he wanted was that his original choice of candidate for the metropolitan see, Bishop Iona of Ryazan', be appointed head of his Church. Indeed, it seems very probable that the synod of six bishops which Vasily II mentioned in his letter to the patriarch was convoked with the purpose not of condemning and deposing Isidor, but of persuading Constantinople to sanction Iona's election as metropolitan in his place.[63]

Why did the appointment of Iona take so long – over seven years after Isidor's departure from Moscow? In the first place, the two patriarchs of Constantinople, Metrophanes II (1440–43) and Gregory III Mammas (1443–51), both ardent supporters of the Union, as well as Emperor John VIII himself, whether or not they were aware of Moscow's wish to appoint Iona, were unlikely to welcome any replacement for Isidor. In their eyes he was still the rightful metropolitan of Russia. And, secondly, events in Russia placed insuperable

---

62. Information on his house arrest is found in the Pskov chronicles. The Tver' Chronicle says that 'he ran to Tver'' to Grand Prince Boris Aleksandrovich, [who] kept him in his presence (*poderzhav . . . u sebe*) and sent him away'. *PSRL*, vol. 15, col. 491.

63. In Lur'e's opinion, it was Archbishop Evfimy II who persuaded Vasily II to break with Isidor. As archbishop of Novgorod he had cause to fear the dangers of the Union. Lur'e also thinks that Evfimy 'sponsored' Simeon's *Tale of the Eighth Council of Florence* when he was in Novgorod after fleeing from Venice in 1439. Source: private correspondence. See, however, above, pp. 177–8 and p. 179 n. 34.

difficulties in the path of the grand prince: in 1441–42 civil war flared up again between Vasily II and his nephew Dmitry Shemyaka; in 1442–43 there were devastating outbreaks of plague, drought and famine;[64] in the winter of 1444 the Mongols again appeared on the scene in Nizhniy Novgorod and Murom; and in July 1445 the Russian armies were soundly defeated by them at the battle of Suzdal' and Vasily II was taken prisoner; later released for a vast ransom, he returned to Moscow and in February 1446 set off on an ill-judged pilgrimage to the Trinity Monastery, only to be replaced in his absence by Dmitry Shemyaka as ruler of Moscow; blinded and led off to Uglich in exile and captivity, Vasily, after swearing to recognize Shemyaka as grand prince, was dispatched to Vologda in the far north (September 1446). As the pendulum of popular support swung back in his favour, Vasily obtained absolution from his oath to Shemyaka in the White Lake Monastery of St Kirill, drew up a treaty with Boris of Tver' and, supported by numerous allies, re-entered Moscow on 17 February 1447, a year and a day after being blinded. It was virtually the end of the civil war. Dmitry Shemyaka fled to the north and after persistent harassment by government troops eventually found refuge in Novgorod, where in 1453 he was poisoned.[65]

There can be no doubt that Vasily had full confidence in the loyalty of his 'metropolitan-elect' – at any rate until 1446. In that year, at the nadir of Vasily's fortunes, Iona became involved in the machinations of Shemyaka. No sooner had Vasily been removed by force from the Trinity Monastery (13 February 1446) than his two sons, Ivan (the future Ivan III), aged 6, and Yury, aged 5, who had been with him in the monastery, managed to escape with their attendants to Yur'ev and thence to Murom. Here they found refuge with many of the grand prince's boyars and with the staunchest of his supporters, the Rya-polovskys, descendants of the princes of Starodub. Fearful lest the princes become the epicentre of opposition, Dmitry Shemyaka decided to lure them by guile from Murom. His own position was by now insecure in the extreme: 'for all the people resented his rule ... wishing to see the grand prince [i.e. Vasily] on his throne'. He therefore sent for Iona 'and promised him the metropolitanate and said to him: "Father, go to your bishopric [i.e. Ryzan' and Murom], to the town of Murom, take the children of the grand prince under

64. Zimin, *Vityaz'*, pp. 96–7.
65. For the events of the latter stages of the civil war, see Crummey, *The Formation*, pp. 73–4; Zimin, *Vityaz'*, pp. 100 ff.

your stole [i.e. as a guarantee of their safety]. And I shall be happy to care for them and I shall release their father the grand prince and I shall grant them a patrimony sufficient for their needs."' Iona went to Murom and conveyed the essence of Shemyaka's proposition to the Ryapolovskys and the grand prince's boyars, who agreed to allow Iona to 'take the children under his stole', after reflecting that refusal to entrust the children to Iona would mean that Shemyaka would come and seize the children, 'do what he likes with them, with their father the grand prince and with all of us' and capture the town of Murom. Iona then went with the children to Pereyaslavl'-Zalesskiy (6 May 1446) where Dmitry Shemyaka was awaiting them. Instead of sending them back to Moscow, he told Iona to take them still further north to Uglich where they were incarcerated with their father.[66] When he returned to Pereyaslavl', Shemyaka, keeping at least a fragment of his promise, ordered him to 'go to Moscow and sit in the court of the metropolitan'.

Not surprisingly, Shemyaka's action aroused widespread resentment in Moscow. Many of his followers abandoned him. Iona, or so we are led to believe by the chronicler, upbraided him daily:

> 'You have broken your word; you have led me into sin and shame; you should have released the [grand] prince, and yet you imprisoned his children with him. You gave me your word and they listened to me. And now I am immersed in falsehood (*a nynche yaz vo vsei lzhi*). Free him and remove this burden from my soul and from your soul . . .'[67]

As we have seen, in September 1446 Vasily II was released from Uglich. In February 1447 he returned victorious to Moscow.

It is not easy to evaluate Iona's role in the complex events of 1446–47. To start with, the narrative which is found in the chronicles derives from a grand-princely – and *not* a metropolitan – codex of the early 1470s[68] and is given entirely from the point of view of Vasily and for all its vivid detail is anything but unbiased. This is the 'grand-

---

66. The sixteenth-century L'vov Chronicle contains a curious addition to the version found in the hypothetical codex of the early 1470s (see below, p. 186 n. 69): '. . . Dmitry Yur'evich . . . sent Bishop Iona of Ryazan' to Murom . . . to fetch the sons of the grand prince . . . he went and took them, but Prince Dmitry wanted to sew them up in skins and drown them in the river Volga. But Bishop Iona prevented him, saying: "I took them on an oath by the Cross; if you transgress the Cross you will receive a greater wound from God." And he hearkened to him and did nothing to them, but sent them to Uglich . . . to their father.' *PSRL*, vol. 20, p. 260.
67. Ibid., vol. 26, p. 204.
68. Ibid., pp. 203–4; vol. 27, pp. 111–12; cf. vol. 25, pp. 266–7 (= the Moscow *svod* of 1479, which derives from the hypothetical *svod* of the early 1470s). See Lur'e, *Obshcherusskie letopisi*, pp. 147–9.

princely' view of what happened – indeed, the preceding description
of Vasily's overthrow and blinding in February 1446 appears for all
the world to be Vasily's own reminiscences dictated by him to his
chronicler at a later date.[69] The picture we are given here of Iona is
hardly a flattering one: he does what Shemyaka tells him to do; he
guarantees the safety of the children, yet delivers them to Vasily's
gaolers in Uglich; no mention is made of any force being used to
oblige Iona to break his guarantee of the children's safety – so much
then for the surety of the stole! – and when Shemyaka orders him 'to
go to Moscow and sit in the court of the metropolitan', Iona obeys
him. Only when Shemyaka's supporters begin to leave him 'on behalf
of the grand prince' and only when Shemyaka himself, realizing at last
the frailty of his situation, begins to consult 'the bishops and the
boyars' on the advisability of releasing the grand prince – only then is
Iona portrayed by the chronicler in a positive light as he berates
Shemyaka for his perfidy.

Although it is clear that whoever wrote the early part of the
chronicle story of Iona's relations with Shemyaka in 1446 considered
his dealings with Vasily's children as proof of his disloyalty,[70] nevertheless there is fairly conclusive evidence to show that after Vasily's
return to power in February 1447 and particularly after his, Iona's,
appointment as metropolitan in December 1448, his attitude to Shemyaka, not surprisingly, approximated to the official 'grand-princely'
line of open hostility. On 29 December 1447 the senior Russian
bishops, including Iona, but excluding the bishops of Novgorod and
Tver', wrote to Shemyaka, accusing him of being 'in contact with
adherents of different faiths (*s inovertsi*), with pagans [?], with many
other lands and planning to destroy [Vasily II] and his little children
and to ruin all Orthodox Christianity'. Finally, after enumerating
further misdeeds, the bishops called on Shemyaka 'to submit to the
will of the grand prince and to repent'. They gave him twenty-three
days ('two weeks after Epiphany') to come to heel, threatening him
with excommunication should he fail to acquiesce.[71] Of course, the
initiative may not have been Iona's – he was, in spite of his rating as
'metropolitan-elect', no more than third in the list of those bishops
who signed the letter. However, no sooner had he been elected
metropolitan than he wrote to the 'Lithuanian princes, *pany*, boyars,

69. *Slovar′ knizhnikov*, vol. 2, I, p. 111.
70. The episode of the upbraiding of Shemyaka may well have been a subsequent –
and clumsy – addition to the narrative.
71. *AI*, No. 40 (quoted pp. 79, 81–2).

governors and people', not only informing them of his appointment but also warning them against Dmitry Shemyaka: 'You know, my sons, what happened because of Dmitry Yur'evich, how much evil and destruction of our land was caused and how much Christian blood was spilled.' He ended the letter by begging them to be watchful and careful, 'so that all should be for the glory of God and not for the destruction of Christianity'.[72] In one of his letters written to Archbishop Evfimy of Novgorod, roughly at the time of Shemyaka's final refuge in the city (1452–53), Iona again expresses his condemnation of Shemyaka: in spite of his demands that Shemyaka send his envoys to Moscow, expressing 'pure repentance', all that he did, Iona complains, was to 'send documents in secret and with great arrogance; but concerning his crime and his guilt – not one befitting word did he send'.[73]

Even after Shemyaka's death in 1453 Iona continued his campaign against him, forbidding any commemoration of his name in Russian monasteries. So incensed was the great Pafnuty, abbot of the Monastery of the Nativity of the Mother of God in Borovsk and lifelong admirer and friend of Shemyaka, that he 'forbade [his monks] to call Iona metropolitan'. Iona countermanded the abbot's order, but Pafnuty refused to submit. Eventually he was forgiven and reinstated. But still he 'continued commemorating Shemyaka until his death'.[74]

What, then, was Iona's true role in the last phase of the civil war? Was he disloyal to Vasily II when Shemyaka was in the ascendancy? Did he betray Vasily's trust by delivering his children to Uglich? And was he motivated in this by Shemyaka's promise of the long-awaited metropolitanate? As is so often the case with such questions, the answer will never be known unless further evidence comes to light. But there can be little doubt that even after Vasily II's return to Moscow in February 1447 both Shemyaka and his close ally Ivan of

72. *RIB*, vol. 6, No. 64, cols. 541, 542. The document appears to consist of two separate letters addressed to the Lithuanians and joined together to make one.
73. *AI*, No. 53, p. 102.
74. *Poslaniya Iosifa Volotskogo*, pp. 365–6; Zimin, *Krupnaya feodal'naya votchina*, pp. 44–5. Yet another disapprover of Iona, Vasily Fedorovich Kutuzov, one of Vasily II's boyars, refused to accept Iona's blessing as metropolitan because of his 'lack of trust (*neverie*)' in him. As a result of his refusal, so we are told in the late sixteenth-century *Stepennaya kniga*, Kutuzov, while in the cathedral of the Dormition in Moscow, was afflicted with a violent toothache. He was summoned by Iona, who gave him a *prosfora*, lectured him and then suddenly struck him on the cheek. Vasily 'cried out, "O woe is me, he has destroyed my last teeth!"', but his toothache disappeared and he went home, 'glorifying God and His Saint, the great bishop Iona' (*PSRL*, vol. 21, p. 514). Iona was canonized locally in 1472 and fully in 1547.

Mozhaysk still relied on him as a possible guarantor of their safety; for at the beginning of June 1447 a document was drawn up by them, investigating the possibility of their being received by 'the grand prince, our elder brother . . . with love and a treaty (*v lyubov' i v dokonchanie*)' and including the clause: '[the grand prince] should not order us to go to him until in our land our father [i.e. Iona] shall be metropolitan'.[75]

Perhaps the most generous explanation of Iona's activities is that in the critical months of 1446 he had little choice of action. With Vasily blinded and a prisoner in Uglich, with the fortunes of the civil war swinging temporarily once again in Shemyaka's favour, had he any alternative but to do what Shemyaka told him to do? And perhaps modern scholars are over-harsh in the accusations of duplicity and treachery they level at him. Lur'e, for example, talks of Iona's 'evident link with the appanage princes of Galich', of which, according to his *Life*, he was a native,[76] of his 'peculiar intermediary position between the two warring princes' and of his 'betrayal' of Shemyaka in the autumn of 1447;[77] while Zimin describes him as 'breaking his oath on the Cross and surrendering Vasily II's children to Shemyaka for the promise of appointment to the metropolitanate', and then, after Vasily's fourth and final assumption of power, of 'serving Vasily II in faith and in truth'. To this he adds the rider: 'The strong of this world love adherents of a dubious reputation; for they are the ones who always strive to be dedicated to power.'[78]

Iona was at last elevated to the rank of metropolitan on 15 December 1448. The appointment took place in Moscow. Four bishops (Efrem of Rostov,[79] Avraamy of Suzdal', Varlaam of Kolomna and Pitirim of Perm') elected him. The archbishop of Novgorod and the bishop of Tver' were not present; they merely sent 'documents agreeing to his appointment'. No reference was made either by the synod of bishops or by the grand prince to Constantinople. The Church of Moscow, Kiev and all Russia – including the dioceses of the Lithuanians and of Little Russia – had become autocephalous.

---

75. *A kn(ya)zyu velikomu . . . ne veleti . . . nam k sobe ekhati, dokole u nas v zemle o(t)ets' nash', mitropolit.* DDG, No. 46, p. 141; see Cherepnin, *RFA*, p. 141.

76. *Dve istorii*, pp. 107–8, § 8.3

77. *Slovar' knizhnikov*, vol. 2, I, p. 423.

78. *Vityaz'*, p. 207.

79. At his enthronement Iona transferred Efrem's bishopric into an archbishopric, 'since Feodor had previously been archbishop' (see above, p. 157, for Abbot Fedor's appointment by Pimen). *PSRL*, vol. 26, p. 208.

CHAPTER FIFTEEN

The Russian Church and the Mongols, 1237–1448

1

While in the early stages of the Kipchak Horde the Mongols kept strict control over the political activities of the Russian princes and their lay subjects (see above, pp. 119–20), their attitude to the Church was strikingly different – one of tolerance and protection. Coming as they did from Mongolia, where they had lived in close contact with established faiths – Christianity (mainly Nestorian), Manicheism, Buddhism, Islam – they held priests and holy men in esteem. Indeed, Chinghis Khan in his Great Yasa, the unrecorded collection of Mongol laws, had laid down that all religions were to be respected equally and that no preference was to be shown to any one of them.[1] The thirteenth-century khans of the Kipchak Horde based on Saray were all, with one exception, benevolent pagans who considered that all religions were equally true, linking all people with one God; and the one non-pagan, Berke (1256–66), who accepted Islam, was singularly lacking in aggression towards Christianity. Like the Polovtsians before them, many of the khans had Christian wives – Nogay, Mangu Temir, Tokhta and Uzbeg – while Uzbeg's sister was married to Yury, prince of Moscow and grand prince of Vladimir.

What did the tolerance shown by the khans to the Russian Church amount to? It goes without saying that deliberate persecution of the Church, interference in its internal administration and seizure of its property were prohibited, or at any rate not practised. There were, of

---

1. On the Great Yasa, see Vernadsky, *The Mongols*, pp. 99–110; Okhotina, 'Russkaya Tserkov'', pp. 70–1.

course, infringements, but they were on the whole fortuitous, perhaps even accidental exceptions to the rule. There were no demonstrable cases of Mongol meddling in senior appointments within the Church in the period under consideration, no known attempts to remove unfriendly or uncooperative hierarchs, or to promote friendly candidates for the prelacy. But above all the khans saw to it that the Church benefited economically from their protection by exempting the clergy from Mongol taxation and by protecting Church property from lay interference, whether Mongol or Russian.

In order to get an idea of the nature of the privileges granted by the khans to the metropolitans and via them to the Church, we must consider for a moment the *yarlyki* or patents, charters of privilege, issued to the metropolitans by the Horde. Six of these have survived in translations into Russian made in the fourteenth century and collected together at the end of the fourteenth or the beginning of the fifteenth century, dating from the earliest, that of Mangu Temir (1 August 1267), to Tyulak's (1379). The collection is by no means complete and it is estimated that at least five are missing, including two preceding that of Mangu Temir,[2] which actually mentions 'the last [i.e. previous] khans bestowing privileges on priests and monks ... and we have not altered their charters'. The reason for this incompleteness is given in a concluding note appended to the collection which states that 'there are many other *yarlyki* which were transmitted to the Church ... by those godless khans' and that of all of the *yarlyki* found in the archives of the metropolitanate 'some we were not able to translate because they were written in a language difficult to interpret'.[3]

The earliest *yarlyki*, that is to say Mangu Temir's and its predecessors, simply enumerate the privileges granted to the Church which the khans' officials (*'baskaki*, princes, army commanders (*pol"chnym knyazem*), tribute collectors, clerks ...') were obliged to observe. These consisted of freedom from 'tribute, customs tax, plough tax [tax on tilled land], *yam* [upkeep of Mongol staging-posts], war tax (*voyna*) [tax in lieu of provision of recruits for Mongol armies], provision of food (*korm*) ...'. Furthermore, the Church's possessions – 'land, water, orchards, vines, mills ...' – were not to be interfered with, and 'anything that was seized they were to give back'. As for 'artisans,

2. In the name of Baty or his son Sartak or his grandson Ulagchi, or, most likely, his brother Berke (1258–66). See Pliguzov and Khoroshkevich, 'Russkaya tserkov'', pp. 89–92. The charters are printed in *PRP*, vol. 3, pp. 465–71.

3. *PRP*, vol. 3, p. 471.

falconers, huntsmen' in the employ of the Church, they were 'not to be touched and not to be kept under guard'. Anyone blaspheming the clergy's faith was to be condemned and put to death. The generosity of the khans even extended to the brothers and sisters of priests, provided they were still dependent upon the priests for food and domicile: they were to enjoy exactly the same privileges. Needless to say, Mangu Temir – and presumably his predecessors – expected some return for their bounty from the metropolitans and the clergy. And yet all they asked for sounds innocuous enough – prayers and blessing: 'that with true heart they pray to God for us and for our race and bless us'.[4]

The remaining five *yarlyki* of the collection, some of which refer to previous non-extant charters (for example, Khan Tokhta's to Metropolitan Petr, which can be dated 12 April 1308), add little to the provisions of Mangu Temir's, although some of the privileges are added to and the number of Mongol officials forbidden to transgress them is increased or specified (for example, 'commanders of 10,000, 1000, 100 and 10', 'senior treasury officers (*darogi*)').[5]

In later years the *yarlyki* were to acquire greater and greater significance in the eyes of the Church hierarchy: the original charters were expanded and clauses were added; even a spurious *yarlyk* – from Khan Uzbeg to Metropolitan Petr – was fabricated. The aim, of course, was to protect the Church's right to landownership and to use the charters as moral justification. In the mid-sixteenth century we find Metropolitan Makary, in an effort to avert secularization of part of his lands, reminding Ivan IV that 'many ... of the impious tsars [i.e. khans] ... took naught from the holy churches and from the holy monasteries, nor did they dare to move things immovable ... but they gave their *yarlyki* to the holy metropolitans ... forbidding anyone to offend or to remove [the monasteries and the churches] to the end of their reign'. After enumerating extant *yarlyki*, with a special mention of Uzbeg's to Petr, Makary exclaims: 'How much more is it befitting for you ... O tsar ... to show great assiduousness towards the holy churches and monasteries! You should not only not remove their immovable possessions, but you yourself should give them the same.'[6] It seems more than likely that Makary and others like him who so valiantly defended the inviolability of their rights and their

4. Ibid., pp. 467–8.
5. Ibid., p. 470.
6. *LRD*, pp. 129–36.

lands from the greedy State were inspired in the first place by the original short collection of translated *yarlyki*. For there they read: 'the holy Church, right up to the present day, has received favour (*milost'*) from the unbelievers and the pagans. But strive, O Orthodox princes and boyars, to show charity to the holy churches so that you may not be put to shame on the day of judgement by those barbarians. For as the Lord said in the Gospel: "The queen of the south shall rise up in the judgement with this generation, and shall condemn it, for they repented not at the preaching of Jonah." '[7]

It must not be imagined, however, that the attitude of the Mongols to the Russian Church in the two hundred and six years from 1242 to 1448 was inflexible. It wasn't: it varied according to the changing political circumstances, to the idiosyncrasies of the khans and to the Church's shifting attitude to the Horde. If we assume that Mangu Temir's charter faithfully reflects the preceding charters of, say, Baty (1224–55/6) and Berke (1256–66), then we have a fairly clear idea of the khans' treatment of the Church from the establishment of the Horde in 1242 to the death of Metropolitan Kirill II in 1281. There is no evidence to show that Berke's conversion to Islam or the popular uprisings against the Mongol tax-collectors in Suzdalia of 1262[8] had any effect on Saray's relations with the Church. The only hint of anti-Christian behaviour is the curious case of the 'renegade' monk turned Moslem, Zosima, who in 1262, as the agent of one of the khan's envoys, 'caused grave offence to the Christians' and perhaps even attempted to extract taxes from the clergy.[9] But this was an isolated incident. There is nothing to show that Berke did anything to lessen Mongol support of the Church. Indeed, in 1261 Metropolitan Kirill and the Mongol authorities founded a new diocese in Saray itself by appointing one Mitrofan as its first bishop.[10] This was a move of vast importance for both the Church and the Mongols, for the bishop could be, and was, used as an ambassador not only between the metropolitan and the patriarch, but also between the khan and the emperor, as well as providing a vital source of information on Mongol affairs for the grand prince.[11]

7. *PRP*, vol. 3, p. 471. The quotation is a conflation of Matthew 12: 42, 41.
8. On the uprisings, see Fennell, *The Crisis*, pp. 119–20.
9. Ibid.
10. *PSRL*, vol. 1, col. 476. Who Mitrofan was is not known. Possibly he was previously – or even simultaneously – bishop of Southern Pereyaslavl', for in 1269, when Mitrofan took the *skhima* and retired to a monastery, 'Metropolitan [Kirill] appointed Feognost bishop of Russian [i.e. Southern] Pereyaslavl' and Saray'. *TL*, p. 330.
11. See Golubinsky, *IRTs*, vol. 2, I, pp. 41, 61.

It is hard to judge from the extant *yarlyki* to what extent Mongol privileges altered during the remainder of the thirteenth century and throughout the fourteenth. Clearly there was a charter issued by Khan Tokhta (1290–1312) to Metropolitan Petr – this is evident from the text of two of the extant *yarlyki*.[12] It confirms Petr's freedom from all dues and taxes. But there is nothing to show whether it was more or less favourable to the Church than its predecessors. Unfortunately, there are no extant *yarlyki* issued either by Uzbeg (1312–42) to Metropolitans Petr or Feognost or by Jani-Beg (1342–57) to Metropolitans Feognost or Aleksiy. However, it is likely that relations between khan and metropolitan were at a somewhat lower level during Uzbeg's and part of Jani-Beg's khanates than before: the beginning of Uzbeg's reign coincided with the strengthening of the Kipchak Horde after the ending of the lengthy struggle between the khans of Saray and the Nogay Horde;[13] and Uzbeg's conversion to Islam may well have led to initial intolerance towards his Christian subjects. As for the *yarlyki* of Uzbeg's brother and successor, Jani-Beg, in so far as their contents can be conjectured from an analysis of the charters of Uzbeg's widow Taydula (especially that of 4 February 1351 to Metropolitan Feognost), they seem to have been slightly less liberal in the protection of the Church and its employees than those of Uzbeg's precedessors.[14]

The chronicles bear vivid witness to the strained relations between khan and metropolitan at the very beginning of Jani-Beg's khanate – clear evidence of the difficulties which the Church suffered under Uzbeg's rule. In 1342, when a number of princes, including Grand Prince Semen, went to pay homage to the new khan and renew their patents, Metropolitan Feognost also went, perhaps simply to bow down to the new khan and renew his *yarlyk*, but also, according to the Novgorod Fourth Chronicle, to settle the affairs of the 'church people' (*za prichet tserkovnyi*):[15] to this the Nikon Chronicle adds: 'for the metropolitan and the bishops [had] had charters for their church people'.[16] Whatever the reason for Feognost's visit – to discuss the privileges of the 'church people', i.e. all those dependent on the Church, or just to pay his respects to the new 'tsar' and renew his

12. Berdibeg's (1357) and Tyulak's (1379). *PRP*, vol. 3, pp. 471–2, 478.

13. Pliguzov and Khoroshkevich, 'Russkaya tserkov'', pp. 93–4. On the conflict between the Kipchak and Nogay Hordes, see Fennell, *The Crisis*, pp. 144–5.

14. See Pliguzov and Khoroshkevich, 'Russkaya tserkov'', p. 94; *PRP*, vol. 3, pp. 477–8.

15. *PSRL*, vol. 4, I, p. 275.

16. Ibid., vol. 10, I, p. 215.

charter – the earliest version, that of the Novgorod First Chronicle, describes in no uncertain detail the shabby treatment meted out to the metropolitan by the Mongols:

> In that year Metropolitan Feognost went to the Horde to the pagan tsar Jani-Beg, and Kalantay falsely accused (*obadisha*) him before the khan; and he was robbed and seized and tortured, and they said: 'Give us yearly tribute (*davay dan' poletnyuyu*).' But he declined to do so and gave them bribes (*polozhi posula*) of 600 rubles and came back to Russia safe and sound.[17]

Some time after this initial display of animosity towards Metropolitan Feognost in 1342, relations between the Mongols and the Church took a turn for the better. It was symptomatic of the beginning of the decline of the Horde. Cracks in the Kipchak edifice were already evident at the end of the 1340s,[18] and by 1357, the year Jani-Beg died, the chronicles announced the beginning of the 'great troubles' (*zamyatnya velika*) which were to wrack the Horde for the next twenty-three years. In the same year Metropolitan Feognost was summoned to Saray, where he healed Uzbeg's widow Taydula of an unspecified illness[19] and returned to Moscow 'safe and sound' and, for sure, laden with gifts. The scribe who reported Jani-Beg's death even went so far as to call him 'the good khan'.[20]

By 1379, the date of the last translated *yarlyk* – Khan Tyulak's to Metropolitan Mikhail-Mityay – all the privileges of the pre-Uzbeg era had been restored to the Russian Church. But times were changing, as relations between the State and the Horde were changing. Ten years after the traumatic sack of Moscow by Tokhtamysh in 1382, Vasily I, having been given the additional patent for Nizhniy Novgorod,

---

17. *NPL*, p. 357. Kalantay was presumably a Mongol official at Jani-Beg's court. This version was copied with insignificant variants in the Novgorod Fourth Chronicle (*PSRL*, vol. 4, I, p. 275), the Ermolinskiy Chronicle (ibid., vol. 23, p. 107) and the Moscow *svod* of 1479 (ibid., vol. 25, p. 175). The version of the Nikon Chronicle has 'certain Russian people' 'slandering Metropolitan Feognost' and saying: 'he has vast revenues, gold, silver and all riches; and he should give you yearly tribute . . .' (ibid., vol. 10, p. 215). In the Tver' Rogozhskiy Chronicle, *s.a.* 1344, Feognost is reported as visiting the Horde 'for the church people' and being 'much tormented' (*mnogu istomu priyat*) by Jani-Beg – but this clearly refers to his trip to Saray in 1342 (also reported in the same chronicle but with no detail). See ibid., vol. 15, I, cols. 55, 54.

18. See Spuler, *Die Goldene Horde*, p. 107.

19. *TL*, p. 376; *PSRL*, vol. 25, p. 180; vol. 10, p. 229. The information found in the chronicles to the effect that Jani-Beg was murdered by his son and successor Berdibeg is discredited by Spuler (*Die Goldene Horde*, p. 108 n. 40).

20. *dobryy tsar'* (*PSRL*, vol. 25, p. 180). The Nikon Chronicle adds that 'Khan Jani-Beg was exceedingly good towards Christianity and gave many privileges to the land of Russia' (ibid., vol. 10, p. 229).

Gorodets, Meshchera and Tarusa and thus saddled with an increase in tribute payable to the Horde, managed to extract tax from part of the metropolitan's estates in order to contribute to the State's payment of Mongol duty. It was, as two Russian historians put it, 'the first legalization of the State taxing the Russian Church in order to pay tribute to the khan'.[21] Twelve years later Vasily I drew up an agreement with Metropolitan Kiprian which for the first time in history provided for the Church's participation in the payment of tribute to the Horde: 'Should we [the grand prince] give tribute to the Tatars, then church people (*tserkovnye lyudi*) shall pay duty; should we not give tribute, then church people too shall not pay duty.'[22]

The Church – or at any rate the metropolitan – must have been alarmed at these, the first groping attempts of grand-princely authority to infringe on the privileges bestowed upon them by the khans. Indeed, it may well be that such unprecedented action persuaded the Church to have the charters translated and to add to them the warning note: '. . . strive, O Orthodox princes and boyars, to show charity to the holy churches so that you may not be put to shame on the day of judgement by those barbarians' (see above, p. 192).

For the Russian episcopacy as well as the abbots of the ever-growing number of monasteries were only too aware of the enormous benefits accruing to them from Mongol patronage: exemption from taxation, immunity of all 'church people' and above all protection from State and Mongol interference. And yet, from 1380 onwards, if not before, they could not but have recognized that, notwithstanding the menace of Tokhtamysh (1382), Tamerlane (1395) and Edigey (1408), the end of the 'Tatar yoke' was at last foreseeable in the not too distant future and that from now on the Church must cooperate with the State in the latter's anti-Mongol policy.

2

As we have mentioned earlier, the only return the Mongols asked for in their charters was that the Russian clergy should 'with true heart pray to God for us and for our race and bless us'. That they did this there can be no doubt. In the *Narration of the Death of Metropolitan*

21. Pliguzov and Khoroshkevich, 'Russkaya tserkov'', p. 99.
22. Ibid., p. 98.

Petr, written shortly after Petr's death (December 1326) and canonization (early 1327), the Moscow-oriented author records that during his last Liturgy the metropolitan prayed for the health of the 'pious tsars [i.e. khans] and for pious Prince Ivan', as well as for 'the defunct tsars and all pious princes'.[23]

But it was not by their prayers alone that the Church recompensed the Mongols. In 1309 Vasily Romanovich, ruler of the small south-western principality of Bryansk on the upper Desna river, was ousted by his uncle Svyatoslav Glebovich. Like his father, Roman Glebovich, Vasily had ruled Bryansk in support of – and in submission to – the Kipchak Horde. His immediate action was to appeal to Khan Tokhta, who provided him with an army. Svyatoslav's rule in Bryansk was unpopular, perhaps because he was attempting a *rapprochement* with the old enemy of the principality, Lithuania. The result was an uprising. At the same time Vasily was at hand with his Mongol army. The situation was grave enough to warrant the intervention of a senior churchman. The newly appointed metropolitan, Petr, came. Who summoned him – the rebellious townsfolk, Svyatoslav or even Vasily – is not known. But he clearly took the side of Vasily and urged Svyatoslav to come to an agreement with his nephew or leave without a struggle. Svyatoslav refused to listen. He was killed fighting, betrayed by the men of Bryansk, and Vasily, supported by the Mongols and the metropolitan, resumed control of the principality.[24]

Curiously enough, Bryansk was also the scene thirty years later of a similar incident, this time involving Petr's successor, Metropolitan Feognost. In 1333 Vasily's brother, Dmitry Romanovich of Bryansk, one of Moscow's staunchest supporters, had attacked Lithuanian-defended Smolensk with a large Mongol force. The campaign ended in defeat for Dmitry, who was replaced in Bryansk by Gleb Svyato-slavich, Svyatoslav Glebovich's son. Gleb's policy, like that of his father, was oriented towards Lithuania: no troops from Bryansk took part in the Russo-Mongol campaign against Lithuanian-held Smolensk in 1339. The population of Bryansk, like their fathers thirty years earlier, had no love for Lithuania, and on 6 December 1340 'assembled a *veche* and slew Prince Gleb Svyatoslavich'.[25] Metropolitan Feognost, who had been summoned perhaps by Gleb's opponents, is described in the chronicles as being unable to pacify the populace. What else he did

23. See Kuchkin, '"Skazanie"', p. 77. 'Pious' as an epithet for the khans is odd, to say the least of it; it may be a later interpolation.
24. *PSRL*, vol. 10, p. 177; *TL*, pp. 353–4.
25. *TL*, p. 364; *PSRL*, vol. 15, I, col. 53.

is not stated. But no doubt he attempted to do what Petr had done under similar circumstances – persuade the prince to toe the Moscow line. Much to Semen's and the khan's satisfaction, Dmitry Roman-ovich was once again installed on the throne of Bryansk.[26]

3

The prayers of the metropolitans and the occasional support of the grand-princely line of non-resistance to, or indeed compliance with, the Mongols were not the only ways in which the Church proved useful to the secular powers and repaid the Horde for its protection. Ideologically, too, the Church was able subtly to influence public opinion concerning the Mongols by its careful handling of the written word.

A scrutiny of the literature of the age, the majority of which we can assume was produced if not by clerics then at any rate by those working in close cooperation with the Church, reveals certain unmis-takable trends. Again and again, in chronicle entries, military tales or hagiographical narratives, we find a tendency to portray the Mongols not as evil-doers, not as anti-Christian, not even, at times, as the enemies of the Russians. Of course, this does not mean that all references to Mongol activities in north-east Russia or at the Horde portrayed the khans and their various agents as benevolent. They did not. As we have seen, the Novgorod chronicler describes the 'accursed' census officials in 1259 as 'wild beasts from the desert', brought by God 'to eat the flesh of the strong and drink the blood of the boyars' (see above, p. 124). And in the troubled years of the internecine war at the end of the thirteenth century, when Russian princes blatantly used Mongol troops to further their own political ends, we find the chroniclers lamenting the sufferings wrought by the 'pagan Tatars'. For instance, in 1293, 'Dyuden''s campaign', as it was called, the great Mongol incursion inspired and led by Aleksandr Nevskiy's son Andrey against his elder brother Dmitry, is described in the Trinity Chronicle with all the available disaster clichés known to the Russians from the chronicles of the eleventh and twelfth centuries: 'they took [the city of] Vladimir and despoiled the church [of the Dormition of the Mother of God] and tore up the wondrous bronze floor, and they

26. See Fennell, *The Emergence*, pp. 201–3.

plundered books, icons, miracle-working Crosses, holy vessels . . .
they laid waste villages . . . monasteries; they humiliated monks and
ravished priests' wives . . .'[27] But this and most other descriptions of
Mongol monstrosities occurring in the unhappy last two decades of
the thirteenth century were written from the point of view of a
champion of Aleksandr Nevskiy's eldest son Dmitry, against whom
the devastating raids were directed. The animosity is directed against
Andrey and represents not so much a condemnation of the Mongols as
an indictment of the *Russian* prince.

At the end of the chronicle entry under the year 1281 describing
Andrey's first irruption into Suzdalia with a Mongol army, the scribe
rounds off his tale of woe and suffering caused by the pagans with the
words: 'this evil happened because of our many and great sins'.[28] In
The Tale of the Battle of the River Kalka, which described the first clash
of the Russians with the Mongols in 1223, this concept of divine
retribution is prominently expressed. The *Tale* in fact begins with the
well-worn cliché: 'Because of our sins there came unknown
people . . .', and ends on precisely the same note: 'And so for our sins
(*za grekhy nasha*) God brought confusion upon us and a great multitude
of people perished.' At the same time the 'godless sons of Ishmael' and
the 'accursed' Polovtsians, who are portrayed as the real villains of the
piece, are *themselves* punished for their sins against the Christian
Russians. At the end of his introduction to the story the author is
quite explicit: 'and they [the Polovtsians] died, *killed by the wrath of
God and of His most pure Mother*, for those accursed Polovtsians did
much evil to the land of Rus', and for this reason all-merciful God
wished to destroy the Cumans [i.e. the Polovtsians], the godless sons
of Ishmael, in order to avenge Christian blood.' And when the
Mongol envoys arrive to inform the Russians that they are fighting
the Polovtsians and to urge the Russians to make peace, they are made
to say to the Russians: 'We have come, *sent by God*, against our slaves
and grooms, the pagan Polovtsians.'[29]

Much the same attitude to the Mongols is found in the *Life* of
Aleksandr Nevskiy, written in all probability by Metropolitan Kirill II
in the early 1280s. Here the Mongols appear in anything but an
unfavourable light. At the beginning of the description of Aleksandr's

27. TL, p. 346. Cf. also the descriptions of Andrey's use of Mongol troops in 1281,
1282 and 1285 (*TL*, pp. 338–9, 339; *NPL*, pp. 325–6).
28. TL, p. 339.
29. NPL, pp. 61–3, 264–7. On the *Tale*, see Fennell and Stokes, *Early Russian Literature*, pp. 81–8.

first visit to the Horde, Khan Baty is portrayed as follows: 'There was at that time a certain powerful tsar in the eastern land, to whom *God had subjected* many peoples.' As if to stress the divine role of the Mongols still further, Baty's envoys are made to say to Aleksandr, 'O Aleksandr, do you know that God has subjected many peoples to me?', while Baty himself, in his encounter with Aleksandr, is described in almost chivalric terms. There are none of the derogatory epithets – 'foul', 'thrice-accursed', 'evil', etc. – which in later literature were fastened to the Mongols. The 'tsar' and the Mongols are viewed as some sort of benevolent force in the background, just as they were in the description of the battle on the Kalka river.[30]

The many Mongol punitive expeditions which were sent against various Suzdalian districts in the first half of the fourteenth century are treated dispassionately, coolly and objectively by the contemporary chroniclers, and their raids are seldom described in terms more lurid or emotive than the conventional: 'they did much evil, harm, caused much suffering',[31] nor are the perpetrators given anything but the stock epithets: 'fierce' or 'evil'. They are there, in the background, ready to enter the scene when summoned and to redress 'wrongs' committed by the erring Russians. In a way, of course, this is a reflection of what Eremin[32] has called the traditional medieval Russian philosophy of history, the traditional attitude towards disaster and catastrophes as found in the eleventh- and twelfth-century chronicles: the earliest chroniclers tend to explain away major national diasters as the result of God's wrath at the sins of the people, His punishment for the evil done by this or that prince. Heathen invaders are looked upon as 'God's scourge' (*batog Bozhiy*), and phrases like 'God punishes us with the invasion of the heathens, for this is His scourge' (*kaznit ny Bog nakhozheniem poganykh: se bo est' batog Ego*) occur frequently in the early chronicles.

In the first half of the fourteenth century, however, the Mongols were not regarded by the churchmen merely as a stick to beat errant Christians with. They are time and again depicted, as it were, with God on their side, working in cooperation with Him as His agent. More than once the words 'rewarded by God and the tsar' (*pozhalovan Bogom i tsarem*) are used to describe a prince, particularly a prince of

---

30. On the *Life* of Aleksandr Nevskiy, see ibid., pp. 107–21.

31. See, for instance, *s.a.* 1315, 1316, 1318 (*PSRL*, vol. 1, col. 529); 1321 (ibid., vol. 10, p. 187; vol. 15, I, col. 41); 1322 (ibid., vol. 10, p. 188; vol. 18, p. 89; vol. 25, p. 163); 1325 (*NPL*, pp. 97, 340; *PSRL*, vol. 25, p. 167); 1338 (ibid., vol. 15, I, col. 48).

32. Eremin, 'Povest'', pp. 51 ff., 64 ff.

Moscow, returning from the Horde.[33] In 1339, for instance, Aleksandr Mikhaylovich of Tver', who had been grand prince of Vladimir from September 1326 to August 1327, met a wretched death at the Horde; the Muscovite chronicler, after drily recording his execution and that of his son, emphasizes the triumphant return from Saray of the princes of Moscow: 'On 28 October Prince Aleksandr Mikhaylovich of Tver' and his son Prince Fedor were killed at the Horde and their bodies were cut to pieces; *but* Prince Semen and his two brothers were sent back to Rus' *with love*, and they arrived in Rus' from the Horde *favoured by God and the khan.*'[34]

There is no lack of examples of the tendency of the chroniclers to exculpate the Mongols in their dealings with the Russians and to portray them at times in a chivalrous light reminiscent of the depiction of Baty in the *Life* of Aleksandr Nevskiy. When, for example, in 1325 Dmitry Mikhaylovich of Tver' murdered Yury of Moscow at the Horde 'without the khan's permission' (*bez tsareva slova*), Uzbeg's righteous indignation and disapproval is stressed by one of the chroniclers: Dmitry is placed 'in great disgrace' and orders are given to convey Yury's corpse to Russia and 'bury him in his patrimony Moscow'.[35] In the following year, 'Khan Uzbeg ordered Prince Dmitry . . . to be put to death for [his execution of] Grand Prince Yury . . .' The khan's behaviour is explained by the fact that he was 'exceedingly angry with all the princes of Tver''.[36] Such transparently spurious motivation, whether indicative of the chronicler's ignorance or deliberate concealment of the facts, clearly reveals his unwillingness to allow any moral censure to fall on the Mongols. The fault, as the chronicler would have us believe, is on the side of the Russians.

Again, take the story of the events leading up to the execution of Aleksandr Mikhaylovich of Tver' in 1339. A sober investigation of all the known facts makes it quite clear that Aleksandr was deliberately removed from the political scene by the khan, aided and abetted by Ivan I of Moscow.[37] Yet only the relatively neutral and objective

---

33. e.g. *s.a.* 1329 (twice) (*TL*, pp. 362–3); 1344 (*PSRL*, vol. 15, I, col. 56; *TL*, p. 367). Cf. 1334 (*PSRL*, vol. 10, p. 206); 1336 (ibid., vol. 15, I, col. 47).

34. *TL*, p. 363. In one of the accounts of the murder of Aleksandr's father Mikhail (*Ubienie velikago knyazya Mikhaila Yaroslavicha*), the latter is made to say to Yury of Moscow in 1317: 'O my dear cousin, if God and the khan gave you the grand principality, then I yield it to you (*Brate, yazhe tebe dal Bog i tsar' knyazhenie velikoe, to az otstupayu tebe*)' – *Otdel rukopisey Rossiyskoy Gosudarstvennoy Biblioteki, Troitskoe sobranie*, No. 671, fo. 115v.

35. *PSRL*, vol. 10, p. 189.

36. Ibid., p. 190.

37. See Fennell, *The Emergence*, pp. 167 ff.

Novgorod First Chronicle distributes the blame where it should be – between Uzbeg and Ivan.[38] The Moscow account makes no mention of who killed Aleksandr, and the reader is left to guess the identity of the murderer; while the Tver' version – fearing Moscow censorship – carefully avoids any implication of Ivan and removes all guilt from Uzbeg. Indeed, when describing the confrontation between Aleksandr and Uzbeg in 1337, the Tverite chronicler makes Aleksandr confess his readiness to die for the sins he has committed against Uzbeg and the latter magnanimously spares his life and restores him to his principality.[39] The scene is expanded and embellished in the later version of the Nikon Chronicle: 'And Khan Uzbeg was amazed at the sweetness of his words and his humility, and he said to his princes: "See how Prince Aleksandr Mikhaylovich of Tver' has saved himself from death by his humble wisdom!"'[40] When in the following year Uzbeg decides to summon Aleksandr once more to the Horde, the chronicler resorts to that well-worn hagiographical topos – Satanic provocation: responsibility is shifted to the 'all-cunning evil counsellor, the Devil', who urges unspecified 'lawless people' to lay false accusations against Aleksandr before the khan.[41]

A striking example of the general attitude of the early fourteenth-century ecclesiastical writers to the Mongols is found in the various accounts of the execution of Mikhail Yaroslavich of Tver' in 1317–18.[42] If they are stripped of later accretions such as prayers, apostrophes, biblical quotations, monologues, dialogues and emotional epithets, we are left with a factual, objective account of Mikhail's trial and execution. Mikhail is tried and found guilty on three specifically stated and entirely plausible charges. Neither Khan Uzbeg nor his *posol* Kavgady (later to be decorated with such standard epithets as 'accursed', 'lawless', 'impious', etc.) are shown as fulfilling more than their normal functions as supreme ruler and judge on the one hand and chief witness-cum-prosecutor on the other. Indeed, when Mikhail arrives at

38. Ibid., p. 167; *NPL*, pp. 349–50.
39. *PSRL*, vol. 15, I, col. 48.
40. Ibid., vol. 10, pp. 207–8.
41. Ibid., vol. 15, I, cols. 48–9. This time the Nikon Chronicle merely states that 'certain people slandered Prince Aleksandr . . . before Khan Uzbeg'. As the previous sentence but one mentions Ivan's arrival at the Horde, there can be little doubt who the 'certain people' were. Ibid., vol. 10, p. 208.
42. For the basic manuscript version of the Tale, see above, p. 200 n. 34 (abbr. *Ubienie*); the version of the Sofiyskiy First Chronicle (*PSRL*, vol. 5, pp. 207–15) is close to this. See Fennell, 'The Ermolinskij Chronicle', pp. 33–8; idem, 'Princely Executions'.

the Horde, Uzbeg is reported as behaving with extreme correctness: he provides him with an escort, 'which allows no one to offend him';[43] while after the execution Kavgady is made to rebuke Yury Danilovich for not paying sufficient respect to Mikhail's naked corpse: 'Kavgady seeing his naked body cast on the ground said with wrath to Prince Yury: "Is not your elder brother the same as your father? Why does his body lie naked cast on the ground?"'[44] The real enemies, we are given to believe, are not the Mongols: it was a Russian, we are told, who committed the murder ('by the name of Romanets');[45] Mongols *and* Russians plunder Mikhail's tent;[46] and even Mikhail's own boyars are described as 'unmerciful' in their treatment of the pious merchants who met the funeral cortège on its way back to Russia.[47]

In 1327, in the last days of Aleksandr Mikhaylovich's brief 'rule' as grand prince, Uzbeg suddenly sent a Mongol army under his cousin Chol-Khan to Tver'. After the inhabitants of Tver' had been subjected to considerable provocation and persecution, they rose up in revolt and slaughtered Chol-Khan, his troops and all the Mongol merchants in the town. The various accounts of the massacre of the Mongols and of the subsequent bloody Mongol reprisals afford a vivid example of this passive, almost benevolent, attitude towards the Mongols, even when they are portrayed in what was a purely aggressive role. All three main versions of the chronicle account – the Tver', Novgorod and Moscow versions – reveal an astonishingly neutral attitude. None show the Mongols as anything but a sort of impartial punishing force, sent by God (*pushcheniem Bozhiem*) because of the sins of the Russians (*mnozhestva radi grekh nashikh*). Such sentiments might be understandable coming from the pen of a Muscovite; but for a Tverite cleric to show no animosity whatsoever towards the enemy who had virtually destroyed the principality of Tver' is little short of amazing.[48]

Of course, in texts dealing with events in the first half of the fourteenth century we do find the Mongols described as vile, evil, pagan, lecherous, etc., and aggressively anti-Christian intentions are ascribed to them. But these are rarely, if at all, contemporary. In the description of Chol-Khan's mission to Tver' in 1327, for instance,

43. See *Ubienie*, fo. 133.
44. Ibid., fo. 138.
45. Ibid., fo. 137v.
46. Ibid., fo. 138.
47. Ibid., fo. 139v.
48. For a detailed study of the various sources, see Fennell, 'The Tver' Uprising'.

there is a vivid, cliché-ridden and entirely spurious scene inserted into one of the narratives in an attempt to motivate subsequent events. Chol-Khan, 'the wicked, accursed instigator of all evil, the destroyer of Christians', is made to say to Uzbeg: 'O master tsar, if you order me I shall go to Rus' and destroy Christianity, and I shall kill their princes and bring their princesses and children to you.'[49] Another version has Chol-Khan planning to murder all the princes of Tver', to put himself and other Mongols on all the Russian thrones and to convert the entire population to Islam.[50] On closer examination it will be found that these evil attributes, these wicked (and highly improbable) intentions, these repetitive clichés are nearly all later interpolations, inserted towards the middle of the fifteenth century, when the attitude of churchmen towards the Mongols was very different from what it was during the first half of the fourteenth century.

4

If we look at the contemporary and near-contemporary Russian chronicles from as early as the 1350s we find that the tone has changed. Gone is the exculpation of the deeds of the Mongols, the chivalrous examples of the khans, the portrayal of their magnanimity. No longer do the scribes eschew moral censure of the Mongols and no longer are the princes 'favoured by God *and the khan*' as they return from their visits to the Horde.[51] The Mongols are now painted with the blackest of colours and an abundance of derogatory epithets: 'accursed pagan Moslems', 'godless Ishmaelites', 'devilish, impious sons of Hagar', and so on and so on. In the place of chivalry and magnanimity we find deceit, treachery and dishonesty. Of course, God still punishes them for their sins with inroads of the heathen, as well as with pestilence and conflagrations.[52] It is by Him that the fleeing – or merely withdrawing – Mongols are pursued: when the mighty Tamerlane ('the accursed and godless Temir Aksak') suddenly left the borders of Ryazan' in 1395, 'it was not we that chased them,

49. *PSRL*, vol. 15, I, cols. 42–3.
50. See *PSRL*, vol. 25, p. 168.
51. Cf., however, *PSRL*, vol. 15, I, col. 164, where *s.a.* 1396 Vasily I is described as returning to Moscow and 'seated [on the throne] by God and the khan [Tokhtamysh]'.
52. e.g. *PSRL*, vol. 15, I, col. 76 (pestilence – 1364); col. 97 (conflagrations).

but merciful God that drove them away by His invisible power',[53] just as He 'scared the sons of Hagar by His invisible power' at the battle of Kulikovo in 1380[54] and Bulak Temir after his defeat on the river P'ana (1367) 'fled to the Horde, chased by the wrath of God'.[55] In the introduction to *The Tale of the Invasion of Edigey* (1408), the writer explains away the cunning and deceit of the 'wolflike sons of Hagar' by 'God punishing us and visiting our transgressions with his staff'.[56]

A new spirit was abroad. It seems as though the Church's voice, as far as its mitigation of the Mongols' motives is concerned, had indeed become muted. God may punish the Russians for their various sins by inflicting on them a Tokhtamysh, a Tamerlane and an Edigey, but now the times have changed and there is no longer any need to show that God is on the side of the enemy.

---

53. Ibid., vol. 15 (1st edn.), col. 454.
54. Ibid., vol. 15, I, col. 139; *TL*, p. 420.
55. *PSRL*, vol. 15, I, col. 85.
56. Ibid., col. 178. See Lur'e, 'Povest' o nashestvii Edigeya', in *Slovar' knizhnikov*, vol. 2, II, pp. 197–201.

CHAPTER SIXTEEN

Landownership by the Church and the Monasteries

1

In the second half of the fifteenth century and during much of the sixteenth the question of Church landownership was to play an increasingly large role in Russian society. Within the Church itself there were those who defended the Church's right to own land and those who claimed that monastic landed possessions could and did lead to the corruption of the monasteries and the 'downfall of monks'. But as well as being divided by the so-called conflict between the 'Possessors' and the 'Non-Possessors', the Russian Church was also to find itself under bitter attack from the State. The huge lands amassed by the monasteries and by the metropolitans and bishops whetted the appetite of the land-hungry grand princes.

How came it that the monasteries and the prelates acquired their vast estates? Let us consider first of all the monasteries. As we have seen, there is little written evidence to show that in the pre-Mongol period the monasteries were endowed with immovable property. There can of course be little doubt that the majority of them, like the Kievan Monastery of the Caves, did in fact acquire lands by divers means to prop up their economy. But the true growth of monastic – and to a lesser extent episcopal – landownership took place in the fourteenth and fifteenth centuries, as did the expansion and spread of the monasteries themselves.

Monasteries in Russia increased in size and number, first and foremost as the result of the Mongol invasion and the overall control exercised by the Kipchak Horde, as well as of the interminable, destructive and seemingly pointless civil wars and power-struggles which rent Russia in the last quarter of the thirteenth and the first quarter of the fourteenth centuries. For not only did men and women turn to the spiritual life and the discipline of the monasteries in order to escape the intolerable stress of everyday existence, but many fled to their shelter simply in order to avoid death or capture in warfare. There were of course innumerable other, purely temporal, reasons for the influx of laymen into monastic life: to escape, for instance, the frequent outbreaks of the plague which caused such havoc amongst the population of Russia during the fourteenth century – in many cases the monasteries were the only places where any sort of medical care could be provided; to opt out of lay life, failed careers, disgrace, family obligations; to side-step the law, the multiple dues and taxes, to avoid conscription in the Mongol forces. Often, too, it was simply the reputation of the abbot – his sanctity and sometimes his acquisitiveness – that attracted new recruits to the community. But, above all, the monasteries for many afforded a haven of safety and a guarantee of protection from outside interference, whether it came from the State or from the infidels. Once within the walls of the monastery, the neophyte knew he or she was safe. The outside world was no longer a menace. Furthermore, it should be pointed out that the choice of monastic life did not necessarily entail tonsure. According to the *Life* of St Sergy of Radonezh, for example, the new inmate of the Trinity Monastery, even if he begged the abbot to tonsure him, was first 'ordered to don the long cassock of black cloth and to spend sufficient time with the [other] brethren until he learned all the rules of the monastery'. Only then would Sergy 'clothe him in the monkish habit as one who has been tested in all things, and having tonsured him would invest him with both mantle and cowl (*klobuk*). And if by his purity of life he excelled in his calling, then he [Sergy] would permit such a one to accept the [supreme tonsure, the] holy *skhima*.'[1]

The growth of the monastic fraternity led to the increase in the number of monasteries. Monasteries begat monasteries. Monks would leave their communities, sometimes singly, sometimes in groups, sometimes as the result of a dispute with the abbot, through dissatisfaction at the strictness – or the laxity – of the rule. Sometimes monks left simply to find peace in hermitages of their own making. At the same time princes and wealthy laymen, anxious to leave a memorial to their names or to found a house where their kin could be buried and prayed for in perpetuity, used their wealth to create ever new communities on their lands.

---

1. *PLDR, XIV–seredina XV v.*, p. 338.

The most remarkable example in the fourteenth and fifteenth centuries of the spread of monasticism from one mother foundation is without any doubt the multiplication of monastic houses issuing from St Sergy Radonezh's Trinity Monastery. In 1337 Varfolomey (Bartholomew) Kirillovich, the son of an impoverished Rostov boyar whose family moved to the village of Radonezh 47 versts to the north–north–west of Moscow, established a hermitage in the neighbourhood and, in the early 1340s, took the tonsure under the name of Sergy. Some ten years or more later, after a number of brethren had joined the hermitage, Sergy was ordained priest and made abbot (*igumen*). The Trinity Monastery, as the foundation was then known from the name of its first church, attracted more and more inmates and grew in renown. Eventually, at the request of Patriarch Philotheus and Metropolitan Aleksiy, Sergy, like his predecessor Abbot Feodosy (see above, p. 67), established the coenobitical rule in his monastery.

Many of Sergy's disciples and close associates followed his example and set off in search of remote sites for their own hermitages, often in the desolate far north of the country where conditions were harshest. Again, like Sergy himself, they attracted brethren who settled in cells and formed small communities. These in their turn grew into monasteries. And so the great spread of hermitages grew from the seed sown by Sergy. At the same time monks from the Trinity Monastery set off to towns – Kolomna, Serpukhov, Zvenigorod and, above all, Moscow – and founded their own houses, which again became the starting points for the establishment of yet more monasteries. Precise numbers are hard to substantiate, but the great Russian historian Klyuchevsky estimated that in the fourteenth and fifteenth centuries as many as twenty-seven hermitages and eight town monasteries sprung from Sergy's Trinity Monastery and its offshoots.[2]

Four years after Sergy's death in 1392 Kirill, the ex-abbot of the Simonov Monastery, set off to the White Lake district (Beloozero) and, some 600 versts north-east of Novgorod, founded a hermitage which was later to grow into the greatest of the northern monasteries of Russia and the centre of monastic colonization in the forests of the north in the fifteenth and sixteenth centuries. His travelling companion Ferapont found conditions too austere and set up his own hermitage 15 versts away, which in turn became one of the major monasteries of the north (the Ferapontov Monastery). Kirill was soon joined by local

---

2. Klyuchevsky, *Sochineniya*, p. 249.

peasants and by monks from the Simonov Monastery, and his hermitage grew into a coenobitic monastery. Kirill insisted on stringent observance of the rule, which was based on that of the Simonov Monastery. According to his *Life*, written in 1462 by Pakhomy the Serb, who visited the monastery some time after Kirill's death in 1427 and used as his informants two of Kirill's close followers, Abbot Kassian and Martinian (later himself abbot of the Ferapontov and Trinity Monasteries), life in the monastery was harsh: monks were not even allowed drinking water in their cells; mead and wine were strictly forbidden in the refectory; monks were not allowed to approach outsiders for alms; and Kirill himself is alleged to have expressed strong views on the evils of monastic landownership. Kirill's reputation was such that not only was he canonized some twenty years after his death but his monastery bore his own name (the Kirillo-Belozerskiy Monastery) rather than that of its church (the Dormition of the Mother of God).[3]

Many of the monasteries which sprung up in the lands north of the Volga in the fifteenth century had close connections with the Kirillo-Belozerskiy, if they did not owe their origins to Kirill himself. Ferapont's monastery in the fifteenth century became a magnet for anchorites whose huts and caves proliferated in the neighbourhood. Further south, the heavily forested districts of Vologda and Kostroma attracted innumerable hermits, some of whom lived in total isolation. St Pavel Obnorskiy (Pavel of the Obnora river district), for example, lived, so we are told in his *Life*, for several years in the hollow of a lime-tree before building himself a cell, which in its turn attracted brethren and became a strictly coenobitic monastery (the Pavlo-Obnorskiy Monastery).[4]

To the south-east of Kirill's monastery, on a rocky island near the eastern shore of Lake Kubena (Ozero Kubenskoe) lay the thirteenth-century Spaso-Kamennyy Monastery, the first known abbot of which, Dionisy, came from Mount Athos during the reign of Dmitry Donskoy. Numerous monastic colonies were founded in the area of Lake Kubena by his disciples, notably by St Dionisy Glushitskiy (died 1437, canonized 1547), who resuscitated a former monastery on the shores of the Lake and then set up a hermitage on the river Glushitsa; from it no less than seven monastic colonies were founded in the area of the

3. On St Kirill, see Borisov, *I svecha*, pp. 280 ff.; Fedotov, *Svyatye*, pp. 143 ff.; Klyuchevsky, *Drevnerusskie zhitiya*, pp. 158–61.
4. On Pavel Obnorsky, see *Slovar´ knizhnikov*, vol. 2, I, pp. 313–17.

Lake. The link between the Spaso-Kamennyy and the Kirillo-Belozerskiy Monasteries was forged in the middle of the fifteenth century,
when Abbot Kassian moved to the Spaso-Kamennyy and became its
abbot.

Still further to the north, two members of the Kirillo-Belozerskiy
Monastery established further bases for colonization and the spread of
Christianity: Aleksandr Oshevenskiy (1427–79), who founded the
Oshevenskiy Monastery in the Kargopol' area, and Savvaty, whose
name is linked with that of Zosima of the Valaam Monastery on Lake
Ladoga in the founding of the great monastery of Solovki on Solovet-
skiy Island in the White Sea.

Limitations of space unfortunately forbid further investigation of
the spread of monastic life in Russia; but it is hoped that this brief
sketch of the Trinity and Kirillo-Belozerskiy Monasteries and their
offshoots will give some idea of how monastic colonization took place
in the fourteenth and fifteenth centuries in Russia.

2

How did the monasteries in Russia acquire their landed wealth? As we
have already seen (see above, pp. 190 ff.), the Mongols did much to
protect Church property from secular – including Mongol – interference. By showing no inclination to hinder the safeguarding of monastic
land, their policy also fostered its growth. For lay landowners, enjoying no such privileges and fearing perhaps for the safety of their
estates, showed considerable generosity towards the monasteries. Their
action, needless to say, was not always disinterested: many grants were
made 'for the mentioning of the soul' (*na pomin dushi, dlya pominoveniya
dushi, v vechnyy pominok dushi*) that is to say, conditional or unconditional grants of land in exchange for which the brethren would
guarantee to pray for the donor's soul for a limited or unlimited
period after his death – sometimes even during his lifetime. This urge
to save one's soul by means of generous donations, an urge doubtless
encouraged by acquisitive abbots, was responsible for a considerable
flow of property from landowners into the hands of the monks. And
even when the initial stress of the Mongol occupation and the dangers
of inter-princely strife had quietened down, still the custom lived on.
By the beginning of the sixteenth century, Iosif, abbot of the Volokolamsk Monastery, found it necessary to write in great detail to a secular
'client' of his, Princess Maria Golenina, on the various 'remembrances'

– offices for the dead (*panikhidy*), requiem litanies (*zaupokoynye ekten'i*), etc. – performed by his monastery in return for land, cash or divers gifts, and he was careful to point out that 'everybody knows, and you know too, that a priest never serves a single liturgy or a memorial service (*panufida* – i.e. *panikhida*) for nothing'.[5] So great, indeed, was the transfer of land from secular to monastic ownership that from the reign of Ivan III onwards there is constant evidence of the efforts of the State (i.e. the grand princes/tsars of Moscow) to prevent further bequests 'for the soul' (*po dushe*) without its approval and even to redeem those lands already donated.[6]

The generosity of individuals and of the State in bequeathing land to the monasteries was, however, due not only to religious motives. There were other reasons as well, economical and political, for the munificence of donors, particularly princely donors. For landownership was practically the only generally recognized source of income for the monasteries. Voluntary contributions for the upkeep of the monks – tithes, tolls and taxes – had existed from the earliest days of Christianity in Russia. But they were never a reliable or universally applied means of support and frequently merely proved an additional source of income for the senior hierarchy. Consequently it was often considered the responsibility of the princes or landowners in whose territory or on whose initiative a monastery had been founded to guarantee the means of subsistence for that monastery by bestowing on it lands or other appendages from their own possessions. Likewise, princes held themselves responsible for the upkeep of self-established, needy or war-damaged monasteries on their territories by the granting of *rugi* –contributions in cash or kind, usually bread, salt, wax, honey and flour – or by the donation of immovable possessions. The responsibility for the maintenance of that class of society which was unable to support itself – the paupers and the beggars – was also removed from the shoulders of the State; 'the wealth of the Church is the wealth of the poor' is a phrase which defenders and opponents of Church property never tired of repeating. And there can be little doubt that the State had other than purely philanthropical aims in distributing its lands to the monasteries. It was to the advantage of the princes to increase the fertility and yield of their territories by granting the monasteries – especially the colonizing monasteries – uninhabited,

---

5. *Poslaniya Iosifa Volotskogo*, p. 181.
6. See Golubinsky, *IRTs*, vol. 2, I, p. 636; Pavlov, *Istoricheskiy ocherk*, pp. 120, 140, 141, 142; Veselovsky, *Feodal'noe zemlevladenie*, p. 91 n. 1.

untilled lands?[7] and it was also to their advantage to buy the political support of the monasteries with rich gifts of land, especially in times of fratricidal strife.

The monasteries' role in the acquisition of territories was not always a passive one. Far from it. The many documents relating to the transfer of land to monastic ownership from the fourteenth century onwards show a lively interest on the part of the abbots in the process of transfer and any number of means of acquisition – from seizure of land and the eventual recognition of the rights of ownership to direct purchase and the practice of wearing down and rendering insolvent debtors by high rates of interest and thus legally acquiring their hypothecated lands.

The period of the 'gathering together' of the State of Moscow from the reign of Ivan I onwards and the gradual fragmentation and dissolution of privately owned estates was clearly the most profitable one for the monasteries as far as the accumulation of territories was concerned. For not only was the acquisition of land by the monasteries encouraged and aided for political purposes by the rulers of Moscow, but also the dissolution of large and small patrimonies caused by their constant division and subdivision between successive generations of ever-multiplying heirs led to the very real enrichment of the watchful monasteries. There was often little need for the latter to take an active part in collecting the fruits of the disintegrating patrimonies; they merely had to wait for these fruits to fall into their hands. Veselovsky's monographic sketches of the dissolution of five estates in the fourteenth and fifteenth centuries show not only the process of fragmentation but also the extraordinary facility with which the monasteries acquired their property at the expense of the impoverished descendants of once-rich landowners. The large estate of Yakov Voronin, for instance, which in the second half of the fourteenth century covered some 2,500 *desyatiny* (6,750 acres) of the district of Pereyaslavl'-Zalesskiy, was split up amongst his sons and grandsons and, within two generations only, had been sold or bequeathed piecemeal to the Trinity Monastery.[8]

7. On the colonizing role of the monasteries in the fourteenth–sixteenth centuries, see Klyuchevsky, *Sochineniya*, pp. 244–62; El'yashevich, *Istoriya*, ch. 6.
8. Veselovsky, *Feodal'noe zemlevladenie*, pp. 165–9.

Far less is known about the landed estates of the metropolitans – and still less, unfortunately, about those of the bishops. If Kirill II, as metropolitan, owned lands, they were if anywhere in south Russia, possibly also in south-west Russia. His successor Maksim seems to have been the first to have acquired any territory for the 'Metropolitan's Estate' (*mitropolichiy dom*) in the north: on arrival in Vladimir-on-the-Klyaz'ma in 1299, he transferred the local bishop to the vacant bishopric of Rostov[9] and may well have taken over any estates belonging by right to the local diocese.[10] Not much more is known about Metropolitan Petr, except that he bought the somewhat remote district of Aleksin on the right bank of the Oka river, outside the principality of Moscow.[11]

It was only during the primacy of Feognost and Aleksiy, the age of mutual support and close cooperation between metropolitan and grand prince, that the domain of the metropolitanate in north-east Russia grew, mostly, it would seem, from princely donations, but perhaps also from purchases. Most is known about their estates and the relationship of these estates with the grand prince from an existing formulaic document which was evidently used as a pattern for all future treaties between newly appointed metropolitans and the rulers of Moscow and which, as Veselovsky puts it, virtually converted the 'Metropolitan's Estate' into a 'semi-independent vassal principality'.[12] It lays down the juridical and fiscal rights of the metropolitans in their own territories and the limitations of the State's authority *vis-à-vis* the metropolitan's subjects. Only in the event of war are the latter obliged to serve under the supreme command of the grand prince: 'as for war, should I myself, the grand prince, mount my horse, then so too will the metropolitan's boyars and servants, but under the metropolitan's general and under my grand-princely banner.'[13]

The locations of the 'Metropolitan's Estate' during its main period

9. Bishop Tarasy, Simeon's predecessor in Rostov, appears to have been captured (and killed?) in Ustyug by Prince Konstantin Borisovich of Rostov and Ustyug in 1295 (*PSRL*, vol. 1, col. 527; vol. 37, p. 71). However, see the Nikon Chronicle *s.a.* 1304, where 'in that year Tarasy, bishop of Rostov, died' (ibid., vol. 10, p. 230).
10. *PSRL*, vol. 1, col. 528; vol. 10, p. 172; *TL*, p. 348.
11. Veselovsky, *Feodal'noe zemlevladenie*, pp. 332–3, 337; *PSRL*, vol. 10, p. 230 ('the holy wonder-worker Petr's town of Aleksin').
12. Veselovsky, *Feodal'noe zemlevladenie*, pp. 334–6, 339 n. 2. The document is printed in *PRP*, vol. 3, pp. 421–3.
13. *PRP*, vol. 3, pp. 422–3.

of growth under Metropolitans Feognost and Aleksiy were in the
Vladimir-on-the-Klyaz'ma district (i.e. the old possessions of the erstwhile bishop of Vladimir) and in the principality of Moscow, that is
to say the original principality of Moscow and the territories annexed
up to the death of Dmitry Donskoy in 1389. There are no acquisitions
recorded in the principalities of Tver', Ryazan' and Yaroslavl' or in
the territories of Novgorod, while in the districts of Suzdal', Nizhniy-
Novgorod and Gorodets no lands were acquired by the metropolitans
before the second half of the fifteenth century.

In the last twenty-two years of the fourteenth century and the first
forty-eight of the fifteenth territorial donations from the State virtually
dried up. This is not surprising when one considers that it was an age
in which the metropolitans appeared to be acting in the interests more
of the oecumenical patriarch than of the grand prince, when there was
less political or ideological assistance required by the State from the
Church and when the Church often seemed relatively indifferent to
purely Muscovite grand-princely problems. Furthermore, in these
seventy years there were long periods during which the metropolitanate was vacant or the metropolitan absent on his peregrinations. True,
Metropolitan Kiprian in 1399 acquired the district of Karash Svyato-
slavl' in the principality of Rostov, but this was given him by Vasily I
in exchange for Aleksin on the Oka, Metropolitan Petr's purchase,
and there were no other recorded grants to Kiprian from the grand
prince, from any other prince or from private individuals.

The Greek Metropolitan Foty (1409–31) was of a quite different
calibre to Kiprian. By means of shrewd management and true business
acumen he succeeded in building up and renovating much of the
metropolitan's estates that had been destroyed or stolen during the
catastrophic twelve years of ecclesiastical confusion following Aleksiy's
death – a task which Kiprian had clearly been unable, or perhaps
unwilling, to perform. In his will, Foty describes the calamitous state
of the landed possessions of the metropolitanate which he found on his
arrival in Moscow: 'when I arrived at this most sacred metropolitanate
after [the demise of] my brother Kiprian, metropolitan of Kiev and all
Russia, I found nothing in the "metropolitan's house" (*v domu . . .
mitropol'stem*): there was rack and ruin, dissipation everywhere. In my
humility I toiled much in this [field].'[14] The Nikon Chronicle paints a
vivid picture of his efforts:

14. *PSRL*, vol. 12, p. 14.

Metropolitan Foty began to refurbish the acquisitions and the income of his metropolitanate: he set about searching for all that had been dissipated, all that had been ruined by princes and boyars or appropriated by usurers – villages, districts, moneys, taxes due to the house of Christ and of His most pure Mother and of the holy great wonder-workers Petr and Aleksiy. All this he retrieved from them and secured . . . in the sacred metropolitanate of all Russia – the moneys, the taxes, the land, the waters, the villages and the districts.[15]

Again, in his will, he talks of his many acquisitions, all of which he entrusts to the safe-keeping of the grand prince:

Whatever accrued to me . . . in the patrimony of your [i.e. Vasily II's] great State, and from other lands and other grand principalities and from the Lithuanian land and from noble and pious princes and boyars and grandees and merchants and Orthodox Christians, men and women, whosoever gave to the House of Christ and His most pure Mother, for the expiation of their sins – gold, silver, pearls, jewels, silver vessels, lands, waters – all this I entrust to my son, Grand Prince Vasily Vasil'evich, and to your children and your grandchildren, so that all this may be preserved and not tampered with by anybody. For all this was given to God and His most pure Mother, the Mother of God, to the House [of the metropolitan, to expiate] for the sins of the Christians.[16]

Foty undoubtedly was successful in amassing landed property – and other wealth too – from princes, boyars, merchants and wealthy individuals: his lands were distributed throughout the various regions (*uezdy*) of the grand principality, in Moscow, Vladimir, Zvenigorod, Kolomna and Kostroma. But, curiously enough, for all his cooperation and amicable relations with Vasily I and Vasily II, neither grand prince is known to have given him a single kopeck, let alone an acre of land. The only act of generosity on the part of the grand princes of Moscow seems to have been Vasily II's – he permitted him to buy one grand-princely hamlet in the Vladimir region.[17] Perhaps, as Veselovsky points out, 'the Moscow government did not find it necessary to enrich the already well-endowed metropolitan'.[18] Perhaps, too, the grand princes felt that so tough a businessman had no need of contributions from the grand-princely estates or treasury. The Nikon Chronicle, which, as has already been pointed out above (p. 163), shows considerable sympathy for Foty, stresses his generosity: 'he bought many things . . . for the feeding of the wretched and the

15. Ibid., vol. 11, p. 213.
16. Ibid., vol. 12, p. 14
17. *AFZ*, No. 226, p. 200.
18. Veselovsky, *Feodal'noe zemlevladenie*, p. 388.

poor.'[19] Foty is also known to have helped the Nevinskiy Presentation (*Vvedenskiy*) Monastery, which he himself founded as part of his metropolitanate estate, by endowing it with a village and six hamlets.[20]

From Foty's death to the appointment of Iona as metropolitan in 1448 no more is known about the state of the landed possessions of the metropolitanate. It is, however, unlikely that there were any sizeable accretions during the civil war or the brief metropolitanate of Isidor.

The growth of monastic territorial possessions was not unaccompanied by protests against the moral right of the Church to own land. Already in the last quarter of the fourteenth century opposition to Church landownership was making itself felt. In the 1370s and 1380s the so-called *Strigol'niki* (lit. 'Shearers'),[21] a heretical sect which amongst other things was accused of denying the validity of the hierarchy on the grounds that preferment in the Russian Church was simoniacal, appear, according to one of their main clerical detractors, the great missionary bishop St Stefan of Perm', to have accused the clergy of acquisitiveness ('they gather together numerous possessions') and to have taught that 'it is not befitting to sing [requiem offices] for the dead, nor to perform memorial services, nor to accept gifts . . . for the soul of a dead person'.[22] Furthermore, he claimed that 'the Strigol'niki say about the present-day bishops and priests: "their services are of no worth, for they do not refrain from acquisitions and they accept estates (*imeniya*) from the Christians, offerings for the living and the dead"'.

4

In the early days of the 'Tatar Yoke' the patents issued by the khans clearly guaranteed the monasteries – and perhaps, too, the estates of the metropolitans – a certain degree of security. But how did the Church protect its land against would-be violators when Mongol protection was less heeded and less effective?

By law the monasteries had unlimited right not only to acquire land but also to dispose of it at will; but from the first the land-owning

19. *PSRL*, vol. 11, p. 213.
20. Veselovsky, *Feodal'noe zemlevladenie*, p. 358.
21. On the possible meanings of the term, see Klibanov, *Reformatsionnye dvizheniya*, pp. 133–6.
22. *AED*, p. 241.

abbots, as well as the metropolitans and bishops, realized the need for more than a *legal* right to their land. Physical defence was out of the question. In his Testament of 9 July 1427 addressed to Vasily II's uncle Andrey Dmitrievich, in whose patrimony his monastery lay, Kirill Belozerskiy wrote: 'We, your poor ones, have nothing to protect ourselves with against those who offend us, except for God and the most pure Mother of God and your charter (*tvoim zhalovaniem*).'[23] Moral defence of Church property against violation was, then, essential. And, little by little, churchmen elaborated their theory of the inviolability and inalienability of their lands.

There were many means of guaranteeing the moral right to ownership: legal documents were drawn up, signed, countersigned and confirmed; a false canon 'against the abusers of the holy Churches of God' was composed and ascribed to the fathers of the Fifth Oecumenical Council ('Should anyone seize Church property by force, he is an offender; against such people the sacred canons impose an anathema (*klyatva*)';[24] the threat of anathema was no doubt widely used to dissuade would-be violators of Church property; and even the *Lives* of the saints were sprinkled with anecdotes relating to the dire fate befalling robbers of Church possessions.[25]

But who then were these violators, these 'offenders of the holy Churches of God'? One has only to examine the complaints of the hierarchy and the abbots to realize that nearly all violations of Church property prior to the reign of Ivan III were of a local and isolated nature; and that on every occasion the action of the Church was sufficient to restore the wrong done. It was a case of local princes illegally annexing monastic lands, destroying churches in their campaigns, demanding undue taxes from the clergy; in the fifteenth century the offenders were as often as not appanage princes (especially in Novgorod), desperately in need of land and finding the competition of the monasteries in the estate market too great. It was not yet a case of *national* threat to Church land, but of isolated violations, in most cases easily dealt with by the ecclesiastical authorities concerned. And it is not therefore surprising to note that before the second half of the

---

23. *AI*, No. 32, p. 62.

24. See tract entitled 'I have heard many say that it is no sin to take anything away from a monastery' attributed to Iosif of Volokolamsk. Malinin, *Starets*, app., No. 20.

25. In the tract 'I have heard many say . . .', Iosif, quoting the *Life* of the eleventh-century St Leonty of Rostov, describes the penalty meted out by God to the boyar Zakhar who appropriated part of the lands of the Rostov diocese. He also quotes from the *Lives* of St Feodosy of the Monastery of the Caves, St Euthymius the Great and St Stephen the Serb.

fifteenth century the Church did not consider it necessary officially to formulate its rights to acquire, retain and dispose of land. It was only in the beginning of the sixteenth century that any sort of theory of the inviolability and inalienability of the Church's possessions was for the first time fully expressed; for only then did it become evident that Church lands were in danger – no longer of local, individual violation, but of secularization at the hands of a land-hungry State.

CHAPTER SEVENTEEN
Politics and the Church

1

If the Church's involvement in the life of the State in the Kievan period was relatively modest and in the main limited to mediation and peace-keeping, its role in the subsequent age was strikingly greater. The influence of the clergy, especially the senior clergy, grew as the Church itself grew – with the increase in the number of churches and monasteries and with the growth of the wealth, above all the landed wealth, of the prelates and the monasteries. Few of the princes could afford to ignore the power of the Church, not only in the early decades of the 'Tatar Yoke' when the Church alone benefited from Mongol protection, but also from the second half of the fourteenth century onwards when the Church's support for the overall anti-Horde policy of the State was needed; and it is not uncommon to find the rulers relying on clerical support to achieve their political ends. This is particularly the case in those frequent situations when inter-princely military activity fizzled out or simply failed to succeed. For the Church had many and powerful weapons at its disposal: moral persuasion, spiritual intimidation, excommunication, proscription, anathema, the issuing – and indeed the deliberate breaking – of safe-conducts, the closure of churches, the administering of oaths and the granting of absolution from them, the power to sanction contracts and to withhold consent for them. Not surprising, then, that the rulers of the land learned to rely on their spiritual leaders and that much of their success and their failure was due to the amount of support the clergy was prepared to give them.

The first instance of the active use of the Church as a weapon in local conflicts took place in 1270 during the rule of Aleksandr

Nevskiy's brother, Yaroslav Yaroslavich, as grand prince of Vladimir. After five years of simmeringly tense relations with Novgorod, Yaroslav found himself faced with one of the many upheavals (*myatezhi*) which marked the city's history. With a formidable army from Suzdalia he threateningly faced the Novgorodians south of the city. As was so often the case in military confrontations between Russians, an attempt was made to settle the conflict first by parleying. But the Novgorodians were in no mood to accept Yaroslav's offer of a compromise and showed themselves only too ready to fight. Yaroslav, however, had the ultimate weapon. A message was sent by Metropolitan Kirill to the Novgorodians: it started, 'God has entrusted me with the archiepiscopate of the Russian land; it is for you to hearken to God and to me.' He then enjoined them to refrain from fighting ('spill no blood'). The account found in the contemporary Novgorod First Chronicle, whose author clearly had no time for Yaroslav, ended with the words 'And God did not allow the Christians to spill blood'. Another version of the incident, however, adds to the metropolitan's enjoinder to spill no blood, 'If you do not do this [i.e. obey me], then I shall place upon you a heavy burden and shall withhold my blessing' – in other words: 'I shall excommunicate you.' Needless to say, the threat was effective. Novgorod capitulated without a blow.[1]

This, the threat of excommunication by Kirill, is the only known instance of the powers that be using a churchman as an instrument of purely inter-Russian political manipulation in the sixty years from 1240 to 1300. No doubt there were other similar incidents during this period, but they were not recorded. As for Kirill's successor to the metropolitanate, Maksim, very little is known of his dealings with the Russian authorities in the years of his sojourn in north-east Russia from 1299 to his death in 1305. But there can be no doubt that he was fully *au fait* with all the complexities of the inter-princely rivalry which raged in Suzdalia from 1302 onwards and aware of the claims of both Tver′ and Moscow to the grand principality of Vladimir: he is reported as being present at the Congress of Pereyaslavl′ (Zalesskiy) in 1303, which was attended by the major contestants for power.[2] And when Grand Prince Andrey Aleksandrovich died in 1304, he made an attempt to prevent Yury Danilovich of Moscow from going to the Horde to claim the patent. On his way to Saray, Yury was stopped in

1. *NPL*, pp. 88–9, 320–1. Cf. *PSRL*, vol. 25, p. 149; vol. 23, p. 88; vol. 20, p. 167; vol. 10, p. 149.
2. *TL*, p. 351.

Vladimir by the 'blessed and ever-memorable metropolitan of Kiev and All Russia, [who] with much entreaty endeavoured to prevent him from going to the Horde, saying: "Together with Grand Princess Oksinia [Ksenia], the mother of Grand Prince Mikhail, I guarantee that you will be granted whatever you wish for from your patrimony."' His efforts were in vain, for Yury paid no heed, and, in spite of being ambushed on the way by Tverites, managed to reach the Horde, where in fact the patent was given to Mikhail of Tver'.[3]

Metropolitan Petr's exploits in the political field are not hard to understand. Like most of his fourteenth-century successors, he was firmly on the side of Moscow as far as relations with Tver' and Lithuania were concerned. This is not surprising; as we have seen above (see pp. 134–5), he was more or less pushed into the arms of the Moscow princes by the reaction of the grand prince of Vladimir, the Tverite Mikhail Yaroslavich, to whose own candidate for the metropolitanate he had been unexpectedly and inexplicably preferred by the emperor and patriarch in Constantinople; and Petr's first recorded act on arrival in north-east Russia – his intervention in Bryansk on the side of Vasily Romanovich against the latter's pro-Lithuanian uncle Svyatoslav Glebovich (see above, p. 196) – may well have aroused the suspicions of the authorities in Tver'. But it was after the bishop of Tver', instigated no doubt by the grand prince, had publicly accused him of simony that Petr demonstratively showed where his political allegiance lay. In 1311, the same year that he emerged triumphantly exonerated from the charges levelled against him at the Council of Pereyaslavl' (1310 or 1311), he showed in no uncertain manner just where he stood between Tver' and Moscow and just how effective his intervention in matters of State could prove for Yury of Moscow. Nizhniy Novgorod, which was now in Yury's hands, was too vital a strategic centre for Mikhail to be deprived of as grand prince, situated as it was on the confluence of the Oka and the Volga. So Mikhail sent a large army ('many warriors') under – of all people – his 12-year-old son Dmitry 'to wage war (*iti rat'yu*) against Nizhniy Novgorod and against Prince Yury'. The expedition, however, was stopped in Vladimir by Petr. He simply refused to give the army his blessing. After waiting three weeks – for the metropolitan to change his mind?

3. Maksim's attempt to stop Yury is mentioned in one of the accounts of Mikhail's subsequent murder at the Horde in 1318. See *PSRL*, vol. 5, p. 207; cf., vol. 25, p. 161. See Kuchkin, *Povesti*, p. 227. For the Tverites' ambush of Yury, see *PSRL*, vol. 25, p. 393; vol. 23, p. 96; vol. 10, p. 174.

– Dmitry disbanded his army and the soldiers all went home.⁴ The metropolitan's veto was sufficient to nullify Mikhail's attempt to command the eastern gateway to the Volga and the Oka rivers.

Equally effective in his opposition to Tver' was Petr's handling of the prelates of his province. The troublesome bishop of Tver', Andrey, who, after his failure to have Petr convicted at Pereyaslavl', persevered with his accusations of malpractice and even attempted to win over the patriarch to his side, suddenly left his see in 1316, at a time when Mikhail was fully occupied in the affairs of Novgorod, and retired to a monastery. It would not be pushing conjecture too far to hazard Petr's influence. Indeed, Andrey was quickly replaced by an appointee of the metropolitan, Varsanofy. Simeon of Rostov, the only other bishop known to have been present at the Council of Pereyaslavl' and perhaps an accomplice of Andrey called in to add weight to his accusations of simony, also left his see for an unknown destination immediately after the Council. In his place Petr appointed his closest of associates, Prokhor, who later wrote an oration in praise of Petr at the Council of Vladimir (1327) on the occasion of Petr's canonization.⁵ Yet a third bishop consecrated by Petr, David of Novgorod (1309), was to cause Mikhail Yaroslavich difficulties in Novgorod during the troubles of 1314 when the latter's governors were arrested and held in the archiepiscopal palace.⁶

Altogether it would be no exaggeration to say that many of the political crises which Mikhail of Tver' had to cope with in the last seven years of his reign were to some extent attributable to Petr's influence and authority.

2

Of all the metropolitans who headed the Russian Church during the fourteenth and the first half of the fifteenth centuries, the most politically active and the most cooperative as far as Ivan I and Semen the Proud were concerned was Petr's successor, the Greek Feognost.⁷

4. *TL*, p. 354.
5. See Kuchkin, ' "Skazanie" ', pp. 66–7.
6. *NPL*, p. 94, 335. See above, p. 135.
7. For a very different view of Feognost, see Borisov, *Tserkovnye deyateli*, pp. 42–60. Borisov talks of Feognost's 'diplomatic cunning' and 'Byzantine wiliness', his 'indifference to Muscovite affairs' (!) and his 'inhibitive influence on the formation of the Russian centralized State'.

Apart from his relentless campaign to block the establishment of rival metropolitan sees on ethnically Russian territory (the metropolitanates of Little Russia and Lithuania) and apart from his probable support of Moscow's ally Dmitry Romanovich of Bryansk in the latter's feud with his pro-Lithuanian cousin Gleb Svyatoslavich, both of which we have discussed above,[8] he time and again furthered the cause of the Moscow princes in their struggle against Tver' and Lithuania.

It was soon after his arrival in Russia as metropolitan that Feognost not only displayed his political mettle but also showed just how effectively he could be used as a weapon of persuasion. It will be remembered that in 1327, while Grand Prince Aleksandr Mikhaylovich was in his native Tver', the city rose up in revolt against the provocatively aggressive Mongol occupying force under Chol-Khan which had been sent by Khan Uzbeg.[9] The slaughter of Chol-Khan and his troops in Tver' was immediately reported to the Horde by Ivan of Moscow, only too anxiously waiting in the wings to see his rival for the grand-princely throne discredited by the only dispenser of the supreme patent. Ivan returned from the Horde with a 50,000-strong army under one Fedorchuk with explicit instructions to deliver Aleksandr Mikhaylovich to the khan. But when Tver' was sacked, Aleksandr Mikhaylovich managed to flee to Pskov, then a focal point of Lithuanian influence. Why Ivan and the Mongol army failed to march against Pskov at the time is hard to explain: perhaps Pskov was too far from Tver'; perhaps it was considered impregnable; or perhaps Fedorchuk's troops, sated with the destruction of the cities of Tver' and other districts in north-east Russia (excluding, of course, Moscow), simply preferred to return to the Horde with their booty and their prisoners. Having failed to carry out Uzbeg's instructions, Ivan first of all attempted diplomacy: his envoys to Pskov included no less a figure than Archbishop Moisey of Novgorod in whose diocese Pskov lay. 'Order [Aleksandr] to go to the Horde' was the message they conveyed. They were met with a curt refusal. Ivan then moved with an impressive army ('all the land of Russia' – *vsyu zemlyu Ruskuyu*) to confront Pskov. As was so often the custom in local confrontations, parleys were set in motion before military action. But threats were of no avail. The Pskovites, assured no doubt of Lithuanian support,

8. For the closings of the metropolitanates of Little Russia (1331, 1347 and 1349) and of Lithuania (post 1330), see above, pp. 136 ff.; for the Bryansk encounter of 1340, see above, pp. 196–7.
9. On the probable reasons for Chol-Khan's mission to Tver', see Fennell, *The Emergence*, p. 109.

persuaded Aleksandr not to leave. But by this time the army had been joined by Metropolitan Feognost, and Ivan, ever the cautious warrior and aware of the danger of attempting to storm Pskov, decided to use him as his ultimate arm: '[He] saw that they could not extract Prince Aleksandr nor drive him out by force, and so he persuaded Metropolitan Feognost [to help]; and the metropolitan fulminated a curse and an excommunication against Prince Aleksandr and against all Pskov.'

Feognost's anathema – or rather his threat of an anathema – was successful only in so far as Aleksandr left Pskov. The metropolitan, the archbishop and of course Ivan had hoped that the result of the threatened anathema would be the surrender of Aleksandr to the Moscow army. But there was no painless extraction of Aleksandr. Instead of meekly surrendering to Ivan or proceeding to the Horde, he slipped out of Pskov unobtrusively and took refuge where he knew he would be safe – in Lithuania. There was nothing Ivan could do but accept the Pskovites' offer of homage ('All Pskov, young and old, bows down to you, our master') and, with the blessing of Feognost and Moisey, conclude an 'everlasting peace' with Pskov.[10]

Feognost was soon to become once more involved in the affairs of Pskov. In March 1331 he sent to Novgorod summoning the archbishop--elect, Vasily Kalika,[11] to be consecrated by him in Vladimir-in-Volynia, where he was engaged in dealing with the affairs of the recrudescent metropolitanate of Little Russia.[12] For some reason or other Vasily was in no hurry to set off. He put off his departure for three months. According to one group of chronicles (the Novgorod Fourth Chronicle, the Moscow *svod* of 1479 and the Ermolinskiy), he and two senior Novgorodian boyars were stopped on the way 'in Lithuanian territory' (probably in Lithuanian-occupied Polotsk) by Grand Prince Gedimin, and under duress (*v . . . tyagote*) agreed that the latter's son Narimunt (Lithuanian: Narimantas) be granted patrimonial rights to several important northern Novgorodian districts.[13] It was an extraordinary concession for the future archbishop of Novgorod and his party to make. Whether or not any pressure was brought to bear on them is hard to say. The chronicles which report the incident all use the same paradoxical phraseology: 'Prince Gedimin peaceably (!) seized them (*iznima ikh*

---

10. *PL*, vol. 1, pp. 16–17.
11. Moisey retired from the see of Novgorod in 1330 but was reinstated on Vasily's death in 1352.
12. See above, pp. 137.
13. *PSRL*, vol. 4, I, pp. 263–4; vol. 25, p. 170; vol. 23, p. 103. No mention is made of the incident in the Tver´ chronicles or in the Novgorod First Chronicle.

na miru) and under such stress (*v takovoi tyagote*) they granted his son Narimunt [the right to] Ladoga, Orekhov, Korela and the land of Korelia.' The contemporary chronicler of Novgorod (Novgorod First Chronicle), on the other hand, who may well have been a member of Vasily's entourage, simply expunged the incident from his report for the year 1331, with a view perhaps to protecting the archbishop-elect's reputation or simply to avoid compromising himself.

Feognost, evidently ignorant of Vasily Kalika's concessions to Gedimin, duly consecrated him in Vladimir. But before Vasily had had time to set off back to Novgorod, a party of emissaries from Pskov arrived at Feognost's residence, sent not only by Gedimin and 'all the Lithuanian princes', but also by – of all people – Aleksandr Mikhaylovich of Tver', who by now had returned to Pskov. The aim of their mission was to have a certain Arseny who came with them appointed the first bishop of Pskov. Not surprisingly the request was summarily rejected by Feognost: a separate bishopric of Pskov was intolerable; it would release the vulnerable territory of the diocese from the ecclesiastical control of the archbishop of Novgorod and would make it, bordered as it was by the lands of the Teutonic Knights to the west and the Lithuanian-controlled principality of Polotsk to the south, an obvious target for any future 'metropolitans of Lithuania' – and Feognost had only just succeeded in closing the first metropolitanate of Lithuania after its last incumbent's demise in 1329 or 1330.[14] Besides, as the Novgorod First Chronicle points out, Pskov had 'betrayed its oath on the Cross to Novgorod by taking Prince Aleksandr from Lithuanian hands and placing him on the throne'; and more unlikely sponsors for Arseny than 'Prince Aleksandr and Gedimin . . . and all the princes of Lithuania' it would be hard to imagine. Of course, Feognost sent them packing.[15]

Aleksandr Mikhaylovich's eventual murder at the Horde in 1339[16] looked like the final episode in the eclipse of Tver' as a power to be reckoned with in north-east Russia. Fragmentation further weakened the principality, for there were no less than ten male descendants of Aleksandr Mikhaylovich's father alive at the time, all of whom had or were to have claims on various parts of the district of Tver'. Still, Aleksandr's brother Konstantin, who in 1339 returned to Tver', where he had formerly ruled with docile neutrality and submissiveness with

14. See above, pp. 138–9.
15. *NPL*, pp. 343–4; *PSRL*, vol. 4, I, p. 264; vol. 25, p. 170; vol. 23, p. 104. For a fuller interpretation of the events of 1331, see Fennell, *The Emergence*, pp. 130–4.
16. See ibid, pp. 164–9; Fennell, 'Princely Executions', pp. 15–17.

regard to Ivan I during Aleksandr's sojourn in Lithuania and Pskov, now dissociated himself from Moscow and showed no inclination to come to heel during the last days of Ivan I and the early years of Semen the Proud. The subsequent decline and enfeeblement of Tver′ was brought about not only by the proliferation of the warring princelings, but also, in no mean measure, by the influence of the Church.

Feognost's contribution to the neutralization of Tver′ was considerable and consistent. In 1343 or 1344 he appointed Fedor, later known as 'Fedor the Good', as bishop of Tver′ to replace the previous incumbent (also a Fedor), who died in 1342. The choice was significant, for Fedor hailed 'from the Holy Trinity [Monastery?] in Kashin',[17] the patrimony of Vasily, the strongly pro-Moscow brother of Aleksandr Mikhaylovich. In the extraordinary and complex imbroglio which followed Konstantin's death (1346) and the granting of the Tver′ patent to Aleksandr Mikhaylovich's son Vsevolod of Kholm rather than to the senior Tverite prince, Vasily of Kashin, we find Fedor – and Feognost – firmly on the side of Vasily. And when in 1357 the conflict between Vasily and Vsevolod flared up again, both Fedor and Metropolitan Aleksiy had no hesitation in standing by Vasily:[18] indeed, it was Bishop Fedor who engineered the ousting of Vsevolod from the throne of Tver′ in 1349 in favour of Vasily. As for the last political act of Fedor's episcopacy, it is not surprising to find him refusing to 'render honour' or even to speak to Metropolitan Aleksiy's rival metropolitan of Lithuania and Little Russia, Roman, when the latter visited his native Tver′ in 1360.[19]

Feognost's uncompromising attitude to the Tver′ question is best illustrated by his reaction to Semen of Moscow's marriage to Vsevolod's sister Maria in 1347. The marriage, Semen's third, was certainly not politically – nor perhaps morally[20] – acceptable to Feognost. According to the Tver′ Rogozhskiy Chronicle, the wedding took place in secret from the metropolitan, who, when he learned the truth, not only refused to give his blessing to the union but locked the

---

17. *PSRL*, vol. 15, I, col. 55.

18. For a detailed account of the inter-princely squabbles in Tver′, see Fennell, *The Emergence*, pp. 227–39.

19. See above, pp. 141–2. Later in 1360 Fedor retired to the Tver′ Otroch′ Monastery, where he died in 1366. On Fedor, see also Klibanov, *Reformatsionnye dvizheniya*, pp. 135 ff.

20. Semen's first wife died in 1345; his second was sent back to her father in 1346, probably on account of her sexual frigidity (see Fennell, *The Emergence*, p. 206 n. 2). His third marriage, therefore, was an adulterous one.

churches of Moscow in protest.[21] Eventually a compromise was reached. Semen needed a wife to produce a male offspring – his only two sons by his first marriage had died in infancy – and Feognost, for all his irritation, could hardly dissociate himself from the grand prince. So, after a 'certain spiritual counselling (*posovetova nechto dukhovne*) with his son Grand Prince Semen Ivanovich,'[22] a message, together with a huge bribe, was sent to the patriarch requesting his blessing for the *fait accompli*. Feognost was obliged to accept what he considered Semen's politically unacceptable gaffe, but, as we have seen above (pp. 137–8), he was richly rewarded by the patriarch with the return of the Little Russian sees to his metropolitanate of 'Kiev and all Russia'.

If further evidence were needed of Feognost's hostile attitude to Moscow's prime political opponents of the 1330s and 1340s, namely Tver' and Lithuania, we have only to consider his dealings with Novgorod at the beginning of the 1340s. At the end of Ivan I's reign Novgorod could be described as being in a state of political suspension, Ivan's governors (*namestniki*) having been withdrawn from the city probably as a result of the preponderance of the pro-Lithuanian faction's authority amongst the boyars. In 1340, while Semen was still at the Horde waiting to receive the patent for the grand principality of Vladimir, Novgorodian river pirates (*ushkuyniki*) had attacked the northern principality of Beloozero in retaliation for its prince's recent abandonment of the anti-Moscow bloc of Tver' and Lithuania.[23] Semen clearly took this as a measure of Novgorod's striving towards independence. One of his first actions after his enthronement as grand prince in October 1346 was to gather an army and, with Metropolitan Feognost in his headquarters, to march on Torzhok. The Novgorodians immediately started negotiations, having already barricaded their city in anticipation of the possible breakdown of the customary peace-feelers put out before the opening of hostilities. This delegation was headed by Archbishop Vasily, who, even if he had any desire to oppose the reimposition of Moscow's authority in Novgorod, could now hardly resist the arguments and persuasive powers of both the grand prince and the metropolitan. The Novgorodians, of course, had no alternative but to sue for peace. Little help could be expected from

---

21. *PSRL*, vol. 15, I, col. 57 – the Tver' Rogozhskiy Chronicle. *Not* mentioned, needless to say, in the Moscow sources (i.e. the Trinity Chronicle and the Moscow *svod* of 1479).
22. Ibid., vol. 10, p. 218.
23. See Fennell, *The Emergence*, pp. 244–5.

any Lithuanian source (Narimunt had proved a feeble ally and Gedimin showed no inclination to intervene). As was to be expected, a treaty was drawn up 'according to the old documents', and Semen, having dispatched his governors to Novgorod, returned to Moscow with his army.[24]

What exactly Feognost's role was in this, the reestablishment of Muscovite control over Novgorod, is not difficult to assess. No sooner had the terms of the treaty been settled than he entered Novgorod with a suite so large that the Novgorod chronicler grumbled at the expense and the trouble involved: 'it was burdensome for the archbishop and the monasteries,' he wrote, 'on account of the provisions of food and gifts.'[25] Feognost remained in the city for nearly two years. It was time well spent from the point of view of Muscovite influence, as he and Archbishop Vasily seem to have worked amicably together in spite of the heavy expenses incurred by his entourage. When, for example, in 1342 Luka, the son of the *posadnik* Varfolomey Mishinich, undertook an irresponsible campaign in the area of the Northern Dvina basin with the aim of increasing the Mishinich family possessions in the Zavoloch'e district of Novgorod's vast northern empire, both Feognost and Vasily refused to give the expedition their blessing – the only recorded case of an episcopal interdict in the period 1240–1448 proving totally ineffectual.[26] All in all, Feognost contributed considerably to the strengthening of Semen's grip on Novgorod throughout his reign.

3

If Feognost's main contribution to the bolstering up of the principality of Moscow lay in his defence and consolidation of the metropolitanate, then Aleksiy's lay more in direct political action taken against Tver' and Lithuania as well as in settling the affairs of Nizhniy Novgorod. Compared with Feognost's victorious struggle to maintain his authority over all the Russian Orthodox believers in his province, Aleksiy, as we have seen, did remarkably little to protect those of his flock who from time to time came under the aegis of Lithuania and Poland

24. Ibid., pp. 245–8.
25. *NPL*, p. 353.
26. Ibid., pp. 355–6. See also Bernadsky, *Novgorod*, p. 17.

and were served by Orthodox metropolitans hostile to Moscow or by proselytizing Latin bishops. It was a flabby attitude. He had little to do with the closing of Metropolitan Roman's metropolitanates of Lithuania and Galicia – it was all done for him by Roman dying in 1362 and by Patriarch Callistus (see above, pp. 142-3); he took no steps to investigate the ecclesiastical situation in the lands annexed by Casimir in the 1350s and the 1360s (see above, pp. 143 ff.); he did nothing to stop Antony from being appointed metropolitan of Galicia in 1372 (see above, pp. 144-5). Indeed, Patriarch Philotheus went so far as to accuse Aleksiy of 'forsaking all the Christians [in Little Russia]' and leaving south-west Russia 'without the law' and with 'no high priest' (see above, p. 145). But when it came to dealing with the complex affairs of Nizhniy Novgorod to the advantage of Moscow and to defending Moscow against a resurgent Tver' and an ever-hostile Lithuania, then Aleksiy showed his true mettle as a dedicated supporter of the by now firmly established authority of the descendants of Daniil of Moscow.

It was perhaps the circumstances of his inheritance – the Byakonty were of boyar stock – and the fact that Ivan II virtually appointed him as regent for his 9-year-old son Dmitry (the future Dmitry Donskoy)[27] that converted Aleksiy into a statesman-prelate.

The first serious political problem that faced him was that of the vast, sprawling, semi-independent principality of Suzdal', Gorodets and Nizhniy Novgorod. It was originally the patrimony of Aleksandr Nevskiy's brother Andrey Yaroslavich, but the eastern section of Nizhniy Novgorod and Gorodets had passed temporarily to Ivan I at the death of Andrey's great-grandson Aleksandr Vasil'evich in 1332. In 1341, however, Aleksandr's brother Konstantin was recognized, presumably by Khan Uzbeg, as ruler of all three districts,[28] with the title of 'grand prince of Nizhniy Novgorod', a title which stuck to all future independent rulers of the area. It was the beginning of the upsurge of the new grand principality: six years later it received its first bishop, Nafanail (Nathaniel);[29] and in 1353 Nizhniy Novgorod was strong enough to compete with Ivan II – albeit unsuccessfully – for the grand-princely patent of Vladimir.

In the early 1360s, the beginning of the 'great disorders' in the

27. *RIB*, vol. 6, app., col. 165.

28. 'In that year [1341] Konstantin Vasil'evich sat upon the grand-princely throne in Nizhniy Novgorod and in Gorodets.' *PSRL*, vol. 15, 1, col. 54.

29. Ibid., cols. 57-8; *TL*, p. 369. Named only 'bishop of Suzdal'', but Nizhniy Novgorod and Gorodets were almost certainly part of his diocese. See Presnyakov, *Obrazovanie*, p. 262 n. 2.

Horde (see above, pp. 128-9), we first hear of Metropolitan Aleksiy's involvement in the affairs of Nizhniy Novgorod. In 1360, the year after Dmitry Donskoy's accession to the throne of Moscow, Konstantin's second eldest son Dmitry was unexpectedly given the patent for the grand principality of Vladimir. After considerable manœuvring between the two Dmitrys, Dmitry of Moscow was at last given the *yarlyk* in 1362 and some sort of a pact was drawn up between him and Dmitry Konstantinovich, later to be sealed by a handy dynastic marriage.[30] The latter's younger brother Boris, however, taking advantage of the general preoccupation with the quest for the grand-princely patent and with direct aid and encouragement from the Horde, had unobtrusively settled in Nizhniy Novgorod. Now Boris, who was married to Ol'gerd of Lithuania's daughter, was the last person the authorities in Moscow, to say nothing of his brother Dmitry, wanted to see ensconced in Nizhniy Novgorod.

The crisis came to a head in 1365 when Dmitry Konstantinovich attempted to take his seat on what he considered to be his rightful throne of Nizhniy Novgorod. But Boris, armed with credentials from Saray, refused to budge. It was the metropolitan's turn to act. Envoys were sent to Nizhniy Novgorod, but Boris would not listen to them. The metropolitan then removed the diocese of Nizhniy Novgorod and Gorodets from the jurisdiction of their bishop (Bishop Aleksiy of Suzdal'), suspecting him perhaps of collaboration with Boris. Finally, Sergy of Radonezh, abbot of the Trinity Monastery, was sent to urge Boris to go to Moscow. But even the great Sergy's persuasive powers had no effect. Sergy then 'closed all the churches [in Nizhniy Novgorod] according to the word [i.e. instructions] of Metropolitan Aleksiy and Grand Prince Dmitry Ivanovich'. For the second time in the history of Russia (see above, pp. 225-6) church closure was used where arguments failed. This time it succeeded. Boris met his brother, who was advancing with an army towards Nizhniy Novgorod. 'Together with his boyars he bowed [in homage], submitted to him, asked for peace and yielded the [grand principality] to him.'[31]

Aleksiy's dealings with Tver' began shortly after his investiture as metropolitan in 1354. Now, Tver' had been in a state of turmoil ever since the early years of Ivan II's reign as grand prince of Vladimir. The

30. Dmitry Donskoy married Dmitry Konstantinovich's daughter Evdokia (Eudoxia, *dim.* Avdot'ya) in January 1387. *PSRL*, vol. 15, I, col. 83; *TL*, p. 384.
31. Accounts of the event in the various chronicles are conflicting and confusing. The fullest version (and the best for chronology) is that of the Nikon Chronicle (*PSRL*, vol. 11, pp. 2–5). See Presnyakov, *Obrazovanie*, pp. 265–71.

civil wars, which had been so carefully fostered by Semen the Proud and Khan Jani-Beg, had resulted in the principality being split into two rival factions, one headed by Aleksandr Mikhaylovich's younger brother, the pro-Muscovite Vasily of Kashin, the other by Aleksandr's son, the pro-Lithuanian Vsevolod, prince of Kholm and grand prince of Tver´ since 1348. As we mentioned above (see p. 142), Metropolitan Aleksiy first became involved in the conflict between the two sides in 1357. In that year Vsevolod went to Vladimir-on-the-Klyaz´ma to complain to the metropolitan about the behaviour of his uncle Vasily, who had evidently broken some contract or other between them (*chto sya . . . uchinilo ot nego cheres dokonchanie*). The result was that, 'on Metropolitan Aleksiy's instructions (*po mitropolichiyu slovu*)', as the Tver´ chronicler took care to point out, Vasily concluded a peace treaty with Ivan II, who in the first four years of his reign had evidently supported the Lithuanian faction headed by Vsevolod.[32] It was an important step for Aleksiy to take, for it meant a complete reversal of Ivan II's attitude towards Lithuania and brought him into line with the policy of his two predecessors. More was to come.

In 1365 the Black Death struck Tver´. The first of the princes to die was Aleksandr Mikhaylovich's nephew Semen, who, childless, left his small patrimony of Dorogobuzh to his widow and to his cousin Mikhail Aleksandrovich. In January 1366 Vsevolod Aleksandrovich of Kholm and two of his brothers died. Vasily of Kashin, certain no doubt that the metropolitan would support him, lodged a complaint against Mikhail Aleksandrovich 'on account of Prince Semen's patrimony'. But Bishop Vasily of Tver´, whom Metropolitan Aleksiy had put in charge of the case, acquitted not Vasily but Mikhail: after all, Dorogobuzh had been legally bequeathed to him by Semen.[33] In the following year Bishop Vasily paid dearly for his judgement in the case: he was summoned to Moscow by the metropolitan's bailiff, judged by Aleksiy himself and suffered 'much trouble and distress'.[34]

Mikhail's acquittal led inevitably to the heightening of tension in Tver´ and to the beginning of a major set-to between Mikhail, by now grand prince of Tver´, and Moscow. In 1367 the Muscovites, 'on the advice of Metropolitan Aleksiy', so a seventeenth-century source tells us,[35] embarked on the building of stone fortifications in place of

32. For Ivan II's policy of peaceful relations with Lithuania (and hostility with the Horde) from his accession in 1354 to 1357, see Fennell, *The Emergence*, pp. 296–7.

33. *PSRL*, vol. 15, I, cols. 78–9, 81.

34. Ibid., col. 84.

35. See Golubinsky, *IRTs*, vol. 2, I, p. 200 n. 2.

the old wooden Kremlin in Moscow. At the same time Moscow began to 'put pressure on Grand Prince Mikhail Aleksandrovich'[36] with the result that he immediately set off to Lithuania in search of reinforcements. The long-drawn-out war between Moscow and Tver' had started. Not only Vasily of Kashin's troops but a Muscovite force as well set about harassing Mikhail Aleksandrovich's supporters.

In the autumn of 1367 Mikhail Aleksandrovich returned to Tver', his army now stiffened with Lithuanian troops. His first reaction was to set off to Kashin to deal with his uncle Vasily. He was met, however, by Vasily's envoys and by Bishop Vasily of Tver', duly chastened by the metropolitan's recent reprimand, and some sort of reconciliation was agreed to.

By now Moscow was fully aware of the danger of Mikhail Aleksandrovich and his Lithuanian connections. It was decided to get rid of him. So, rather than risk a military defeat in Tver' territory, the grand prince and the metropolitan invited Mikhail and his close associates to 'peace talks' in Moscow. Mikhail would never have risked the journey without a guarantee of his safety. But the Moscow authorities, intent on luring him to the Kremlin without an army and without a bodyguard, issued a safe conduct in the name of the supreme head of the Church in Russia, Aleksiy, the most sacred and inviolable gage of his immunity.

This 'evil plan', as the Tver' chronicle called it,[37] worked. 'Trusting in God and in [the metropolitan's] oath on the Cross', Mikhail fell into Aleksiy's trap. On arrival in Moscow he was 'arrested and held under duress' along with the boyars who accompanied him. He was, however, soon released, not because the metropolitan thought better of his deceit, but because Mongol envoys were reported approaching Moscow, and the authorities there had no wish for the Horde to interfere at this stage of international affairs in Moscow–Tver' relations.

Indignation at the metropolitan's duplicity was widespread. Even the Trinity Chronicle, the mouthpiece of Aleksiy's successor Kiprian, notes the resentment of Mikhail: 'he complained against the metropolitan in whom he had believed more than all others as a true bishop.'[38] Ol'gerd of Lithuania even wrote to Patriarch Philotheus in 1371 complaining of Aleksiy's guile: 'They invited my brother-in-law

36. *PSRL*, vol. 15, I, col. 84.
37. Ibid., col. 87. But *not* – not surprisingly – the Moscow Trinity Chronicle (*TL*, p. 386).
38. *TL*, pp. 386–7.

Mikhail [to Moscow] by means of a pledge [of his safety], and the metropolitan removed all fear from him, [saying] that he could come and go at will. But he was arrested.'[39] Although no reply of Philotheus to Ol'gerd's letter has survived, the patriarch wrote in the same year to Aleksiy rebuking him for his attitude to Mikhail: 'I see nothing good in the fact that you have scandals and conflicts with the king of Tver', Mikhail . . . As his father and teacher, try to make peace with him. If he has sinned against you in any way, then forgive him and accept him as your son and have peace with him as you have with the other princes.'[40]

Needless to say, in the conflict with Tver' and Lithuania Aleksiy also made use of excommunication, not so much as a threat but as a punishment for those who had sided with 'the enemies of the faith, the foes of the Cross', that is to say for those Russian princes who had taken part in Ol'gerd's first invasion of Moscow in 1368. The main culprit of course was Mikhail Aleksandrovich of Tver', but Svyatoslav Ivanovich of Smolensk was also included in Aleksiy's anathema. Patriarch Philotheus, who was kept well in touch by Aleksiy with the political affairs of his province, confirmed the excommunications. In June 1370 he addressed a letter to all the Russian princes who broke their oaths of allegiance to Dmitry of Moscow and allied themselves with the 'impious Ol'gerd': 'in as much as [they] were excommunicated by the most sacred metropolitan of Kiev and all Russia . . . Our Humility [i.e. Philotheus] . . . also holds them excommunicated, since they have acted against the sacred community of Christians.' Only when they repent to the metropolitan, he added, would they receive pardon from the patriarch.[41] Svyatoslav of Smolensk's 'treachery' was evidently considered even more heinous, for he received a separate letter from Philotheus in which he was accused of 'transgressing oaths on the Cross . . . and taking up arms together with Ol'gerd against the Christians'. For this, the patriarch continued, 'the most sacred metropolitan of Kiev and all Russia, our beloved brother and concelebrant, excluded you from the Church. And well and rightly he did so.'[42] Again Philotheus confirmed that he too held Svyatoslav excluded from the Church and that his ban would only be lifted when Aleksiy

39. *APC*, vol. 1, p. 580; *RIB*, vol. 6, app., col. 135; Meyendorff, *Byzantium*, p. 288.

40. *APC*, vol. 1, pp. 320–1; *RIB*, vol. 6, app., col. 157; Meyendorff, *Byzantium*, p. 290.

41. *APC*, vol. 1, pp. 523–4; *RIB*, vol. 6, cols. 117, 119; Meyendorff, *Byzantium*, pp. 285–6.

42. *RIB*, vol. 6, app., cols. 121, 123.

informed him of Svyatoslav's contrition.

If further proof were needed of Aleksiy's commitment to the policies of Moscow, we have only to consider the canonization of the three Lithuanian martyrs, Evstafy (Eustathius), Antony and Ioann. These Christian members of Ol'gerd's court were put to death in 1347 at Ol'gerd's command, allegedly for refusing to share his pagan beliefs and customs.[43] In all probability it was Metropolitan Aleksiy who canonized them, possibly in 1364, and with the blessing of Patriarch Philotheus, although the evidence for this comes from sources dating from the seventeenth century.[44] It is, however, certain that Philotheus did in fact approve of the canonization and that in 1374 parts of their relics were translated to the cathedral of St Sophia in Constantinople at his request.[45]

4

Of the remaining metropolitans of Kiev and all Russia prior to 1448 only two are known to have exploited their 'spiritual weapons' to further the aspirations of the rulers of Moscow: Kiprian and Foty.

For all his activity in the political field, Metropolitan Kiprian is only once reported as having recourse to excommunication in order to gain his ends – and they were *his* ends rather than those of the State. It occurred in 1391 when Kiprian came to Novgorod to plead with the Novgorodians, who six years earlier had virtually declared their ecclesiastical independence from Moscow by refusing not only to accept the metropolitan's judgements but also to allow him to hear appeals against their archbishop. Kiprian spent two weeks in Novgorod arguing his case with the inhabitants of the city and urging them to revoke their decision to accept neither his judgements nor his demands that they present themselves at his court in Moscow for the administration of justice – in other words, comply with the immemorial juridical dependence of the Church of Novgorod on the metropolitan. The Novgorodians' refusal to accept the traditional judicial prerogatives of the metropolitan meant, of course, a considerable loss of income for his treasury. But that was not Kiprian's main concern. It

---

43. *PSRL*, vol. 5, p. 226; vol. 25, p. 177; vol. 23, p. 109; vol. 20, p. 185.
44. See Golubinsky, *Istoriya kanonizatsii*, p. 70.
45. For more detail, see Meyendorff, *Byzantium*, pp. 187–8 and especially n. 8.

was rather for the unity of the Church. He took the strongest measure available – he excommunicated them. He left Novgorod 'without blessing their [arch]bishop Ioann and all the Novgorodians for their trampling on that which was entrusted to God'.[46] For two years the proscription, confirmed by the patriarch, remained technically in force. Whether the Novgorodians observed it is another question. The archbishop's chronicle makes no reference to the enforcement of the ban. At last, in 1394, Kiprian returned with a high-grade ecclesiastical delegation from Constantinople. The archbishop this time gave in and agreed to the metropolitan's demands. Kiprian 'blessed him' together with 'all great Novgorod'.[47]

As we have said above, Kiprian worked tirelessly for peaceful relations between Moscow, Lithuania and Poland: he may well have persuaded Yagaylo/Jagiełło of Lithuania – later king of Poland – not to join Mamay's force on the eve of the battle of Kulikovo (see above, pp. 152-3), and in 1391 he perhaps negotiated – and certainly officiated at – the wedding of Vasily I to Vitovt's daughter Sofia (see above, p. 158). Furthermore, it seems more than probable that in 1384 Kiprian was behind the treaty between Yagaylo and Dmitry Ivanovich which had as its aim the proposed marriage between Yagaylo and a daughter of Dmitry, a project which, as Meyendorff rightly remarked, would have changed the course of history.[48] But in all these instances we know nothing of whatever methods Kiprian may have used to gain his ends.

As for that most energetic of metropolitans, Foty, we have already discussed his ambivalent relations with Vitovt and his struggle to protect the unity of his province by preventing the appointment of Lithuanian-backed outsiders to the metropolitanates of Lithuania and Galicia. As an active intervener in the political life of the State, however, he is only known to have come into his own at the death of Vasily I in 1425.

The situation was tense. Vasily's sole surviving son, Vasily II, was only 9 years old at the time. His eldest uncle, the 50-year-old Yury

---

46. *PSRL*, vol. 10, pp. 126–7; *NPL*, pp. 384–5.

47. *NPL*, p. 387; Meyendorff, *Byzantium*, pp. 246–8. Note that in his letter to Sergy of Radonezh of 1378, Kiprian stated that his reaction to his 'arrest, imprisonment, dishonour and ridicule' on his arrival in Moscow was to excommunicate 'all those who plotted these acts', i.e. Dmitry Donskoy and his advisers. See above, pp. 148–9. Cf. Skrynnikov, *Gosudarstvo*, pp. 63–4.

48. Meyendorff, *Byzantium*, p. 248. The marriage never came off. Jagiełło married Jadwiga, the daughter of Louis of Hungary, on becoming king of Poland. On the treaty, see Cherepnin, *RFA*, p. 51.

Dmitrievich, prince of the widely separated Zvenigorod and Galich,[49] considered that according to Dmitry Donskoy's will he was the rightful heir to the grand-princely throne (see above, pp. 130-1). But Vasily Vasil'evich was well provided with support. His mother Sofia – the daughter of Grand Prince Vitovt of Lithuania – three uncles, Andrey, Petr and Konstantin Dmitrievichi, and above all his father's faithful metropolitan, Foty, had no intention of allowing Yury to claim the throne. The initiative was taken by Foty himself. On the night of Vasily I's death he sent one of his boyars, Akinf Oslebyatev, to Yury's western capital Zvenigorod, summoning him to Moscow. But Yury refused. Instead he set off to his remote north-eastern appanage of Galich. To gain time, he offered Vasily a temporary truce (*peremirie*) to St Peter's Day (29 June) and immediately set about raising an army. A Muscovite force was sent to Kostroma, while Yury's troops concentrated in Nizhniy Novgorod. As was so often the case in inter-princely conflicts in medieval Russia, nothing happened. Neither side attacked. Yury retreated to Galich, while the Muscovite army returned to Moscow. It was merely a show of strength on both sides. But neither was prepared to abandon the struggle.

In order to gain time once again, Yury suggested another temporary truce, this time to last a year. His proposal had little effect. Foty, Vasily, Sofia Vitovtovna, Vasily's three uncles and his grandfather Vitovt, as well as 'all the princes and boyars', held what can only be described as a major council of State to decide on how to cope with Yury, who with his three sons constituted a major threat to the grand principality.[50] It was decided 'to send their father the metropolitan, Foty, to Prince Yury'. Foty, the chronicle narrative avers, 'had no hesitation. He straightway set off with joy to Galich concerning peace.' On the way to Galich he stopped at Yaroslavl' on the Volga, no doubt in an attempt to engage the support of the numerous hitherto uncommitted princes of Yaroslavl'.[51]

On arrival at Galich Foty was confronted with a vast mass of as many of his subjects as Yury could muster to impress him. Negotiations between the two soon broke down. Foty urged Yury to conclude

49. i.e. Galich in the land of Merya – not to be confused with Galich in south-west Russia.
50. Whether Vitovt was actually present in Moscow or whether he was simply notified by the council is not clear from the wording of the chronicle account. See *PSRL*, vol. 26, p. 183; vol. 25, p. 246.
51. 'He came to Yaroslavl' on the festival of the birth of John the Baptist [24 June] ... but he only dined with Prince Ivan Vasil'evich. The princes of Yaroslavl' begged him to hear morning Mass with them ... but he set off for Galich.' Ibid.

a peace treaty with Vasily, 'so as to avoid bloodshed between him and the grand prince'. But Yury was only prepared to go as far as yet another temporary truce: time was needed to prepare for hostilities and to negotiate for the *yarlyk* with the Horde.[52]

The breakdown of the talks left Foty with no alternative but to use his ultimate weapon: excommunication. 'In a fury the metropolitan refused to bless [Prince Yury] and his city and departed.' His departure coincided with an outbreak of the Black Death in Galich. Faced with a possible decimation of his forces and no doubt urged by the populace and clergy to beg Foty to lift his ban, Yury set off after Foty on horseback, caught up with him in the nearby village of Pasynkovo beyond the Lake of Galich and bowed to the ground in submission. Foty returned to Galich, blessed Yury and the city and resumed talks. This time he was successful. Yury sent his envoys to Moscow, where a peace treaty was concluded. There were, however, reservations. Yury agreed 'not to seek the grand principality of his own accord' – in other words, not by military force – 'but according to the [will of the] khan: whosoever is favoured by the khan shall be grand prince of Vladimir, Novgorod the Great and all Russia'.[53] At least it meant peace for the time being. Whether this was due entirely to Foty's diplomacy or whether the disastrous spread of the plague made warfare a virtual impossibility for Yury we cannot tell. But in any case there were no serious clashes between uncle and nephew for the remainder of Foty's life (he died in 1431),[54] and on 11 March 1428 a non-aggression treaty 'with the blessing of our father Foty, metropolitan of Kiev and all Rus'' was concluded between Vasily II and Yury,[55] who agreed to be named as 'younger brother' of his nephew the grand prince. Foty's efforts had secured six years of non-aggression between the two contestants. It was only after his death that the bitter civil war began in earnest.

Only one other churchman in this period, apart from the metropolitans, is held up by historians – not by all but by many – as 'influencing the course of Russian history' by his political activities, namely St Sergy of Radonezh, abbot of the Trinity Monastery. There can be no doubt that, like his predecessor Abbot Feodosy

---

52. Zimin, *Vityaz'*, p. 35.
53. *PSRL*, vol. 26, p. 184; vol. 25, p. 247.
54. In 1430, perhaps when Foty and Vasily II were in Lithuania as Vitovt's guests (see above, p. 169), Yury 'broke the peace with Grand Prince Vasily Vasil'evich'. No fighting is reported. *PSRL*, vol. 26, p. 186; vol. 23, pp. 146–7.
55. *DDG*, No. 24, pp. 63–7.

of the Kievan Monastery of the Caves, he profoundly influenced the course of Russian monasticism. But as for his incursions into the political life of the State, some caution is required before we can talk of his 'intervention . . . in the fate of the young State of Moscow'.[56]

His reputation as an intermediary in the affairs of State is built largely on the episode of the closure of the churches in Nizhniy Novgorod in 1365, on his successful mission to Oleg of Ryazan' in 1385 and above all on his 'blessing' and encouragement of Dmitry Donskoy on the eve of the battle of Kulikovo in 1380.

As we have seen above (p. 229), Sergy was sent to Nizhniy Novgorod to talk Boris Konstantinovich into yielding the throne of the principality, which belonged by right to his brother Dmitry. When oral persuasion failed, Sergy closed all the churches in the town – perhaps in the whole principality – and when Dmitry appeared on the horizon with a threatening army, Boris gave up the throne. It must, however, be borne in mind that the report of the incident found in the Nikon Chronicle states that Sergy, in closing the churches, was acting specifically as the agent of the metropolitan and the grand prince: 'according to the instructions of Metropolitan Aleksiy and Grand Prince Dmitry Ivanovich' are the words used.[57] No source in fact mentions that Boris gave up the struggle *as a result of* Sergy's ban. However, it was probably the combination of the closure of the churches and the fact that Dmitry was approaching with an army reinforced by troops from Moscow that obliged Boris to yield.

Twenty years later, in 1385, Sergy set off on another mission of appeasement. This time the wayward prince was Oleg of Ryazan', who in March of that year, not content with having allied himself to Mamay before the battle of Kulikovo, had seized and sacked Moscow's southern possession of Kolomna, which prior to the fourteenth century had been an integral part of the principality of Ryazan'. Sergy was now 63 years old. It was clearly not going to be an easy assignment, for 'before that time many people had gone to [Oleg] and it had not been possible to assuage him', so the contemporary chronicle tells us. This time, however, no coercive measures were needed. 'With gentle

56. Fedotov, *Svyatye*, pp. 140–1.
57. Note that the Trinity Chronicle (completed in 1408 at the court of Metropolitan Kiprian) and its main source, the Tver' Rogozhskiy Chronicle, make no mention of the episode. The Moscow *svod* of 1479 (*PSRL*, vol. 25, p. 183) merely states that Dmitry Donskoy sent Sergy and that Sergy 'closed the churches'. Only the Nikon Chronicle says that he closed the churches *on the instructions of Aleksiy and Dmitry* (*PSRL*, vol. 11, p. 5).

talk and quiet speech and didactic words . . . he talked with him for a long time about the good of his soul, about peace and about love.' The results were all that Dmitry Donskoy could have wished for: 'Prince Oleg exchanged ferocity for gentleness . . . having been put to shame by so holy a man.' Not only did he conclude a permanent peace treaty with Moscow, but he married off his son Fedor to Dmitry's daughter Sofia.[58]

Much of Sergy's reputation as the 'influencer of the course of history', the 'agent of the prince of Moscow', the 'motivator' of Dmitry Donskoy and the 'source of his inspiration' and so on, is of course founded on the legends which describe him as playing a leading role in the preliminaries to the battle of Kulikovo. In the accounts of the numerous – usually victorious – campaigns of the warriors of medieval Russia against external enemies, princes rarely took to the field without being blessed by abbot, bishop or metropolitan and encouraged to fight the good fight. So it was with Dmitry Donskoy in 1380. In various sources – none of them contemporary – he is portrayed as visiting the Trinity Monastery, asking the abbot's opinion as to whether he should 'march against the godless ones', being blessed by Sergy, inspired by him to fight and prophetically assured of victory. Furthermore, the abbot provides him with two 'monks' (Peresvetov and Oslyabya) – more likely professional soldiers – to assist him in battle. After the battle Dmitry Donskoy returns and out of gratitude to Sergy founds a church – later incorporated into a monastery – on the river Dubenka near Sergy's Trinity Monastery.

Much of this comes from various fifteenth-century versions of the tale of the 'battle beyond the Don river' and from the *Life* of Sergy Radonezhskiy, the original of which, written by Epifany Premudryy ('the very wise'), has not survived and is only known in later fifteenth-century redactions rewritten by Pakhomy Logofet, or Pakhomy the Serb, as he is often known.[59] Many of the details of the various accounts are clearly inaccurate. Dates are wrong. Some facts are contradictory. Dmitry, for instance, is said to have arrived at the Trinity Monastery on Sunday, 18 August 1380, whereas 18 August in that year fell on a Monday; the church and monastery on the Dubenka

58. *PSRL*, vol. 15, I, cols. 150, 151. According to the Nikon Chronicle, it was Dmitry Donskoy who persuaded Sergy to go to Ryazan´ and talk Oleg into agreeing to peace. *PSRL*, vol. 11, pp. 86–7.

59. On the various redactions of the *Life* of St Sergy, see Müller, 'Einleitung', in *Die Legenden*, pp. v ff. For the text of the *Life*, see *PLDR, XIV–seredina XV v.*, pp. 256–429; for the various literary Tales, see *Skazaniya i povesti, passim*.

river were built and consecrated on 1 December 1479 and *not* after Kulikovo. According to the extended chronicle version of the battle found in the Novgorod Fourth Chronicle, it was Bishop Gerasim of Kolomna who blessed Dmitry Donskoy before the battle,[60] while Sergy merely sent an epistle containing the blessing and a command 'to fight the Tatars' which reached him just before action began.[61] In the *Tale of the Battle with Mamay*, much of which is based on Epifany's *Life* of Sergy, Dmitry Donskoy twice visits Metropolitan Kiprian: the first time he is advised to 'satisfy the impious ones with gifts'; the second 'to oppose them in the name of the Lord'.[62] Kiprian, however, was either in Kiev or Lithuania at the time (see above, pp. 152-3). Could it be, then, that, as one Russian medievalist has recently suggested, Sergy of Radonezh's much acclaimed blessing of Dmitry Donskoy on the eve of the battle of Kulikovo never took place? And that if a blessing took place at all, it was before the battle on the Vozha river, two years earlier?[63]

Perhaps, then, we should beware of exaggerating St Sergy's role in the history of the close interaction between Church and State in medieval Russia. After all, it was in his profound influence on the development and spread of Russian monasticism that his great contribution to the history of the early Russian Church consisted. With St Sergy the spiritual outweighed the political.

---

60. *PSRL*, vol. 4, I, p. 315.
61. Ibid., p. 316.
62. *Skazaniya i povesti*, pp. 28, 29.
63. See Kuchkin, 'Dmitriy Donskoy i Sergiy Radonezhskiy'; Skrynnikov, *Gosudarstvo*, pp. 77 ff. For a refutation of Kuchkin's views, see Borisov, *I svecha*, pp. 223–30.

Bibliography

Acta patriarchatus Constantinopolitani (APC), ed. F. Miklosich and I. Müller, 2 vols (Vienna, 1860–62).

Akty feodal'nogo zemlevladeniya i khozyaystva XIV–XVI vekov, vol. 1, (*AFZ*) ed. L. V. Cherepnin (Moscow, 1951).

Akty istoricheskie, vol. 1 (*AI*) (St Petersburg, 1841).

Akty, otnosyashchiesya k istorii Zapadnoy Rossii, vol. 1 (St Petersburg, 1846).

Alef, G., 'Muscovy and the Council of Florence', *Slavic Review*, vol. 20 (Seattle, 1961), pp. 389–401; repr. in *Rulers and Nobles in Fifteenth-Century Muscovy* (London, 1983), No. III.

Alekseev, M. P., 'Anglo-saksonskaya parallel' k Poucheniyu Vladimira Monomakha', *TODRL*, vol. 2 (Moscow–Leningrad, 1935), pp. 39–80.

Die altrussischen hagiographischen Erzählungen und liturgischen Dichtungen über die heiligen Boris und Gleb, Nach der Ausgabe von Abramovič (AHE), ed. L. Müller, Slavische Propyläen, vol. 14 (Munich, 1967).

Angold, M. J., *The Byzantine Empire, 1025–1204: A Political History* (London, 1984).

Annales de Saint-Bertin (Annales Bertiniani), ed. F. Grat, J. Vieillard, S. Clémencet and L. Levillain, Publications de la Société de l'Histoire de France, vol. 131 (Paris, 1964).

Antifeodal'nye ereticheskie dvizheniya (AED), ed. N. A. Kazakova and Ya. S. Lur'e (Moscow–Leningrad, 1955).

Arrignon, J.-P., 'A propos de la lettre du pape Grégoire VII au prince de Kiev Izjaslav', *Russia Mediaevalis*, vol. 3 (Munich, 1977), pp. 5–18.

Arrignon, J.-P., 'La Rus' entre la Bulgarie et l'empire byzantin de la fin du Xe au début du XIIe siècle', in: *Proceedings*, pp. 702–13.

Arrignon, J.-P., 'La Création des diocèses russes des origines au milieu du XIIe siècle', *Mille ans de christianisme russe, 988–1988* (Paris, 1989), pp. 27–49.

Auty, R. and Obolensky, D. (eds.), *An Introduction to Russian History*, Companion to Russian Studies, vol. 1 (Cambridge, 1976).

Barrick, C. L., 'Andrey Yur'evich Bogoljubsky, a Study of Sources', unpublished D.Phil. thesis (Oxford, 1984).

Belyakova, E. V., 'K istorii uchrezhdeniya avtokefalii russkoy tserkvi', in: *Rossiya na putyakh tsentralizatsii* [in honour of A. A. Zimin] (Moscow, 1982), pp. 152–6.

Bernadsky, V. N., *Novgorod i Novgorodskaya zemlya v XV veke* (Moscow–Leningrad, 1961).

Borisov, N. S., *Russkaya tserkov' v politicheskoy bor'be XIV–XV vekov* (Moscow, 1986).

Borisov, N. S., *Tserkovnye deyateli srednevekovoy Rusi XIII–XVII vv.* (Moscow, 1988).

Borisov, N. S., *I svecha by ne ugasla* . . . (Moscow, 1990).

Cherepnin, L. V., *Russkie feodal'nye arkhivy XIV–XV vekov,* vol. 1 (*RFA*) (Moscow–Leningrad, 1948).

Chichurov, I. S., '"Khozhdenie Apostola Andreya" v vizantiyskoy i drevnerusskoy tserkovno-ideologicheskoy traditsii', in: *Tserkov'*, pp. 7–23.

Codex diplomaticus nec non epistolaris Silesiae (*CD*), vol. 1 (Wrocław, 1951).

Constantine Porphyrogenitus, *De caeremoniis aulae byzantinae,* vol. 1, *CSHB* (Bonn, 1829).

Constantine Porphyrogenitus, *De administrando imperio,* ed. Gy. Moravcsik, transl. R. J. H. Jenkins, Corpus fontium historiae byzantinae, vol. 1 (Washington, DC, 1967).

Corpus scriptorum historiae byzantinae (*CSHB*) (Bonn).

The Council of Constance, the Unification of the Church, transl. L. R. Loomis, ed. J. H. Mundy and K. M. Woody, Records of Civilization, Sources and Studies, LXIII (New York–London, 1961).

Crummey, R. O., *The Formation of Muscovy, 1304–1613,* Longman History of Russia, vol. 3 (London–New York, 1987).

Długosz, J. [Ioannis Dlugossii], *Annales seu Cronicae Incliti Regni Poloniae,* ed. J. Dąbrowski, vols 5–6 (Warsaw, 1973).

Dmitriev, L. A., 'Rol' i znachenie mitropolita Kipriana v istorii drevnerusskoy literatury (k russko-bolgarskim literaturnym svyazyam XIV–XV vv.)', *TODRL*, vol. 19 (Moscow–Leningrad, 1963), pp. 215–54.

Dubler, C. E., *Abū Ḥāmid el Granadino y su relación de viaje por tierras eurasiáticas* (Madrid, 1953).

Dukhovnye i dogovornye gramoty velikikh i udel'nykh knyazey XIV–XVI vv. (*DDG*), ed. L. V. Cherepnin (Moscow–Leningrad, 1950).

El'yashevich, V. B., *Istoriya prava pozemel'noy sobstvennosti v Rossii,* vol. 1, *Yuridicheskiy stroy pozemel'nykh otnosheniy v XIII–XVI vv.* (Paris, 1948).

Eremin, I. P., 'Literaturnoe nasledie Feodosiya Pecherskogo', *TODRL*, vol. 5 (Moscow–Leningrad, 1947), pp. 159–84.

Eremin, I. P., 'Literaturnoe nasledie Kirilla Turovskogo', *TODRL*, vol. 11 (Moscow–Leningrad, 1955), pp. 342–67; vol. 12 (1956), pp. 340–61; vol. 13 (1957), pp. 409–25; vol. 15 (1958), pp. 331–48.

Eremin, I. P., '"Povest' vremennykh let" kak pamyatnik literatury', in: idem, *Literatura Drevney Rusi* (Moscow–Leningrad, 1966), pp. 42–97.

Featherstone, J., 'Olga's Visit to Constantinople', *Harvard Ukrainian Studies*, vol. 14 (Cambridge, Mass., 1990), pp. 293–312.

Fedotov, G. P., *Svyatye Drevney Rusi (X–XVII st.)* 2nd edn (New York, 1959).

Fennell, J. L. I., 'The Tver' Uprising of 1327: A Study of the Sources', *Jahrbücher für Geschichte Osteuropas*, NS, vol. 15 (Wiesbaden, 1967), pp. 161–79.

Fennell, J. L. I., *The Emergence of Moscow 1304–1359* (London, 1968).

Fennell, J. L. I., 'The Ermolinskij Chronicle and the Literary Prelude to "Tale of the Murder of Mixail of Tver"', in: *Studies in Slavic Linguistics and Poetics in Honor of B. O. Unbegaun* (New York–London, 1968), pp. 33–8.

Fennell, J. L. I., 'K voprosu ob istochnikakh tret'ey chasti Moskovskoy Akademicheskoy letopisi', in: *Problemy izucheniya kul'turnogo naslediya* [in honour of D. S. Likhachev] (Moscow, 1985), pp. 140–8.

Fennell, J. L. I., 'Princely Executions in the Horde 1308–1339', *Forschungen zur osteuropäischen Geschichte*, vol. 38 (Berlin, 1986), pp. 9–19.

Fennell, J. L. I., 'The Canonization of Saint Vladimir', in: *Tausend Jahre Christentum in Russland, Zum Millenium der Taufe der Kiever Rus'* (Göttingen, 1988), pp. 299–304.

Fennell, J. L. I., *The Crisis of Medieval Russia 1200–1304*, Longman History of Russia, vol. 2 (London–New York, 1983); Russian translation: Fennel (*sic*), *Krizis srednevekovoy Rusi, 1200–1304*, ed. A. L. Khoroshkevich and A. I. Pliguzov (Moscow, 1989).

Fennell, J. L. I., 'When was Olga Canonized?', in: *Christianity and the Eastern Slavs*, vol. 1, *Slavic Cultures in the Middle Ages*, ed. B. Gasparov and O. Raevsky-Hughes, California Slavic Studies, 16 (Berkeley–Los Angeles–Oxford, 1993), pp. 77–82.

Fennell, J. L. I. and Stokes, A., *Early Russian Literature* (London, 1974).

Froyanov, I. Ya., 'Nachalo khristianstva na Rusi', in: G. L. Kurbatov, E. D. Frolov and I. Ya. Froyanov, *Khristianstvo: Antichnost', Vizantiya, Drevnyaya Rus'* (Leningrad, 1988), pp. 189–329.

Giedroyć, M., 'The Arrival of Christianity in Lithuania: Between Rome and Byzantium (1281–1304)', *Oxford Slavonic Papers*, NS, vol. 20 (Oxford, 1987), pp. 1–33.

Gill, J., *The Council of Florence* (Cambridge, 1959).

Giraudo, G., 'Voprošanie Kirikovo: remarques sur la vie d'une communauté paroissiale dans la Rus´ kiévienne du XIIe siècle', in: *Proceedings*, pp. 743–60.

Golubinsky, E. E., *Istoriya Russkoy Tserkvi (IRTs)*, 2 vols in 4 books (Moscow, 1900–11).

Golubinsky, E. E., *Istoriya kanonizatsii svyatykh v russkoy Tserkvi*, 2nd edn (Moscow, 1903).

Graham, H. F., *The Moscovia of Antonio Possevino S.J.*, *with Critical Introduction and Notes*, UCIS Series in Russian and East European Studies, vol. 1 (Pittsburgh, 1977).

Gramoty velikogo Novgoroda i Pskova (GVNP), ed. S. N. Valk (Moscow–Leningrad, 1949).

Grekov, I. B., *Vostochnaya Evropa i upadok Zolotoy Ordy (na rubezhe XIV–XV vv.)* (Moscow, 1975).

Halecki, O., 'From Florence to Brest (1439–1596)', in *Sacrum Poloniae Millenium* (Rome, 1958), pp. 13–444.

Hannick, C., 'Kirchenrechtliche Aspekte des Verhältnisses zwischen Metropoliten und Fürsten in der Kiever Rus´', in: *Proceedings*, pp. 727–41.

Honigmann, E., 'Studies in Slavic Church History. A: The Foundation of the Russian Metropolitan Church according to Greek Sources', *Byzantion*, vol. 17 (Brussels, 1945), pp. 128–62.

Hurwitz, E. S., *Prince Andrej Bogoljubskij: The Man and the Myth*, Studia historica et philologica, XII, Sectio Slavica, vol. 4 (Florence, 1980).

Kartashev, A. V., *Ocherki po istorii russkoy Tserkvi*, vol. 1 (Paris, 1959)

Kazakova, N. A., 'Pervonachal´naya redaktsiya "Khozhdeniya na Florentiyskiy sobor"', *TODRL*, vol. 25 (Moscow–Leningrad, 1970), pp. 60–72.

Khoroshkevich, A. L. and Pliguzov, A. I.: see Fennell, *The Crisis*.

Klibanov, A. I., *Reformatsionnye dvizheniya v Rossii pervoy poloviny XVI v.* (Moscow, 1960).

Kloss, B. M., *Nikonovskiy svod i russkie letopisi XVI–XVII vekov* (Moscow, 1980).

Klyuchevsky, V. O., *Drevnerusskie zhitiya svyatykh kak istoricheskiy istochnik* (Moscow, 1871).

Klyuchevsky, V. O., *Sochineniya*, vol. 2 (Moscow, 1957).

Knoll, P. W., *The Rise of the Polish Monarchy, Piast Poland in East-Central Europe 1320–1370* (Chicago–London, 1972).

Kuchkin, V. A., 'Dmitriy Donskoy i Sergiy Radonezhskiy v kanun Kulikovskoy bitvy', in: *Tserkov´*, pp. 103–26.

Kuchkin, V. A., '"Skazanie o smerti mitropolita Petra"', *TODRL*, vol. 18 (Moscow–Leningrad, 1962), pp. 59–79.

Kuchkin, V. A., *Povesti o Mikhaile Tverskom, istoriko-tekstologicheskoe issledovanie* (Moscow, 1974).

Kuz´min, A. G., '"Kreshchenie Rusi": kontseptsii i problemy', in: *'Kreshchenie Rusi' v trudakh russkikh i sovetskikh istorikov* (Moscow, 1988), pp. 3–56.

Kyyevo-Pechers'kyy pateryk, ed. D. Abramovich, Pam'yatky movy ta pys'men-stva davn'oy Ukrayiny, vol. 4 (Kiev, 1931).

Lampert of Hersfeld, *Annales Weissenburgenses*, ed. O. Holder-Egger, *MGH, SSRG* (Hanover–Leipzig, 1894).
Lenhoff, G., *The Martyred Princes Boris and Gleb: A Sociocultural Study of the Cult and the Texts*, UCLA Slavic Studies, vol. 19 (Columbus, Ohio, 1989).
Leo Diaconus, *Historia, CSHB* (Bonn, 1828).
Letopisets Pereyaslavlya-Suzdal'skogo, sostavlennyy v nachale XIII veka (mezhdu 1214 i 1219 gg.) (LPS), ed. M. A. Obolensky (Moscow, 1851).
Letopisi russkoy literatury i drevnosti (LRD), ed. N. Tikhomirov (Moscow, 1859–63).
Lilienfeld, Fairy von (ed. and transl.), *Der Himmel im Herzen, Altrussische Heiligenlegenden* (Freiburg im Breisgau–Basel–Vienna, 1990).
Litavrin, G. G., 'O datirovke posol'stva knyagini Ol'gi v Konstantinopol'', *Istoriya SSSR*, 1981 (Moscow), No. 5, pp. 173–84.
Litavrin, G. G., 'Puteshestvie russkoy knyagini Ol'gi v Konstantinopol', Problema istochnikov', *Vizantiyskiy vremennik*, vol. 42 (Moscow, 1981), pp. 35–48.
Litavrin, G. G., 'K voprosu ob obstoyatel'stvakh, mester i vremeni kreshcheniya knyagini ol'gi', in: *Drevneishie gosudarstva na territorii SSSR. Materialy i issledovaniya 1988 g.* (Moscow, 1986), pp.49-57.
Litavrin, G. G. and Florya, B. N., 'Obshchee i osobennoe v protsesse khristianizatsii stran regiona i Drevney Rusi' in: *Prinyatie Khristianstva narodami Tsentral'noy i Yugo-Vostochnoy Evropy i kreshchenie Rusi* (Moscow, 1988).
Liutprand, bishop of Cremona, *Relatio de legatione Constantinopolitana*, in: *Die Werke Liudprands von Cremona*, 3rd edn, *MGH, SSRG* (Hanover–Leipzig, 1915).
Lur'e, Ya. S., *Obshcherusskie letopisi XIV–XV vv.* (Leningrad, 1976).
Lur'e, Ya. S., *Dve istorii Rusi XV veka, Rannie i pozdnie, nezavisimye i ofitsial'nye letopisi ob obrazovanii Moskovskogo gosudarstva* (Moscow–Paris, forthcoming).

Malinin, V., *Starets Eleazarova monastyrya Filofey i ego poslaniya, istoriko-literatur-noe issledovanie* (Kiev, 1901).
Mango, C., *The Homilies of Photius, Patriarch of Constantinople* (Cambridge, Mass., 1958).
Matuzova, V. I., *Angliyskie srednevekovye istochniki IX–XIII vv.*, Drevneyshie istochniki po istorii narodov SSSR (Moscow, 1979).
Meyendorff, J., *Byzantium and the Rise of Russia: A Study of Byzantino–Russian Relations in the Fourteenth Century* (Cambridge, 1981).
Mezentsev, V., 'The Territorial and Demographic Development of Medieval Kiev and other Major Cities of Rus': A Comparative Analysis based on Recent Archeological Research', *The Russian Review*, vol. 48 (Columbus, Ohio, 1989), pp. 145–70.

Monumenta Germaniae historica, Scriptores rerum germanicarum in usum scholarum (*MGH, SSRG*).

Monumenta Poloniae historica, vol. 1 (Lwów, 1864).

Moshin, V. A., 'Russkie na Afone i russko-vizantiyskie otnosheniya', *Byzantinoslavica*, vol. 9 (Prague, 1947–48), pp. 55–85.

Müller, L., *Zum Problem des hierarchischen Status und der jurisdiktionnellen Abhängigheit der russichen Kirche vor 1039*, Osteuropa und der deutschen Osten, Beiträge aus Forschungsarbeiten und Vorträgen der Hochschulen des Landes Nordrhein-Westfalen, Reihe III, vol. 6 (Cologne–Braunsfeld, 1959).

Müller, L., *Die Legenden des Heiligen Sergij von Radonež, Nachdruck der Ausgabe von Tichonravov*, Slavische Propyläen, vol. 17 (Munich, 1967).

Müller, L., *Die Werke des Metropoliten Ilarion*, Forum Slavicum, vol. 37 (Munich, 1971).

Müller, L., *Des Metropoliten Ilarion Lobrede auf Vladimir den Heiligen und Glaubensbekenntnis, nach der Erstausgabe von 1844 neu hggb (MIL)*, Slavische Studienbücher, vol. 2 (Wiesbaden, 1982).

Müller, L., *Die Taufe Russlands, die Frühgeschichte des russischen Christentums bis zum Jahre 988*, Quellen und Studien zur russischen Geistesgeschichte, vol. 6 (Munich, 1987).

Nazarenko, A. V., 'Kogda zhe knyaginya Ol'ga ezdila v Konstantinopol'?', *Vizantiyskiy vremennik*, vol. 50 (Moscow, 1989), pp. 66–83.

Nazarenko, A. V., 'Rus' i Germaniya pri Svyatoslave Igoreviche', *Istoriya SSSR*, 1990 (Moscow), No. 2, pp. 60–74.

Novgorodskaya pervaya letopis' starshego i mladshego izvodov (NPL), ed. A. N. Nasonov (Moscow–Leningrad, 1950).

Obolensky, D., 'Byzantium, Kiev and Moscow: A Study in Ecclesiastical Relations', *Dumbarton Oaks Papers*, vol. 11 (Cambridge, Mass., 1957), pp. 21–78; repr. *Byzantium and the Slavs* (London, 1971), No. VI.

Obolensky, D., *The Byzantine Commonwealth, Eastern Europe 500–1453* (London, 1971).

Obolensky, D., 'A *Philorhomaios anthropos*: Metropolitan Cyprian of Kiev and all Russia (1375–1406)', *Dumbarton Oaks Papers*, vol. 32 (Washington, DC, 1978), pp. 79–98; repr. *The Byzantine Inheritance of Eastern Europe* (London, 1982), No. XI.

Obolensky, D., 'A Late Fourteenth-Century Byzantine Diplomat: Michael Archbishop of Bettleem', in: *Byzance et les Slaves: Mélanges I. Dujčev* (Paris, 1979), pp. 299–315; repr. in *The Byzantine Inheritance*, No. XIII.

Obolensky, D., 'The Baptism of Princess Olga of Kiev: The Problem of the Sources', *Byzantina Sorbonensia*, vol. 4 (Paris, 1984), pp. 159–76.

Obolensky, D., *Six Byzantine Portraits* (Oxford, 1988).

Obolensky, D., 'Cherson and the Conversion of Rus': An Anti-Revisionist View', *Byzantine and Modern Greek Studies*, vol. 13 (Birmingham, 1989), pp. 244–56.

A History of the Russian Church to 1448

Okhotina, N. A., 'Russkaya Tserkov' i Mongol'skoe zavoevanie (XIII v.)',
in: *Tserkov'*, pp. 67–84.

Ostrowski, D., 'Why did the Metropolitan Move from Kiev to Vladimir in
the Thirteenth Century?', in: *Christianity and the Eastern Slavs*, vol.
1, *Slavic Cultures in the Middle Ages*, ed. B. Gasparov and O.
Raevsky-Hughes, California Slavic Studies, 16 (Berkeley–Los Angeles–Oxford, 1993), pp.
83–101.

Pamyatniki literatury Drevney Rusi (PLDR):
  XI–nachalo XII veka (Moscow, 1978).
  XII vek (Moscow, 1980).
  XIII vek (Moscow, 1981).
  XIV–seredina XV veka (Moscow, 1981).
Pamyatniki russkogo prava (PRP):
  vol. 2: *Pamyatniki prava feodal'no-razdroblennoy Rusi*, ed. A. A. Zimin
  (Moscow, 1953).
  vol. 3: *Pamyatniki prava perioda obrazovaniya russkogo tsentralizovannogo
  gosudarstva, XIV–XV vv.*, ed. L. V. Cherepnin (Moscow, 1955).
Paszkiewicz, H., *Jagiellonowie a Moskwa*, vol. 1, *Litwa a Moskwa w XIII–XIV
  wieku* (Warsaw, 1933).
Pavlov, A. S., *Istoricheskiy ocherk sekulyarizatsii tserkovnykh zemel' v Rossii*,
  part 1 (Odessa, 1871).
Photius, ['Encyclical to the Patriarchs of the East'], in: *Patrologiae cursus
  completus, Series Graeca (PG)*, vol. 102 (Paris, 1900), cols. 721–42.
Pliguzov, A. I. and Khoroshkevich, A. L., 'Russkaya tserkov' i antiordyn-
  skaya bor'ba v XIII–XV vv. (po materialam kratkogo sobraniya khanskikh
  yarlykov russkim mitropolitam)', in: *Tserkov'*, pp. 84–102.
Podskalsky, G., *Christentum und theologische Literatur in der Kiever Rus' (988–
  1237)* (Munich, 1982).
Podskalsky, G., 'Der hl. Feodosij Pečerskij: historisch und literarisch betra-
  chtet', in: *Proceedings*, pp. 714–26.
Polnoe sobranie russkikh letopisey (PSRL):
  vol. 1: *Lavrent'evskaya letopis'*, 2nd edn (Leningrad, 1926–28).
  vol. 2: *Ipat'evskaya letopis'*, 2nd edn (St Petersburg, 1908).
  vol. 4, I: *Novgorodskaya chetvertaya letopis'*, 2nd edn (Petrograd, 1915).
  vols 5–6: *Sofiyskie letopisi* (St Petersburg, 1851–53).
  vols 9–12: *Nikonovskaya letopis'* (St Petersburg, 1862–1901).
  vol. 15: *Tverskaya letopis'* (St Petersburg, 1863).
  vol. 15 (2nd edn), I: *Rogozhskiy letopisets* (Petrograd, 1922).
  vol. 18: *Simeonovskaya letopis'* (St Petersburg, 1913).
  vol. 20, I: *L'vovskaya letopis'*, chast' 1-aya (St Petersburg, 1910).
  vol. 21, II: *Stepennaya kniga, chast' 2-aya* (St Petersburg, 1913).
  vol. 23: *Ermolinskaya letopis'* (St Petersburg, 1910).
  vol. 25: *Moskovskiy letopisnyy svod kontsa XV veka* (Moscow–Leningrad,
  1949).
  vol. 26: *Vologodsko-Permskaya letopis'* (Moscow–Leningrad, 1959).

246

vol. 27: *Nikanorovskaya letopis'*, *Sokrashchennye letopisnye svody kontsa XV veka* (Moscow–Leningrad, 1962).

vol. 35: *Letopisi Belorussko-litovskie* (Moscow, 1980).

vol. 37: *Ustyuzhskie i Vologodskie letopisi XVI–XVIII vekov* (Leningrad, 1982).

Popov, A. N., *Istoriko-literaturnyy obzor drevnerusskikh polemicheskikh sochineniy protiv Latinyan, XI–XV vv.* (Moscow, 1875).

Poppe, A., 'Le Traité des azymes $\Lambda \acute{\epsilon} o \nu \tau o \varsigma$ $\mu \eta \tau \rho o \pi o \lambda \acute{\iota} \tau o \upsilon$ $\tau \widehat{\eta} \varsigma$ $\acute{\epsilon} \nu$ '$P \omega \sigma \acute{\iota} \alpha$ $\Pi \rho \epsilon \sigma \theta \lambda \acute{\alpha} \beta a \varsigma$: quand, où et par qui il a été écrit?', *Byzantion*, vol. 35 (Brussels, 1965), pp. 504–27; repr. in *The Rise of Christian Russia* (London, 1982), No. VII.

Poppe, A., 'L'Organisation diocésaine de la Russie aux XIe–XIIe siècles', *Byzantion*, vol. 40 (Brussels, 1970), pp. 165–217; repr. in *The Rise*, No. VIII.

Poppe, A., 'La Tentative de réforme ecclésiastique en Russie au milieu du XIe siècle', *Acta Poloniae Historica*, vol. 25 (Warsaw, 1972), pp. 5–31; repr. in *The Rise*, No. V.

Poppe, A., 'The Political Background to the Baptism of Rus': Byzantine–Russian Relations between 986–989', *Dumbarton Oaks Papers*, vol. 30 (Washington, DC, 1976), pp. 197–244; repr. in *The Rise*, No. II.

Poppe, A., 'The Building of the Church of St Sophia in Kiev', *Journal of Medieval History*, vol. 7 (Amsterdam, 1981), pp. 15–66; repr. in *The Rise*, No. IV.

Poppe, A., 'How the Conversion of Rus' Was Understood in the Eleventh Century', *Harvard Ukrainian Studies*, vol. 11 (Cambridge, Mass., 1987), pp. 287–302.

Poppe, A., 'Two Concepts of the Conversion of Rus' in Kievan Writings', in: *Proceedings*, pp. 488–504.

Poslaniya Iosifa Volotskogo, ed. A. A. Zimin and Ya. S. Lur'e (Moscow–Leningrad, 1959).

Povest' vremennykh let (*PVL*), ed. D. S. Likhachev and B. A. Romanov, 2 vols (Moscow–Leningrad, 1950).

Presnyakov, A. E., *Obrazovanie velikorusskogo gosudarstva, ocherki po istorii XIII–XV stoletiy* (Petrograd, 1918).

Pritsak, O., 'At the Dawn of Christianity in Rus': East Meets West', in: *Proceedings*, pp. 87–113.

Proceedings of the International Congress Commemorating the Millennium of Christianity in Rus'–Ukraine (*Proceedings*), Harvard Ukrainian Studies, vol. 12/13 (Cambridge, Mass., 1988/1989).

Prokhorov, G. M., *Povest' o Mityae, Rus' i Vizantiya v epokhu Kulikovskoy bitvy* (Leningrad, 1978).

Prosvirin, A., 'Afon i russkaya Tserkov'' [first part], *Zhurnal Moskovskoy Patriarkhii*, 1974 (Moscow), No. 3, pp. 2–25.

Pskovskie letopisi (*PL*), ed. A. N. Nasonov, vol. 1 (Moscow–Leningrad, 1941), vol. 2 (Moscow, 1955).

Ramm, B. Ya, *Papstvo i Rus' v X–XV vv.* (Moscow–Leningrad, 1959).

Rapov, O. M., 'O date prinyatiya khristianstva knyazem Vladimirom', *Voprosy istorii*, 1984 (Moscow), No. 6, pp. 34–47.

Regino of Prüm, *Chronicon cum Continuatione Treverensi*, ed. F. Kurze, *MGH, SSRG* (Hanover, 1890).

Runciman, S., *The Kingdom of Acre and the Later Crusades,* A History of the Crusades, vol. 3 (Cambridge, 1954).

Runciman, S., *The Eastern Schism: A Study of the Papacy and the Eastern Churches during the XIth and XIIth Centuries* (Oxford, 1955).

Runciman, S., *The Fall of Constantinople, 1453* (Cambridge, 1965).

The Russian Primary Chronicle, ed. and transl. S. H. Cross and O. P. Sherbowitz-Wetzor, The Mediaeval Academy of America Publications, vol. 60 (Cambridge, Mass., 1953).

Russkaya istoricheskaya Biblioteka (RIB), vol. 6: *Pamyatniki drevnerusskogo kanonicheskogo prava*, ed. V. N. Beneshevich, part 1, 2nd edn (St Petersburg, 1908); vol. 36: part 2, I (Petrograd, 1920).

Rybakov, B. A., *Russkie letopistsy i avtor 'Slova o polku Igoreve'* (Moscow, 1972).

Rybakov, B. A., *Yazychestvo Drevney Rusi* (Moscow, 1987).

Sapunov, B. V., 'Nekotorye soobrazheniya o drevnerusskoy knizhnosti XI–XIII vekov', *TODRL*, vol. 11 (Moscow–Leningrad, 1955), pp. 314–32.

Sbornik XII veka Moskovskogo Uspenskogo sobora, vol. 1, ed. A. A. Shakhmatov and P. A. Lavrov (Moscow, 1899).

Shchapov, Ya. N., *Knyazheskie ustavy i Tserkov' v Drevney Russi XI–XIV vv.* (Moscow, 1972).

Shchapov, Ya. N., *Vizantiyskoe i yuzhnoslavyanskoe pravovoe nasledie na Rusi v XI–XIII vv.* (Moscow, 1978).

Shchapov, Ya. N., *Gosudarstvo i Tserkov' Drevney Rusi X–XIII vv.* (Moscow, 1989).

Shepard, J., 'Some Remarks on the Sources for the Conversion of Rus'', in: *Le Origini e lo sviluppo della Cristianità slavo-bizantina*, Istituto storico Italiano per il Medio Evo, Nuovi Studi storici, vol. 17 (Rome, 1992), pp. 59–95.

Sinitsyna, N. V., 'Avtokefaliya russkoy Tserkvi i uchrezhdenie Moskovskogo patriarkhata (1448–1589 gg.)', in: *Tserkov'*, pp. 126–51.

Skazaniya i povesti o Kulikovskoy bitve, ed. L. A. Dmitriev and O. P. Likhacheva (Leningrad, 1982).

Skrynnikov, R. G., *Gosudarstvo i Tserkov' na Rusi XIV–XVI vv.* (Novosibirsk, 1991).

Slovar' knizhnikov i knizhnosti Drevney Rusi, vol. 2, *Vtoraya polovina XIV–XVI v.*, 2 books (Leningrad, 1988–9).

Slovo o polku Igoreve, ed. V. P. Adrianova-Peretts (Moscow–Leningrad, 1950).

Smirnov, S., *Materialy dlya istorii drevne-russkoy pokayannoy distsipliny (teksty i zametki)* (Moscow, 1912).

Southern, R. W., *Western Society and the Church in the Middle Ages*, Pelican History of the Church, vol. 2 (London, 1971).

Spuler, B., *Die Goldene Horde: Die Mongolen in Russland 1223–1502*, 2nd edn (Wiesbaden, 1965).

Stokes, A., 'The Status of the Russian Church 988–1037', *Slavonic and East European Review*, vol. 37 (London, 1959), pp. 430–42.

Stökl, G., 'Kanzler und Metropolit', *Wiener Archiv für Geschichte des Slawentums und Osteuropas*, vol. 5 (Vienna, 1966), pp. 150–75; repr. in idem, *Die Russische Staat in Mittelalter und früher Neuzeit*, Quellen und Studien zur Geschichte des östlichen Europa, vol.13 (Wiesbaden, 1981), pp. 98–123.

Tachiaos, A. E., 'The Greek Metropolitans of Kievan Rus´: An Evaluation of their Spiritual and Cultural Activity', in: *Proceedings*, pp. 430–45.

Tatishchev, V. N., *Istoriya Rossiyskaya*, vol. 2 (Moscow–Leningrad, 1963).

Theophanes continuatus, *CSHB* (Bonn, 1838).

Thietmar of Merseburg, *Die Chronik des Bischofs Thietmars von Merseburg und ihre Korveier Uberarbeitung*, ed. R. Holtzmann, *MGH*, *SSRG*, NS, vol. 9 (Berlin, 1935).

Thomson, F. J., 'The Nature of the Reception of Christian Byzantine Culture in Russia in the Tenth to Thirteenth Centuries and its Implications for Russian Culture', *Slavica Gandensia*, vol. 5 (Ghent, 1978), pp. 107–39.

Thomson, F. J., 'The Ascription of the Penitential *Zapovedi svyatykh otets´ k ispovedayushchemsya synom i d´´shcherem* to Metropolitan George of Kiev', *Russia Mediaevalis*, vol. 4 (Munich, 1979), pp. 5–15.

Thomson, F. J.,'Quotations of Patristic and Byzantine Works by Early Russian authors as an Indication of the Cultural Level of Kievan Russia', *Slavica Gandensia*, vol. 10 (Ghent, 1983), pp. 65–102.

Tikhomirov, M. N., *Drevnerusskie goroda*, 2nd edn (Moscow, 1956).

Tinnefeld, F., 'Die russische Fürstin Olga bei Konstantin VII. und das Problem der "purpurgeborenen Kinder"', *Russia Mediaevalis*, vol. 6, I (Munich, 1987), pp. 30–7.

Troitskaya letopis´ (*TL*), ed. M. D. Priselkov (Moscow–Leningrad, 1950).

Trudy Otdela drevnerusskoy literatury (*TODRL*).

Tserkov´, obshchestvo i gosudarstvo v Feodal´noy Rossii (Moscow, 1990).

Udal´tsova, Z. V., Shchapov, Ya. N., Gutnova, E. V. and Novosel´tsev, A. P., 'Drevnyaya Rus´ – zona vstrechi tsivilizatsiy', *Voprosy istorii*, 1980 (Moscow), No. 7, pp. 44–60.

Vasil´evsky, V. G., *Trudy*, vol. 3 (Petrograd, 1915).

Vernadsky, G., *Ancient Russia* (New Haven–London, 1943).

Vernadsky, G., *Kievan Russia* (New Haven–London, 1948).

Vernadsky, G., *The Mongols and Russia* (New Haven–London, 1953).

Veselovsky, S. B., *Feodal´noe zemlevladenie v Severo-vostochnoy Rusi*, vol. 1, *Chastnoe zemlevladenie, zemlevladenie mitropolich´ego doma* (Moscow–Leningrad, 1947).

Vlasto, A. P., *The Entry of the Slavs into Christendom: An Introduction to the Medieval History of the Slavs* (Cambridge, 1970).

Vodoff, V., 'A propos des "achats" (*kupli*) d'Ivan Ier de Moscou', *Journal des Savants*, 1974 (Paris), pp. 95–127; repr. in *Princes et principautés russes, Xe–XVIIe siècles* (London, 1989), No. XIII.

Vodoff, V., *Naissance de la Chrétienté russe, la conversion du prince Vladimir de Kiev (988) et ses conséquences (XIe–XIIIe siècles)* (Paris, 1988).

Vodoff, V., 'Pourquoi le prince Vladimir Svjatoslavič n'a-t-il pas été canonisé?', in: *Proceedings*, pp. 446–66.

Vodoff, V., 'Aspects et limites de la notion d'universalité dans l'ecclésiologie de la Russie ancienne', in: *Il Battesimo delle Terre russe, Bilancio di un Millenio*, Civiltà Veneziana Studi, vol. 43 (Florence, 1991), 143–65.

Ware, T. [Bishop Callistos of Diokleia], *The Orthodox Church* (Harmondsworth, 1963).

Yahia of Antioch, *Histoire*, fasc. 2, ed and transl. I. Kratchkovsky and A. Vasiliev, Patrologia orientalis, vol. 23, III (Paris, 1932). *Patrologia orientalis*, vol. 23, III (Paris, 1932).

Zimin, A. A., 'Pamyat' i pokhvala Yakova Mnikha i zhitie knyazya Vladimira po drevneyshemu spisku', *Kratkie soobshcheniya Instituta slavyanovedeniya*, vol. 37 (Moscow, 1963), pp. 66–75.

Zimin, A. A., *Krupnaya feodal'naya votchina i sotsial'no-politicheskaya bor'ba v Rossii (konets XV–XVI v.)* (Moscow, 1977).

Zimin, A. A., *Vityaz' na rasput'e, Feodal'naya voyna v Rossii* (Moscow, 1991).

Map of medieval Russia showing the principal towns

Index

Abu Hamid al-Gharnati, 84
Abydus (battle of), 38
Adalbert, archbishop of Magdeburg, 26, 29–30
Adrianopolis, 8
Afanasy, abbot, 154
Afanasy, follower of Metropolitan Isidor, 181
Akim, bishop of Novgorod (10th century), *see* Ioakim (Akim), bishop of Novgorod
alcohol, 36n
Alef, G., 172n, 240
Aleksandr Mikhaylovich, prince of Tver', grand prince of Vladimir, 126, 200–1, 202, 222–3, 224–5
Aleksandr Oshevenskiy, founder of the Oshevenskiy Monastery, 209
Aleksandr Vasil'evich, prince of Suzdal', Gorodets and Nizhniy Novgorod, 228
Aleksandr Vladimirovich, prince of Kiev, 171, 178n
Aleksandr Yaroslavich Nevskiy, grand prince of Vladimir, 121–4, 133, 198–9
Alekseev, M.P., 98n, 100n, 240
Aleksin, district, 212, 213
Aleksiy, archbishop of Novgorod, 144
Aleksiy, bishop of Suzdal', 229
Aleksiy Byakont, bishop of Vladimir-on-the-Klyaz'ma, *see* Aleksiy, metropolitan
Aleksiy, metropolitan, 136, 140–8, 193, 207, 212–13, 225, 227–33
    and Lithuania, 232–3
    and Little Russia, 143–6, 227–8

and Nizhniy Novgorod, 228–9, 237
    and Tver', 142, 229–32
    canonization of, 148
Alexander the Great, 107
Alexius I Comnenus, emperor, 96
almshouses, 56, 65, 68, 111
anathema, 166, 216, 218, 223, 232
Andrew, Apostle, 20–1
Andrey, bishop of Tver', 135, 220, 221
Andrey Aleksandrovich, prince of Gorodets, grand prince of Vladimir, 125, 197–8, 219
Andrey Dmitrievich, prince of Mozhaysk, 216, 235
Andrey Ol'gerdovich, prince of Polotsk, 152
Andrey Vladimirovich Dobryy, 21n
Andrey Yaroslavich, prince of Suzdal', Nizhniy Novgorod and Gorodets, grand prince of Vladimir, 120, 122, 123, 133, 228
Andrey Yur'evich Bogolyubskiy, prince of Vladimir, 14, 15, 21n, 54, 102
Andronicus II Palaeologus, emperor, 134
Andronicus IV, emperor, 150–1
Angles, 4
Angold, M.J., 96n, 240
Ann of Savoy, 137
Anna, sister of Emperor Basil II, wife of Vladimir I, 36, 37–8, 39, 40
Anna Vsevolodovna, sister of Vladimir Monomakh, 48
Annales Bertiniani, 5n
Antonio Bonumbre, cardinal, 179
Antonius, metropolitan of Heraclea, 175, 176

252

Index

Index

Index

DATE DUE